R00447 07961

CHICAGO PUBLIC LIBRARY
HAROLD WASHINGTON LIBRARY CENTER

BF
311
.C64
1976
V.3   Con   nd
         se

BF
311
.C64
1976
V.3

Consciousness and
self-regulation

R004470796l

DATE	BORROWER'S NAME	
AUG 2 8 1995		

SOCIAL SCIENCES AND HISTORY DIVISION

THE CHICAGO
EDUCATION

D1117011

© THE BAKER & TAYLOR CO.

Consciousness and Self-Regulation

Advances in Research and Theory

VOLUME 3

A Continuation Order Plan is available for this series. A continuation order will bring delivery of each new volume immediately upon publication. Volumes are billed only upon actual shipment. For further information please contact the publisher.

Consciousness and Self-Regulation

Advances in Research and Theory

VOLUME 3

Edited by

RICHARD J. DAVIDSON

State University of New York at Purchase
Purchase, New York

GARY E. SCHWARTZ

Yale University
New Haven, Connecticut

and

DAVID SHAPIRO

University of California at Los Angeles
Los Angeles, California

PLENUM PRESS · NEW YORK AND LONDON

Library of Congress Cataloging in Publication Data

Main entry under title:

Consciousness and self-regulation.

Vol. 3— has subtitle: Advances in research and theory.
Vol. 3— edited by Richard J. Davidson, Gary E. Schwartz, and David
Shapiro.
Includes bibliographical references and indexes.
1. Consciousness. 2. Self-control. I. Schwartz, Gary E., 1944—   . II.
Shapiro, David, 1924—
BF311.C64   153   76-8907
ISBN 0-306-41214-4 (v. 3)

BF
311
.C64
1976

R0044707941

© 1983 Plenum Press, New York
A Division of Plenum Publishing Corporation
233 Spring Street, New York, N.Y. 10013

All rights reserved

No part of this book may be reproduced, stored in a retrieval system, or transmitted
in any form or by any means, electronic, mechanical, photocopying, microfilming,
recording, or otherwise, without written permission from the Publisher

Printed in the United States of America

Contributors

Bernard J. Baars, Department of Psychology, State University of New York, Stony Brook, New York

Emanuel Donchin, Cognitive Psychophysiology Laboratory, Department of Psychology, University of Illinois, Champaign, Illinois

Marta Kutas, Department of Neurosciences, University of California, San Diego, La Jolla, California

Peter J. Lang, Department of Clinical Psychology, University of Florida, Gainesville, Florida

Daniel N. Levin, Medical School, Duke University, Durham, North Carolina

Gregory McCarthy, Neuropsychology Research Laboratory, Veterans Administration Hospital, West Haven, Connecticut

Gregory A. Miller, Department of Psychology, University of Illinois, Urbana, Illinois

Robert R. Pagano, Department of Psychology, University of Washington, Seattle, Washington

Georges Rey, Division of Humanities, State University of New York at Purchase, Purchase, New York

Walter Ritter, Albert Einstein College of Medicine and Lehman College, City University of New York, Bronx, New York

Stephen Warrenburg, Department of Psychology, Yale University, New Haven, Connecticut

Preface to Volume 3

Six years have passed since the appearance of the first volume of *Consciousness and Self-Regulation: Advances in Research*. Since that time, both the field and the editors of this series have undergone some change. This new preface is intended to provide an update of these recent developments.

Around the time Volume 1 appeared, the scientific study of consciousness was very much in its infancy. While isolated research efforts were directly concerned with the study of conscious and/or volitional processes, little systematic theory or integration was evident. Moreover, research in these areas was, at that time, still not quite considered as lying within the "proper" domain of psychological investigation. Over the past several years, we have witnessed a growing recognition of the importance of the study of consciousness within the behavioral-scientific community. Consciousness is now viewed by many prominent cognitive theorists as a central issue in cognitive psychology. Similarly, an increasing emphasis on conscious processes can be detected within contemporary psychobiological research.

The increasing attention directed toward the study of consciousness and volition has helped to uncover some of the deeper and less obvious assumptions investigators have been making about the precise nature of mind–brain relations. One of the more important recent developments is the contribution which contemporary philosophy has made to this dialogue. A number of philosophers have been quite helpful in exposing the problems and prospects of the various positions regarding mind–brain identity. We intend to represent this interdisciplinary effort in this and in future volumes of the series.

The central focus and orientation of the series remains as it was conceived. Our bias remains with psychobiological approaches to the problems of consciousness and self-regulation. However, our viewpoint is broad and we will continue to include new developments in cognitive science, linguistics, and philosophy as they bear upon the major issues to which this series is addressed. We also expect to maintain a balance, reflected in the previous two volumes, between basic and applied research. The case remains that both basic and clinical research programs continue to contribute to our understanding of consciousness and volition.

As the original preface indicates, the impetus and organization of the series emerged from a number of seminars at Harvard University on the psychophysiology of consciousness, emotion, and self-regulation. In the late 1960s, Gary E. Schwartz was a graduate student at Harvard working under the direction of David Shapiro. Schwartz joined the faculty at Harvard in 1971 and, in 1972, Davidson came to Harvard as a graduate student working under Gary E. Schwartz. The time we spent together at Harvard was an extremely exciting and productive period for all of us, and the data and ideas generated at that time continue to influence our work and our lives. While each of us has moved in somewhat different directions, we continue to be united by our recognition of the centrality of consciousness and self-regulation in the life sciences and by our commitment to a broad psychobiological perspective.

RICHARD J. DAVIDSON
GARY E. SCHWARTZ
DAVID SHAPIRO

Preface to Volumes 1 and 2

> The first and foremost concrete fact which every one will affirm to belong to his inner experience is the fact that consciousness of some sort goes on.[1]
> —William James, 1893

We are witnessing today a mounting interest among behavioral and biological scientists in problems long recognized as central to our understanding of human nature, yet until recently considered out of the bounds of scientific psychology and physiology. Sometimes thrown into the heading of "altered states of consciousness," this growing research bears directly upon such time-honored questions as the nature of conscious experience, the mind–body relationship, and volition. If one broadly views this research as encompassing the two interrelated areas of consciousness and self-regulation, one can find many relevant contemporary examples of creative and experimentally sophisticated approaches, including research on the regulation of perception and sensory experience, attention, imagery and thinking, emotion and pain; hypnosis and meditation; biofeedback and voluntary control; hemispheric asymmetry and specialization of brain function; drug-induced subjective states; and biological rhythms. Because the material is spread over many different kinds of publications and disciplines, it is difficult for any one person to keep fully abreast of the significant advances. The overall aim of the new Plenum Series in *Consciousness and Self-Regulation: Advances in Research* is to provide a scholarly forum for discussing integration of these diverse areas by presenting some of the best current research and theory.

It is our hope that these volumes will enable investigators to

[1] William James, *Psychology: Briefer Course* (New York: Henry Holt and Company, 1893), p. 152.

become more well-rounded in related areas of research, as well as provide advanced students with a ready means of obtaining up-to-date, state-of-the-art information about relevant problems, theories, methods, and findings. By selecting significant developments in theory and research, we also hope that over the years the series can help legitimate the field as a scientific venture as well as delineate critical issues for further investigation.

Psychology and biology are going through a reawakening, and research on the issues to which this series is devoted is helping to bring these fields closer together. History tells us that Wundt founded psychology as the science of consciousness, and James expanded it to encompass "such things as sensations, desires, emotions, cognitions, reasonings, decisions, volitions and the like."[2] But these ideals could not be achieved, or so it seemed, and psychology turned away from questions of experience and volition, as well as from biology, and was replaced with behaviorism. The transformation was arduous, and it required a certain allowance for inconsistency. For example, Edmund Jacobson, one of the pioneers in the psychophysiology of higher mental processes, recalled, "Lashley told me with a chuckle that when he and Watson would spend an evening together, working out principles of behaviorism, much of the time would be devoted to introspection."[3]

In *William James: Unfinished Business* (1969), Mandler summarized the good points, and the bad points, of this era of psychology in his "Acceptance of Things Past and Present: A Look at the Mind and the Brain." He aptly noted:

> I think the Watsonian behaviorist development was inevitable—I think it was even healthy—if we learn not to do it again. Watson and the behaviorists did, once and for all, clean up the problem of the proper data language for psychology. In that sense, we are all behaviorists. The behaviorists inveighed against an establishment which imported theoretical notions and hypotheses into purely descriptive realms of psychology. They successfully excluded vague notions about the causes of behavior—the introspective statements—from the facts of psychology. But in the process the Watsonians felt called upon to do the reverse and to remove complex and imaginative models from psychology. . . . Behaviorism has been one of the most antitheoretical movements in science. . . .

[2] Ibid., p. 1.
[3] Jacobson, "Electrophysiology of Mental Activities and Introduction to the Psychological Process of Thinking." In F. J. McGuigan and R. A. Schoonover (Eds.), *The Psychophysiology of Thinking* (New York: Academic Press, 1973), p. 14.

> . . . I submit that it was this antitheoretical stance that prevented any close attention to physiology. . . . If the mechanisms we postulate are "like" physiological mechanisms, then we will have heeded James in modern terms. But if we are, as we were, afraid to postulate complex mental mechanisms, we will never find the corresponding complex physiological mechanisms.[4]

This series is dedicated to William James, emphasizing the integration and patterning of multiple processes, coupled with the most significant advances in methodology and knowledge. Some of the chapters will be broad-based and theoretical; others will focus on specific research problems or applications. Inclusion of material in all cases is determined by the investigator's focus on or concern with consciousness and related processes, whether in normal or in abnormal populations. While the editors have a decided bias toward biologically oriented approaches to consciousness and self-regulation, papers that deal primarily with cognition or self-report are included when of particular significance to these topics. Since important findings in this area are often derived from the study of clinical populations and are of direct relevance to the assessment and treatment of psychological and psychophysiological disorders, chapters dealing with basic research are interwoven with chapters of more clinical concern. In this way it is hoped that the series can provide a fertile interchange between the basic and applied sides of this area. To help the reader understand the perspective and rationale for the diverse selections comprising a given volume, a brief overview of each volume is presented by the editors.

The impetus for and organization of the series grows out of student response to our interdisciplinary seminars at Harvard on the psychophysiology of consciousness, emotion, and self-regulation, coupled with the enthusiasm and support of Seymour Weingarten, Executive Editor of Plenum. Their input, and prodding, is gratefully acknowledged.

GARY E. SCHWARTZ
DAVID SHAPIRO

---

[4] G. Mandler, "Acceptance of Things Past and Present: A Look at the Mind and the Brain." In R. B. MacLeod (Ed.), *William James: Unfinished Business* (Washington, D.C. American Psychological Association, 1969), pp. 13, 14.

Overview of Volume 3

The first chapter, "A Reason for Doubting the Existence of Consciousness," by Georges Rey presents an important viewpoint represented by contemporary analytic philosophy. Rey attempts to delineate the phenomena to which consciousness refers and uncovers more confusion and less consensus than we might initially have thought to exist. He specifically argues that many of the mental operations linked to consciousness by various prominent theorists and investigators could occur nonconsciously, and furthermore, these mental operations could be instantiated by a machine. This type of analysis is extremely useful in helping to focus on precisely what may be *unique* about processes which are conscious as opposed to nonconscious.

The comparison between conscious and unconscious processes as an aid in distilling the unique properties of conscious activity is a theme continued in the chapter by Bernard J. Baars. He attempts to specify a set of empirical constraints on any theory of consciousness. *Conscious processing* is viewed by Baars as a special operating mode of the nervous system. Conscious processing is characterized by global representation which provides information to the nervous system as a whole. Conscious processes are viewed as computationally less efficient than unconscious processes (carried out by a set of dedicated specialized processors). In addition, conscious processing has a great range and relational capacity, although the quantity of information of which an individual can be conscious at a given moment is quite limited. Conscious events are said to be percepts and input consistent with context, whereas unconscious events include contexts required to organize percepts and input inconsistent with context.

Emanuel Donchin, Gregory McCarthy, Marta Kutas, and Walter Ritter in their chapter, "Event-Related Brain Potentials in the Study of Consciousness," present a critical review of the literature on evoked response concomitants of conscious and unconscious processes. At the outset, they make a number of important methodological points, including the need to recognize the componential nature of the event-related potential (ERP) waveform. Different ERP components may be differentially related to various behavioral processes, and it is inappropriate to consider the ERP waveform as unitary. A fundamental distinction is that between exogenous and endogenous ERP components. An *exogenous component* represents "an obligatory response of the brain to input in sensory channels." *Endogenous components* often follow exogenous components and represent "information processing *invoked* by the psychological demands and the context in which a stimulus is presented, rather than that *evoked* by the presentation of stimuli."

Donchin and his colleagues survey the literature on different endogenous ERP's components and conclude that these brain events are reflections of various types of cognitive operations. Some of these cognitive operations are in turn related to consciousness. A very detailed discussion of the P300, a positive component occurring approximately 300 msec following a stimulus, concludes with the suggestion that whenever P300 occurs, "the subject is conscious of the task-relevant information carried by the eliciting stimulus." They further state that "the P300 can be used to index the occurrence of conscious processing."

The exploration of the physiological concomitants of conscious processing is continued in the chapter by Peter J. Lang, Gregory A. Miller, and Daniel N. Levin entitled "Anxiety and Fear: Central Processing and Peripheral Physiology." These authors describe the theoretical underpinnings and empirical data associated with their program of research on the nature of emotional imagery. They separate emotional responses into three separate categories: verbal response, behavioral acts, and physiological activity. Lang and his colleagues show how these three response systems exhibit complex patterned relations, sometimes varying together and, at other times, varying independently. They describe the results of their research which examines the impact of verbal instructions on autonomic and skeletal-muscular activity. An important element in their research is the distinction between different components of an image. They have utilized recent cognitive approaches to the study of imagery in their own work and conceptualize the structure of an image in terms of different types of propositions. For example, stimulus propositions refer to the descriptions of the stimulus elements (e.g., The large wooden door is tightly closed) while response propositions refer to the manner in which behavior and/or physiology changes (e.g., Your heart pounds wildly).

Lang and his colleagues have demonstrated important differences in physiological responding between groups of subjects trained on stimulus versus response image propositions. They have also found that certain individual differences interact with these basic effects. The data they have collected have important implications for both clinical practice as well as for the developing psychophysiology of consciousness and self-regulation.

The phenomenon of psychophysiological self-regulation is also addressed by Robert R. Pagano and Stephen Warrenburg in their chapter "Meditation: In Search of a Unique Effect." They present a detailed overview of their research program on Transcendental Meditation. The issues which this research addresses include the physiological changes which characterize the state of meditation, whether the state effects of meditation generalize to the nonmeditation state and thereby resemble trait-like effects, and whether certain predispositional factors influence an individual's response to meditation.

One of the important control procedures utilized by Pagano and Warrenburg was the inclusion of a nonmeditation relaxation group against which the data from a meditation group could be compared. They observed that "the state of somatic relaxation obtained during the practice of a variety of meditation/relaxation techniques. . . is qualitatively and quantitatively very similar when these techniques are practiced under optimally relaxing conditions by healthy normal subjects." They also found that while trait effects of meditation did emerge, they were comparable to the trait effects of other procedures which involve "a regimen of taking time out daily to engage in enjoyable restful activity." They examined the possibility that meditation produces a shift in hemispheric dominance toward increased right hemisphere activation. No evidence was obtained to support this hypothesis. Pagano and Warrenburg report on many other effects of meditation and their research is a fine example of a systematic, methodologically sound approach to the study of an altered state of consciousness.

Contents

3 Event-Related Brain Potentials in the Study of Consciousness 81

EMANUEL DONCHIN, GREGORY McCARTHY, MARTA KUTAS, AND WALTER RITTER

4 Anxiety and Fear: Central Processing and Peripheral Physiology 123

PETER J. LANG, GREGORY A. MILLER, AND DANIEL N. LEVIN

5 Meditation: In Search of a Unique Effect 153

Robert R. Pagano and Stephen Warrenburg

1   *A Reason for Doubting the Existence of Consciousness*

GEORGES REY

I. DEFINITIONS

I was asked, as a philosopher, to address an audience primarily of psychobiologists about the nature of consciousness. Many people—among them, quite likely, many readers of the present volume—might find this a little strange: After all, would a conference of physicists really invite a philosopher to address them on the nature of matter? Or of biologists on the nature of life? Perhaps; but why not? Let me first say something about the sort of thing a philosopher may legitimately have to say, before going on to make what I hope will be some useful, substantive claims of my own.

Notwithstanding a long philosophical tradition to the contrary, I shall not attempt to present here anything in the way of so-called "*a priori* knowledge.*" That is, I shall not be presenting anything that purports to be special, "conceptual" knowledge that is, or can be, justified completely independently of any experiments, or that is irrefutable by them. That tradition has fallen on hard times in this century, and I'm sympathetic to many recent philosophers, notably W. V. Quine (1951/1980) and Hilary Putnam (1962/1975a), who seem to me to have faced up to this; they have developed a conception of knowledge that allows that even the most general claims about the world—even, for example, the claims of logic and mathematics, but certainly the claims associated with philosophy—are not *a priori* and may, at least in principle, come to be revised in the light of continuing empirical theory and research.

A particularly important application of this general view, recently urged by Putnam (1970/1975b,c,d) and Saul Kripke (1972/1980), allows that even our understanding of the meanings of our words may evolve and be revised in the light of empirical findings, and, moreover, that this can occur without its being merely a matter of an arbitrary resti-

GEORGES REY • Division of Humanities, State University of New York at Purchase, Purchase, New York 10577.

pulation of the meaning of those words.[1] Rather, we can regard ourselves as coming, through continuing empirical research, to *discover* the
meanings of many words that we are nonetheless antecedently competent to use. Thus, on this view, did we eventually come to give up
the belief that fire and water are basic elements of the world, discovering
instead that water is (best defined as) H_2O, and that fire is no element
whatsoever; and thus, on this view, do we now look to physics and
biology for at least what may be central to the proper definition of *matter*
and *life*. What Putnam and Kripke have shown is how this is possible;
how, in particular, the *reference* of a term (the thing[s] in the world to
which the term refers) can be fixed even when competent users of the
term are ignorant of its meaning. Roughly, what they cite are some of
the external causal and social considerations that enter, often deci-
sively, into establishing reference somewhat independently of the descriptions that the users may associate with a term. What one does in
general in determining the reference of a term is first to theorize about
how the relevant portion of the world is carved up (i.e., do the science
of that portion of the world) and then to determine what actual thing,
if anything, speakers have been "getting at" in their usage of the term,
in particular, what things have been causally linked to (the majority of)
the social usages of the term. Only then might one provide a genuine
definition of the term that can at the same time provide us with an
insight into the nature of the phenomenon that the term refers to.

It is with this view in mind that I shall therefore refrain here from
presenting anything like a definition of what is at the moment so theoretically obscure a term as *consciousness*. If it is anything at all, it is
whatever empirical scientists—psychologists, psychobiologists, but
probably not merely philosophers—will in the course of their researches
discover it to be.[2]

What, then, might there be left for a philosopher to say on the
topic? Well, many people, perhaps especially empirical scientists, might
be left a little uneasy with the view that consciousness, if it is anything,
is whatever they discover it to be. For one thing, they may not be entirely
sure about just how to proceed. In this respect the situation *is* different
from that of *matter* and *life*. These days, anyway, most scientists seem

---

[1] Schwartz (1977) provided an excellent anthology of the main papers that have introduced
and discussed the many ramifications of this view. For an attempt to develop it as a full
semantic theory, see Devitt (1981).

[2] Thus, I'm very sympathetic to Natsoulas (1978, p. 907) when he insisted that the question
of the definition of *consciousness* is "a thoroughly theoretical one." He recounted a story
of Wolfgang Köhler, who, when asked for his definition of *perception*, replied, "If I could
give you an answer, my life's work would be over." Natsoulas remarked that "Köhler
might have been speaking for generations of perception psychologists yet to come," to
say nothing of the psychobiologists of consciousness.

to know where to look—what sorts of research to undertake—to determine at least roughly what the nature of matter or life might be. Physics and biology are, I take it, pretty firmly established. Not so, evidently, psychology or even psychobiology. There seem to be lingering puzzles and confusions about precisely how to go about it: after all, just what sort of thing is consciousness? How do we find out anything about it in our own, and then in anyone else's, case? What sort of relation could it possibly bear to the brain? How might neurophysiological data really ever have any bearing whatsoever on questions of our mental lives? Wittgenstein (1953/1967) nicely described the "giddiness" we feel when we consider the seemingly

> unbridgeable gulf between consciousness and brain process. . . . When does this feeling occur in the present case? It is when I, for example, turn my attention in a particular way on to my own consciousness, and, astonished, say to myself: THIS is supposed to be produced by a process in the brain!— as it were clutching my forehead. (p. 124e)

There are, that is to say, quite general, abstract, and methodological issues to be considered, issues not immediately resolvable by any particular experiments. And, in present society anyway, it is philosophers who are generally expected to consider them. And so I shall—a few of them anyway. However, that a philosopher is presenting them should not for a moment be taken to imply that only a philosopher could or should present them. Divisions among the disciplines are to my mind just another piece of a generally problematic division of labor in society as a whole.

II. THE CARTESIAN INTUITION

Actually, even what I have said so far about the ultimately empirical character of any definition of *consciousness* might strike many people as methdologically puzzling, perhaps even as outrageous. For if there is one area in which certain sorts of *a priori* claims are particularly tenacious, it's with regard to the mental, especially with regard to the conscious. "I see clearly that there is nothing which is easier for me to know than my mind," remarked Descartes (1641/1911, Vol. 1, p. 157). Thought being "whatever is in us in such a way that we are immediately conscious of it" (1641/1911, Vol. 2, p. 52), he took as one of his certainties, his "clear and distinct idea" of himself as "a thinking thing" (1641/1911, Vol. 1, p. 190). And many in the philosophical and popular traditions since then have readily agreed. While they might not quite regard their belief in their own consciousness as *a priori* knowledge, they would certainly conceive it to be in some analogous way "incorrigible," or

unrevisable in the light of further research. "No matter what your theory
and instruments might say," some people will insist, "they can never
give me reason to think that I am not conscious right here, now." Let
us call this the *Cartesian Intuition*. It is something like this intuition that
Eccles (1966) seems to be articulating when he writes:

> Conscious experience is the immediate and absolute reality. . . . My con-
> scious experience is all that is given to me in my task of trying to understand
> myself; and it is only because of and through my experience that I come to
> know of a world of things and events. (p. 315)

Some might even think that it involved the same sort of understanding
that has often been presumed to be involved in claims to *a priori* knowledge, that is, a knowledge of the meaning of the word. For if you really
doubt that you are conscious, it might be argued, then you just don't
understand the meaning of the word.

Partly for the sake of the general rejection of the *a priori* that I
endorsed above, but also for the sake of a richer understanding of our
mental life, I think it's important to consider ways in which this Cartesian intuition might be mistaken. In particular, I should like to consider
a kind of mistake that I think *might* be involved in our attribution of
consciousness to *anything*. If it is a mistake, then it is a mistake that we
would each be making in his or her own case as well. Recognition of
this as at least a *possibility* should have the effect of loosening the hold
of the Cartesian intuition; and that, I submit, cannot but have a salutary
effect on our thinking about thought generally.

Let me first consider, by way of analogy, the kind of mistake I have
in mind. There is an ancient East Indian theory about the sources of
human fortune and misfortune that has lately gained currency in many
Western circles. According to it, a person's fortunes and misfortunes in
a lifetime are the consequences of her or his "karma," or, roughly, the
"inherited" good or ill of the good and bad deeds performed by the
person in previous lives.[3] Thus, when you win at the races, have many
and good friends, enjoy excellent health, and lead a satisfying life, these
are all the consequences of "good karma"; and when you break a leg,
lose at the races, are betrayed in love, and live miserably, this is all the
result of "bad karma." (I once heard one, presumably extreme, adherent
of the view even claim that the horrors that the Vietnamese suffered
beneath American bombs were also due to their "bad karma.")

[3] I do not pretend here to any serious scholarly understanding of the doctrines of karma
(I presume that my point does not turn on any details of them). What I have sketched
here, however, is entirely consistent with the discussions of the topic in the *Encyclopedia
of Philosophy*, Smart (1967), as well as in Hiriyani (1978). I'm indebted to Jonathan Kolleeny
for the latter reference, as well as for intriguing conversations about the matter.

Now, besides being morally repugnant, this view seems to me to be quite preposterous. But I don't have in mind here any of the usual criticisms that might be raised against it. I'm not, for instance, concerned with whether it's "empirically meaningful," or whether it's experimentally verifiable or falsifiable, or whether *karma* is a properly introduced theoretic term, or even whether the attendant doctrine of reincarnation makes any sense. The view does strike me as meaningful; it conceivably might be true; but it's nonetheless quite preposterous. It's simply too *simplistic*. If we consider in full the actual details of people's various fortunes and misfortunes and what we know about at least the proximate causes of them—if we consider, that is, all that we know about the exigencies of ski slopes, the statistics of horse races, the fickleness of the human heart, the various causes of disease, no less the effects of imperialistic foreign policies—if we seriously consider all these things, then the theory that assimilates all these different causes to one kind of thing, much less a kind of thing that plays any significant moral role, seems implausible in the extreme. How in the world could such a single cause work? How could all these enormously diverse effects, distributed in such scattered quarters, involving such intricate relations to multitudes of other events, possibly be coordinated? Once we examine the actual details of human misfortune and place them in a careful, general theory of the world, we see that there's nothing that plays anything like the role that karma was supposed to play. One might, of course, identify karma with, say, those deeds of the child that form the character of the adult, or perhaps with those deeds of the parent that cause the misfortunes of the child, or with some other causal lines that could be traced from the deeds of one lifetime to the events of another. But surely, such identifications (or "reductions") would be highly artificial and misleading. Too many of the beliefs associated with the term would turn out to be false (e.g., in reincarnation, in the significance of these causal links), and certainly, the result would play a very different social role, particularly in moral reasonings, from the one karma was intended to play. It was posited partly to affirm a moral orderliness in the world that, alas, simply does not obtain. There is nothing that will properly serve for what users of the term were "getting at." Consequently, the term fails to refer. It involved a wrong, excessively simplistic way of looking at things.

What I want to propose here is that the term "consciousness" *might* turn out to be subject to a similar objection. That is, it might turn out to involve an excessively simplistic way of looking at our mental lives, a way that attempts to posit a unity that our mental life simply may not possess.

My strategy will be as follows. I shall consider what, in current theories of mental activity, seem to be distinct mental operations and what seem to be plausible theories of them. I shall then consider in each case the plausibility of regarding each particular operation, with or without the others, as a candidate for the role of consciousness. In each case, I shall consider whether the particular operation(s) could occur *unconsciously*. But especially in order to emphasize their status as real operations in the world, as opposed to processes in some mysterious medium that itself might be regarded as already involving consciousness, I shall also consider whether it would be reasonable to regard *a machine* that performed that operation as thereby conscious. I think that we shall find ourselves in each case extremely uneasy with this proposal, just as someone might find himself or herself uneasy, in each case, were a particular cause of human fortunes to be identified with karma. This particular unease about identifying consciousness in this way with any particular mental operations, or with any combination of them, I shall take to be evidence of a problem with the term *consciousness* similar to the problem I found with the term *karma*. And that, then, will provide us with at least *one* reason for thinking that the term fails to refer, that, indeed, there is no such thing as consciousness. There would simply be nothing in the world the speakers can properly be regarded as "getting at" in their uses of the term.

Someone, of course, might insist that the term *consciousness* be defined before we undertake such an investigation, so that there might be a reasonable way of evaluating the comparisons I shall make. But such an approach misconstrues the problem. For part of the problem is that we really don't have any good definition of *consciousness*. We have a wide variety of usages of the term (and its related grammatical forms), each of which can be both assimilated and distinguished from the others, depending on the purposes at hand: the *Oxford English Dictionary* (OED) (1933) lists 10 "definitions" of *conscious*, 7 of *consciousness*, on the latter of which Natsoulas (1978) expanded, although Ryle (1949) considered only 7 for both. The word does not seem to be *straightforwardly* ambiguous in the way that *bank* and *pride* are. Its usages are all quite intimately related, emphasizing now this, now that aspect of our mental life. Whether those usages mark genuine differences in meaning depends upon whether those aspects are themselves genuinely different aspects; and to decide that is to decide upon some or another *theory* of our mental life (quite as our earlier remarks about meaning might lead us to expect). Perhaps in sorting out the usages of the term, we will want to distinguish different sorts of processes that have been confused, each of them involving consciousness "in a different sense." But perhaps we shall find, as I will attempt to argue we might well find, that there is no clear sense at all that can be attached to the word, in terms of any real phenomena in the world. In any case, those who want to insist on definitions can regard the comparisons that follow as just so many efforts to provide one, with a reason in each case to reject it.

But let me emphasize that I shall not be concerned with establishing such claims *conclusively*. The appropriate evidence, much less the appropriate theory, is not yet available in psychology for conclusive claims about much of anything. I mean only to make certain claims *plausible*, to put them seriously in the running, and so, at least, to undermine the hold of the Cartesian intuition, thereby allowing for a greater freedom of thought about mind.

III. THE COMPUTATIONAL-REPRESENTATIONAL THEORY OF MIND

One of the soundest reasons for taking a particular description of an object seriously, it seems to me, is that the object satisfies laws in which the description figures. Amoebas, for example, can be regarded as literally *alive* since they satisfy many of the laws of living things. Similarly, an object can be regarded as literally possessing a mental life insofar (and perhaps only insofar) as it satisfies psychological laws. Now, to be sure, given the still fetal state of psychology as a science, there really aren't any fully developed psychological laws available. But there are law sketches (cf. Hempel, 1965, pp. 423–425). And among them, few strike me as more central and basic than those that attempt to capture what might be called the *Rational Regularities*: these are the regularities among a creature's states whereby it instantiates the steps of inductive (e.g., particular to general), deductive (e.g., general to particular), and practical (e.g., means–ends) reasoning (see Appendix, Part A). For example, many animals seem to be able to learn the spatial layout of their immediate environment, to discover the location of desired objects in it, and to act in ways that might reasonably lead them to acquire those objects. So far, the best explanation of such remarkable capacities seems to be one that postulates mental processes in the animals whereby they are able to perform at least rudimentary inductions and deductions and are able to base their behavior on some or another form of the practical syllogism; that is, they generally act in a way that they believe will best secure what they most prefer. It seems to me that it is these regularities that justify us ultimately in ascribing beliefs and preferences to anything at all. Were an object not to satisfy them, neither in its behavior nor (more importantly) in its internal processing, I see no other reasonable basis for such ascription, and insofar as an object does satisfy them, I see a very firm basis indeed. In any case, it certainly seems to be the basis we ordinarily exploit in ascribing beliefs and preferences, and many other mental states, in the many useful and insightful ways we do. It is a central part of what Max Weber (1922/1980) intended by "Verstehen" or "empathetic" explanation, and it is what many philosophers have recently come to call "intentional explanation," the creatures (or, more generally, the systems) so explained being "intentional systems" (Dennett, 1971).

I don't by any means intend to suggest that we yet fully understand this form of explanation, much less all the behavior of the explicanda. Great strides have been made in the last century in explicating deductive relations by means of formal logic; shorter strides have been made in understanding the practical relations by means of decision theory; and, as yet, no one seems to have gotten very far at all in answering the notorious riddles of induction (Goodman, 1963). But it is worth noting some recent progress.

One of the major insights into the nature of psychology that has emerged in the last 30 years is that is can be regarded as centrally concerned with *syntax*, or the formal properties of representations. This insight is sustained by (and, in turn, begins to explain) two important properties of mentality. On the one hand there is the famous feature of "intensionality," so prized by Brentano (1874/1964) and his followers (e.g., Chisholm, 1957): mental states like beliefs and preferences (what are called the "propositional attitudes") seem to involve a relation not to an existent thing preferred or believed about, but to something else— an idea, a possibility, a proposition—in any case, a *representation* of something that may or may not turn out to be real. This, at any rate, is what seems to be established by the failure of existential generalization and coreferential substitution into the "that . . ." clause following, e.g., *believes* or *prefers* (see Appendix, Part B). A powerful and convenient medium of such representation is afforded by a syntactically specified set of *sentences*, that is, a formal language. (For this particular way of handling the problem of intensionality see Quine, 1956; Harman, 1973; Fodor, 1975.)

On the other hand, the best theories to date with regard to the rational regularities into which these beliefs and preferences essentially enter are also syntactic. According to various completeness theorems (Henkin, 1949/1969; Kripke, 1959), it can be shown that all deductively valid arguments in quantification theory and modal logic are provable within formal systems; that is, they can be generated by transformation rules defined over entirely syntactically specified objects (see Appendix, Part A). Similar hopes, not all of them entirely forlorn, linger for inductive logic and decision theory. (I use *inductive* here broadly, to include not only principles of enumeration but any "reasonable" relations between evidence and explanatory hypotheses, especially those associated with "abduction," "analysis-by-synthesis," and "inferences to the best explanation"; see, e.g., MacKay, 1951; Harman, 1965; Chomsky, 1972). Insofar as we can obtain such results, "thinking" can be increasingly characterized as a very particular kind of computational process, namely, one that involves *syntactic transformations of representations.*

Put another way, intensionality and rationality—the two properties that seem peculiar to psychological beings—seem to suggest a surprising hypothesis: *thinking is spelling* (and transformations thereof). At any rate, it is this hypothesis that is being taken increasingly seriously by various theorists (e.g., Harman, 1973; Fodor, 1975, 1980), who postulate a "language of thought," encoded and computed on in the nervous systems of psychological beings, as a way to explain their intensional rationality. Fodor (1975) especially has presented impressive arguments for such a view. But whether it is actually true for human beings need not concern us here. It will be enough for our purposes that such a hypothesis provides a *possible* analysis of thought, one possible way that something could manage to think. For if that's true, then, regardless of how people actually do manage to think, it would still be true that any system that could consistently spell and transform strings of symbols in accordance with particular rules would qualify thereby as a thinking thing.

An interesting application of this insight arises when we notice that modern computational machinery provides just such systems. As Gödel (1931/1967) showed in the first part of his Incompleteness Theorem, the system of syntactic transformations necessary for logic and any finitely axiomitizable theory expressible in it can be mirrored by functions definable in elementary arithmetic. And any elementary (i.e., primitive recursive) arithmetic function can demonstrably be computed by a Turing machine; that is, it can be computed mechanically (see Appendix, Part C). It follows that, in principle, a machine could generate the theorems of any finitely axiomitizable theory. In particular, it could generate the theorems of almost any system of deduction, induction, or decision theory that anyone cared to construct. Thus, if the above hypothesis about mentality's being syntactic is correct, then one could, in principle, construct a machine that could think.

A perhaps more surprising point is that it might not be so remote a possibility in practice, either. In particular, it seems to me to be entirely feasible (although, for reasons I shall come to, not especially worthwhile) to render an existing computing machine intentional by providing it with a program that would include the following:

1. The alphabet, formation, and transformation rules for quantified modal logic (the system's "language of thought").
2. The axioms for your favorite inductive logic and/or abductive

system of hypotheses, with a "reasonable" function for selecting among them on the basis of given input.

3. The axioms of your favorite decision theory, and some set of basic preferences.
4. Mechanical inputs, via sensory transducers, for Clauses 2 and 3.
5. Mechanical connections that permit the machine to realize its outputs (e.g., its "most preferred" basic act descriptions).

Any computer that functioned according to such a program would, I submit, realize significant Rational Regularities, complete with intensionality. Notice, for example, that it would be entirely appropriate— and probably unavoidable—for us to *explain* and *predict* its behavior and internal states on the basis of those regularities. It would be entirely reasonable, that is to say, for us to adopt toward it what Dennett (1971) has called the "intentional stance." Unlike Dennett, however, I see no reason not to take the resulting ascription of beliefs and preferences entirely *literally*. For, again, what better reason to take a description of an object seriously than that the object satisfies laws into which that description essentially enters? We would seem to have the best reason in the world, therefore, for regarding the computer so programmed as a genuinely thinking thing.

Caveat emptor: for all its rationality and intensionality, there is every reason to think that such a machine would, at least these days, be colossally *stupid*. Although it would certainly shine here and there in deductive logic, and it would always do precisely whatever it deemed best, it would hardly be very worldly wise. And that's mostly because we simply don't know yet how really, to spell out the *reasonable* of the proposed program's Clause 2: we don't yet have any very good idea of what all *our* actual, apparently quite ingenious inductive principles might be. Philosophers have proposed some that, within certain narrow bounds, are fairly plausible (e.g., simple enumeration, Baysian metrics, simplicity orderings, and principles of conservativism and entrenchment); but we know they really aren't in the ballpark for dealing with the full complexity of inputs that our environments provide. But still, they are pretty clearly "reasonable." And they provide, therefore, a fairly rich basis—particularly in conjunction with the far more satisfactory deductive and practical regularities of Clauses 1 and 3—for serious explanation and prediction of the computer's states and behaviors in terms of its preferences and beliefs. Bad reasoning, to a point, is still reasoning. I see no reason to think that we can't right now devise programs like Clauses 1–5 that would be at least good enough to get us up to that point (which is not to suggest that, given the system's stupidity, it would actually be worth doing).

For our purposes here, what the possibility of such a machine does is to underscore a point that has been gradually emerging from a century's work in psychology: that, contrary to the spirit of Descartes, the letter of Locke (1690/1961, Book II, Chapter 1, Para. 19), most of the definitions in the OED, and the claims of many theorists down to the present day (see below), *consciousness must involve something more than mere thought*. However clever a machine programmed with Clauses 1–5 might become, counting thereby as a thinking thing, surely it would not also count thereby as *conscious*. The program is just far too trivial. Moreover, we are already familiar with systems satisfying at least Clauses 1–5 that we also emphatically deny are conscious: there are all those unconscious neurotic systems postulated in so many of us by Freud, and all those surprisingly intelligent, but still unconscious, subsystems for perception and language postulated in us by contemporary cognitive psychology. (Some evidence of the cognitive richness of unconscious processing is provided by the interesting review of such material in Nisbett & Wilson, 1977, but especially by such psycholinguistic experiments as that by Lackner & Garrett, 1973, in which subliminal linguistic material provided to one ear biased subjects in their understanding of ambiguous sentences provided to the other ear.) In all of these cases we are, I submit, quite reasonably led to ascribe beliefs, preferences, and sometimes highly elaborate thought processes to a system on the basis of the Rational Regularities, despite the fact that the systems involved are often not the least bit "conscious" of any such mental activity at all. It is impossible to imagine these psychological theories getting anywhere without the ascription of unconscious content—and it is equally difficult to imagine any animals getting anywhere without the exploitation of it. Whatever consciousness will turn out to be, it will pretty certainly need to be distinguished from the thought processes we ascribe on the basis of the rational regularities.

How easily this point can be forgotten, neglected, or missed altogether is evidenced by the sorts of proposals about the nature of consciousness one finds in some of the recent psychobiological literature. The following seem to be representative:

> Consciousness is usually defined by the ability: (1) to appreciate sensory information; (2) to react critically to it with thoughts or movements; (3) to permit the accumulation of memory traces. (Moruzzi, 1966)

> Perceptions, memories, anticipatory organization, a combination of these factors into learning—all imply rudimentary consciousness. (Knapp, 1976)

> Modern views . . . regard human conscious activity as consisting of a number of major components. These include the reception and processing (recoding) of information, with the selection of its most important elements and retention of the experience thus gained in the memory; enunciation of the task

or formulation of an intention, with the preservation of the corresponding modes of activity, the creation of a pattern or model of the required action, and production of the appropriate program (plan) to control the selection of necessary actions; and finally the comparison of the results of the action with the original intention . . . with correction of the mistakes made. (Luria, 1978)

Consciousness is a process in which information about multiple individual modalities of sensation and perception is combined into a unified, multidimensional representation of the state of the system and its environment and is integrated with information about memories and the needs of the organism, generating emotional reactions and programs of behavior to adjust the organism to its environment. (John, 1976)

What I find astonishing about such proposals is that they are all more-or-less satisfiable by almost *any* information-processing system, for precisely what modern computational machinery is designed to do is to receive, process, unify, and retain information; create (or "call") patterns, models, and subroutines to control its activity; and, by all means, to compare the results of its action with its original intention in order to adjust its behavior to its environment. This latter process is exactly what the "feedback" that Wiener (1954) built into his homing rocket was for! Certainly, most of the descriptions in these proposals are satisfied by any recent game-playing program (see, e.g., Berliner, 1980). And if it's genuine "modalities," "thoughts," "intentions," "perceptions," or "representations" that are wanted, then, as I've argued, supplementing the program with Clauses 1–5 will suffice, but without rendering anything a whit more conscious. (Of course, these terms, especially *sensory* and *experience*, might be interpreted as *presupposing* consciousness; but then the above accounts would be circular. The only terms that may not be applicable to the machines I've so far considered are *sensation* and *emotion*. I'll return to these terms later.)

Something more is required. But what might that be? Well, there are many different sorts of proposals that have been or might be made, but what is disturbing about all of the ones that I have encountered is that they seem to involve either very trivial additions to Clauses 1–5 or absolutely no additions whatsoever. Let's consider some of the more plausible ones.

A natural extension of the notion of an intentional system, of the sort that we have been considering, has elsewhere been developed by Dennett (1976) into what we might call the notion of an "*n*-order intentional system." A "first-order" intentional system is one that has beliefs and preferences by virtue of its satisfying the rational regularities in something like the manner just described. A "second-order" intentional system is a first-order system that, in addition, has beliefs and preferences *about beliefs and preferences*. It is the sort of intentional system that might, for example, engage in deliberately deceptive behavior, attempting to satisfy some of its own preferences by manipulating the beliefs and preferences of some other intentional system. An "n-order intentional system" is just a generalization of these notions: it is a system that has beliefs and preferences about beliefs and preferences about beliefs and preferences . . . to any arbitrary degree n of such nestings.

This might be regarded as a promising suggestion about the nature of consciousness until one reads, as I recently did, about some relatively trivial work in computer science that was done by Brown (1974) and Schmidt and D'Addami (1973) at Rutgers University. They have very neatly devised a program called the "Believer System" that essentially exploits the Rational Regularities as a basis for explaining the behavior of persons in given stories. For example, from descriptions of someone gathering together some logs and rope and subsequently building a raft, the program constructs (by iterations of means–ends reasoning) the motive that the agent wanted to build a raft, as well as a plan to the effect that he believed that gathering together some logs and ropes was the best available means of doing so. The program is hardly very imaginative. But then neither are we much of the time when we ascribe beliefs and preferences to each other on what appears to be similar basis. The perhaps surprising moral of this research would seem to be that if a system is intentional at all, it would seem to be a relatively small matter to render it n-order intentional as well. What one would do, essentially, is allow the program at some juncture to "call" (or access) itself in such a fashion that it is able to ascribe this very same "Believer" program to the agent as part of that agent's plan. Given that every time it would reach that juncture, it would always be able (say, on certain specified conditions) to further call itself in this way, it would be able to ascribe such ascriptions, and such ascriptions of such aspirations, indefinitely, to a depth of nesting limited only by its memory capacity. (Cf. the "bluffing" games, in which one always needs to be prepared to suppose that one's opponent has foreseen the reasoning one has just engaged in.) We might call this extension of the Believer System:

6. The recursive believer system.

It is the very paradigm of the sort of program that is realizable on existing machines. Given that the Rational Regularities afford a sufficient basis for the ascription of beliefs and preferences, it would seem that a machine programmed with Clauses 1–6 would be capable of having beliefs and preferences about beliefs and preferences to any arbitrary depth of nesting. That is to say, it would be relatively trivial to program an existing machine to be n-order intentional.

Would *it* be conscious? I think not. Dennett (1978, pp. 279–280) himself remarks on a number of cases in which the demonstrable presence of such nested reasonings does not at all require the system's consciously entertaining them. On the contrary, people tend to be quite poor at *consciously* entertaining merely third-order intentions. For example, in a famous analysis of meaning, Grice (1957, p. 385) argues that "A meant something by x" is roughly equivalent to "A intended the utterance of x to produce some effect in an audience by means of the (audience's) recognition of this intention"; about which Dennett remarks:

> Before Grice, were one asked: "Did you intend your audience to recognize your intention to provoke that response in him?" one would most likely have retorted: "I intended nothing so devious. I simply intended to inform him that I wouldn't be home for supper" (or whatever). So it seems that if these complicated intentions underlay our communicating all along, they must have been unconscious intentions. Indeed, a perfectly natural way of responding to Grice's papers is to remark that *one was not aware* of doing these things when one communicated. (p. 280)

Or consider an example of the "reciprocal perspectives" that Laing, Phillipson, and Lee (1966) find so crucial in explaining familial interactions:

> From the point of view of the subject, the starting point is often between the second and third order level of perspective. Jill thinks that Jack thinks that she does not love him, that she neglects him, that she is destroying him, and so on, although she says she does not think she is doing any of these things. . . . She may express fears lest he think that she thinks he is ungrateful to her for all that she is doing, when she wants him to know that she does *not* think that he thinks that she thinks he thinks she does not do enough. (pp. 30–31)

These sorts of deeply nested intentions probably affect our behavior efficiently only so long as we are *not* struggling to make ourselves conscious of them. In any case, the authors go on to discuss examples of responses on Rorschach and intelligence tests in which, they argue, the responses were often affected by unconscious reciprocal perspectives (1966, pp. 42–44). It is doubtful that *n*-order intentionality will provide us the condition we are seeking on something's possessing consciousness.

As these last examples also show, the capacity for "*self*-consciousness," or reflection on one's *own* thought processes, will not be much help either. At any rate, having a concept of oneself would seem to involve nothing more than being *n*-order intentional with the ability to refer to oneself, that is, System A's having beliefs and preferences about System A, that is, itself. But if System A can have beliefs and preferences about some System B's beliefs and preferences—that is, if System A is second-order intentional at all—what possible obstacle could there be to its having beliefs and preferences about System A's—that is, its own—beliefs and preferences? At most, it might need a specially functioning phoneme in its language of thought that would serve to link itself as receptor of its inputs to itself as originator of its outputs, rather as "I" does in English (cf. Castaneda, 1968; Perry, 1979). But this is just to put a particular constraint on its use of a particular phoneme, a constraint not different in kind from the sorts of constraints that might be also put on other pronouns and proper names that any first-order intentional system would have to include. So "self-consciousness" would seem to add nothing to the conditions already captured by Clauses 1–6. Moreover, it should be abundantly clear that many of a person's beliefs and preferences about herself or himself are often unconscious, and so the condition fails in any case to capture what we're after.

It is worth pausing here to notice that, contrary to widespread rumor, nothing in the development of modern logic prevents effective self-reference. To be sure, paradoxical sentences can be produced by self-reference—in conjunction with other assumptions about logic and set theory. But what such sentences are standardly taken to show are simply the surprising problems with those other assumptions. Thus, Russell's paradox proved the nonexistence of a certain set, and Gödel's "Incompleteness Theorem," the unprovability within a system of a certain truth. In fact, if modern logic has shown anything about self-reference, it is its relative triviality and *unavoidability* (see especially Smullyan, 1957/1969, but on all of this, the Appendix, Part D). Russell's conclusion depends on a certain slightly surprising property of *any* two-place relation, and Gödel's theorem exploits the fact that, at least *through a numerical code*, sentences of arithmetic can be constructed that quite clearly refer to themselves. Moreover, contrary to Globus (1976, p. 290), this self-reference does not require "a system of extraordinary richness": any system adequate to express arithmetic will do. The machines I have been imagining (almost any existing computers) are more than adequate for that.

Talk of reference, though, might well remind one of natural language. Elsewhere, Dennett (1968, pp. 118–119) regarded this as an indication of consciousness, or what he called "awareness$_1$": "A is aware$_1$ that p at time t if and only if p is the content of the input of A's speech center at time t," as distinct from "awareness$_2$," which involves merely all the unconscious mental capacities we have been so far considering. Perhaps it would be more to our present purposes to put the *p* into the Language of Thought and have it merely be stored in a "buffer memory" to which the speech center has normally reliable access (cf. Dennett, 1978, p. 156); and we might further require that the sentences in such a location include especially second-order self-ascriptions of psychological states (the internal translations of, e.g., "I think the light is on" or "I'd like some lemonade"). Such a proposal certainly accords with our pretty strong intuition that consciousness has something to do with reportability: after all, what persuades us that an agent is *not* conscious of some mental state that we independently see reason to ascribe is his or her inability to report on it. So it would appear that this proposal might plausibly afford a *necessary* condition on consciousness. But would it be sufficient?

Well, it seems to be disturbingly easy to imagine programming existing computational machinery to have the capacity to report in a public language on at least some of its own mental states. Most machines already possess one or another form of external language: the programming languages with which programmers ordinarily interact with the machine, as well as, increasingly often, one or another piece of an actual natural language, such as English—as in Winograd's (1972) SHRDLU program, or in Weizenbaum's (1965) notorious ELIZA program, which is designed to provide roughly the responses of a Rogerian psychotherapist. To be sure, no one has quite yet captured *full English*: its syntax is pretty exasperating, and its semantics seems in general to be inseparable from the worldly wisdom of English speakers. But we have, I believe, pretty good reason to think that the syntax will be recursively generatable, and that at least the fragments of it with which we normally contend are virtually recursive and decidable (else, how do *we* manage to decide it?), and so programmable on existing machines. The problem of our worldly wisdom is simply the aforementioned problem of understanding our complex and ingenious inductions. Pending progress there, one probably wouldn't be able to have a very stimulating and far-ranging conversation with any existing machine (although consider the surprises that Berliner, 1980, describes the programmers themselves as having experienced with regard to the championship moves of their backgammon program!). But one could probably do as well with regard to introspection as one does with the vast majority of human beings. All one would need to do would be to supplement the program that includes Clauses 1–6 with:

> 7. A fragment of English adequate to describe or express the mental states entered in executing Clauses 1–6, descriptions that are produced as a reliable consequence of being in those states.

Indeed, one might just introduce into Clauses 1–6 an instruction to store temporarily in a special, easily accessible location (the aforementioned "buffer memory"?) a description in the machine's language of thought of every mental state it enters, precisely when it enters it. This description could then be compiled into the fragment of English supplied by Clause 7 whenever an "introspective report" is requested (or otherwise motivated). For example, on entering the state of believing that a light is on, the machine might automatically store an internal translation of "I believe a light is on," which translation is accessed and compiled into the fragment of English, and the result printed out, if the machine is requested or otherwise motivated to do so. Moreover, since because of Clause 6 it is already *n*-order intentional, it could even process and respond to, for example, requests with just the sort of complex, nested intentions that, as I mentioned earlier, writers such as Grice (1957) (see also Schiffer, 1972) have argued are essential to the "nonnatural meaning" characteristic of human linguistic communication (that is, it might respond to requests only when, for example, it intended to produce a certain belief in the requester by means of the requester's recognition of this intention as the cause of its response). Remember that the syntax and semantics needed for such communication of at least these sorts of basic introspective reports seem to be quite managably limited, and isolable from the obviously as yet unmanageable syntax and semantics of full English. Conversing with such a machine would be quite like talking with an extremely unimaginative—but unusually self-perceptive—human being, who knew only about his or her own psychological states. But it would be conversing with a fully functioning introspector, nonetheless.

So, would a machine programmed, now, with Clauses 1–7 be *conscious*? It seems preposterous to think so. If one wasn't inclined to think that Clauses 1–6 were sufficient for consciousness, it is extremely difficult to see that just adding Clause 7 should make *that* much difference. One would be adding little more than an odd, special-purpose compiler. Practically every computer in the country could be rendered conscious thereby in about a week!

There are further mechanisms and processes to which one might try to turn for a suitable basis for consciousness. The mechanisms of attention and short-term memory might seem particularly promising. Human beings and many animals seem to be endowed with a capacity to concentrate their cognitive processing in one area or modality or stimulation to the relative exclusion of others. There has been a great deal of research in this respect on short-term memory (Miller, 1956) and on the nature of the selective filtering of signals (Kahneman, 1973), and on the relation of such filtering to feedback and "feedforward" (or plan-related) processes (Pribram, 1980). Some writers, noting the role that conscious activity seems often to play in the deliberate revision of plans, have suggested that this be taken as a defining condition of consciousness. This may have been what Luria had in mind in the passage of his that I quoted earlier, and it seems to be what Piaget (1976) had in mind when he wrote:

If a well-adapted action requires no awareness, it is directed by sensori-motor regulations which can then automate themselves. When on the contrary an active regulation becomes necessary, which presupposes intentional choices between two or several possibilities, there is an awareness in function of these needs themselves. (p. 41)

Indeed, Davidson (1980) adds:

The formulation of new goals and the modification of habitual action patterns may be facilitated by conscious involvement; in fact, they may require it, although an adequate empirical test for this suggestion may be difficult to achieve. (p. 40)

But merely an empirical test won't be sufficient for our purpose. The trouble with these further sorts of processes, at least so described, as candidates for consciousness is that they really don't seem to make any further demands on a machine than those we've already been imagining. Most machines with sizeable memory stores necessarily have a limited number of centralized work addresses, in which material from long-term storage, as well as any present inputs to the system, can temporarily be placed for short-term, "on-line" processing. That the capacity of these addresses is quite limited, and that the selection of content for them is contingent on the plan (or program) being implemented, which in turn is sensitive to feedback, seems to me to go without saying for any but the most modest machines. Certainly any machine equipped to deal with Clauses 1–7 would need to be designed in such a fashion: consider the "buffer memory" supplied to execute Clause 7. Such centralized work addresses might, of course, be precisely the place at which high-level decisions in a program (e.g., whether to continue a particular subroutine or whether to call a new one) might be made, causing the machine to make "intentional choices between two or several possibilities," to "formulate new goals," and thereby to "modify its habitual action patterns." But where in any of this is there any need of consciousness? Again, were it sufficient for consciousness, almost every computer in the country would be conscious already!

"But," the reader has perhaps been anxious to ask from the start of the discussion, "what about *sensations*? Surely any device capable of *them* would thereby qualify as conscious." Here the issues are, to be sure, a little complicated, but still, I think, not, in the end, very helpful. First of all, it should be noticed that we've already allowed, in Clause 3, for sensory transducers that could convert, for example, electromagnetic waveforms into patterns of signals that would presumably be encoded in the machine's Language of Thought. Insofar as these signals might be responsible, by means of the inductive processing involved in Clause 2, for confirming and disconfirming beliefs about the lay of the land and the probable shape of things to come, it would certainly be plausible to regard the entire process as at least a *functional equivalent* of visual perception. Indeed, we might understand Clause 3 to include sensors that would also signal to it the presence of certain sorts of damage to its surface and parts of its interior. These signals might well be processed in such a way as to cause in the machine a sudden, extremely high-preference assignment to the implementation of any subroutine that the machine believed would be likely to reduce the further reception of such signals. That, I submit, would amount to very nearly a functional equivalent of pain. Moreover, insofar as these processes could—either by mistake or by program design—be in various ways self-induced, the machine would be subject to the functional equivalents of hallucinations and/or its own deliberate imaginings.

But, of course, it is the *sensations*—the colors, the pains, the hallucinations—*themselves* that are important, not mere "functional equivalents" of them. Most of us would pretty surely balk at claiming that a machine that ran on Clauses 1–7 alone should be regarded as *really* having the experience of *red* just because it has a transducer that emits a characteristic signal, with some of the usual cognitive consequences, whenever it is stimulated with red light. But I'm not at all sure what entitles us to our reservation. For what else is there? In particular, what else is there that we are so sure is essential to what happens with us? How do we know *we* "have the experience of red" over and above our undergoing just some such process as I have described in this machine? What more do we know about ourselves in this regard than that we, too, enter a characteristic state when certain of our transducers are stimulated with red light? Certainly, it's not because we have some well-confirmed theory of sense experience that distinguishes us from such a machine!

Whether or not it's particularly well-confirmed, something like a theory with a long tradition to it (see Alston, 1971); and for an important recent discussion, Block (1980) claims that we have some sort of "privileged access" to such experiences, that we have, for example, "direct, incorrigible" knowledge of the qualitative feel of our experiences. Now, I'm not sure precisely how this claim is to be made out. If it is the claim that it has often been taken to be (see, e.g., Williams, 1978, pp. 73 & 306) that believing one is having a sensation entails one's having it, then it would seem we would be forced to concede that the machine we've imagined really does have them after all. For, what with its transducers, inductions, and nested self-ascriptions, it could certainly acquire sensory beliefs, for example, that it *seemed* to see red; and *that* belief would be very hard to distinguish from the belief that it's having a red sensation (indeed, in some accounts, e.g., Sellars, 1956/1963, these beliefs *are* indistinguishable). But if something more than that mere belief is required—say, some condition that somehow guarantees the presence of privileged access and/or direct acquaintance—then, the question arises how we can be so sure that *we* satisfy that condition. Or do we have privileged access to our privileged access as well, direct acquaintance not only with our sensations but with *the fact of our direct acquaintance?* I forbear from following out the regress that this particular line of reasoning suggests.

Clearly, some further condition *is* needed, beyond merely believing that one has a sensation or feeling, for one to qualify as genuinely having a sensation or feeling. And it is not implausible to suppose that some such further condition might also serve to distinguish humans with sensations from machines without them. Elsewhere (Rey, 1980) I have argued that one thing that may very likely distinguish us from any computers yet envisaged is some of our emotions. For there is strong psychobiological evidence that the capacity for at least certain of our emotions (e.g., depression, anger, and fear) depends on the presence in our brains of certain hormones and neuroregulators (e.g., norepinepherine and testosterone), or at least on certain as-yet-unknown properties of those substances. We have absolutely no reason to believe that, whatever those properties turn out to be, they will be available in existing computational hardware. To the contrary, given the extraordinarily high level of functional abstraction on which the cognitive processes for which existing machines are designed can be defined, it would be an amazing coincidence if they were. (William Lycan, 1981, has pointed out that in general, one would expect our various psychological faculties to be characterizable on many different levels of functional abstraction from the basic physical properties of the brain.)

Now, I think it would be rash to clutch at these emotions and their associated hormones and neuroregulators as providing the conditions on consciousness that we are ultimately seeking: our feelings, after all, are not always conscious, and moments without feeling are not moments of unconsciousness. However, it is not implausible to suppose that a similar dependence on noncognitive properties of our bodies and brains may be essential to our having the particular sorts of sensations and qualitative states that we seem to have (see Block, 1980; Searle, 1981). But, of course, this dependence would need to be spelt out. At the moment, it is, to my knowledge, utterly obscure how we might do that, much less just what those properties might be.

In any case, a consequence of this possibility would be that we would lose most of the epistemological privileges that have traditionally been attached to our sensory life. For the truth of a person's beliefs about his or her own sensations would depend on the presence of these special bodily properties, and so it would be as open to empirical investigation and doubt as the truth of any neurophysiological claim. There might, of course, be what might be called *empirical privileged access*: by careful correlation of people's reports with the appropriate properties of their brains, we might discover that some people are and some people are not reliable reporters of their qualitative states. But there would always be the very real, if eerie, possibility that a person could be dead wrong: he could swear up and down that he was having even quite painful sensations, but be told truthfully by the best psychobiological theory and examination of his brain that, lacking as he did the appropriate properties in his brain, he was sadly mistaken, that he really wasn't experiencing painful sensations at all, but only "functional equivalents" of them. I remind the reader that this is precisely the position in which we were only too willing to leave our computer, helplessly programmed with merely Clauses 1–7.

IV. THE PROBLEM OF CONSCIOUSNESS

Many of these latter considerations can be applied directly to the issue of consciousness itself. In this chapter, I have sketched a way in which an existing computational machine might come to realize, at least in kind if not in degree, most of what have been proposed as our unique psychological capacities. Supplied with Clauses 1–7, the computer would appear to be capable of having beliefs and preferences (to an indefinite degree of nesting), self-reference, a public language, introspective reports, and of processing transduced information about the state of the world and its own body—all apparently without consciousness. The only significant features of our mental life (other than consciousness) that such a machine would at the present time unquestionably lack are our powers of "induction," our seemingly limitless ingenuity in appreciating the world (although see Chomsky, 1976); and, as I lately mentioned, it would also lack the capacity for many of our emotions. But surely, those emotions are not essential to consciousness (they can be unconscious, and we can be conscious without them); and as for induction, well, it is somehow difficult to believe that our consciousness consists merely in our *cleverness*. How clever do we have to be? What does each of us know about our own cleverness that gives us such confidence in our consciousness? (Remember that, as shown in Berliner, 1980, at least with respect to backgammon, the cleverness of machines seems now to exceed that of humans.) In any case, if you are the slightest inclined—as I must confess that I am—to doubt that the machine that I have described possesses consciousness, then I submit that you ought to begin to be equally inclined to doubt that you possess consciousness yourself. For the question seems to me unavoidable: What in the world makes you so sure that you are not just such a machine, cleverly constructed out of fleshlike plastics at MIT and surreptitiously slipped to your parents on the day that they say you were born? What particular kind of capacity do you know that you have that the machine lacks—or could not come to have by essentially trivial modifications— that is arguably relevant to being conscious? To be sure, it *seems* vividly to you, as it did to Descartes, that you are not such a machine, that you are not a mere "automaton," but, in addition, a consciously thinking, sensing thing. But, of course, so might it seem precisely to any such machine. Indeed, one could surely, with very little trouble, supplement Clauses 1–7 with

8. The Cartesian intuition and related claims of epistemological privilege.

(They are hardly very subtle, complex, or dependent on ingenious in- ductions about the world!) The machine could print out "I see clearly that there is nothing which is easier for me to know than my own mind" and proceed to insist that "No matter what your theory and instruments might say, they can never give me reason to think that I am not conscious right here, now." After all, these latter beliefs are just so many more, relatively trivial second-order beliefs.

I see no way to rule out *a priori* the possibility that I am not such a machine. Insofar as I cannot rule out the possibility that such a machine would not be conscious, I certainly cannot rule out the possibility that I am not conscious right here, now, either. Reflections on the possibility of programming an existing computer with Clauses 1–8 provide, then, at least one way in which the Cartesian intuition might begin to be undermined.

It is worth pausing here to consider some of the more traditional suggestions that people have made about consciousness, especially as they are designed to distinguish persons from machines. Descartes begat a long line of metaphysical "dualists"—of whom Popper and Eccles (1979) are perhaps the most recent proponents—who would locate con- sciousness in the presence of some special, "immaterial" substance or "emergent" property, which inheres somehow in our heads and may be the source of our "free will" and "creativity." Apart from what seems to be an inescapable vagary that attaches to such suggestions, there is the embarrassing lack of evidence of any such special substance, or even of any causal breaks or insufficiencies in the physical processes that appear to produce our behaviors. It may be (although I doubt it) that a necessary condition for moral responsibility and genuine creativity is that the agent's acts be produced, say, by the spontaneous activity of some special substance, in a fashion "free from causal law." If so, then, perhaps, so much the worse for moral responsibility and genuine creativity. Or, at any rate, so much the worse for our ordinarily knowing just which of whose acts, and when, fill such a bill. If it be insisted that we do "just know" that we *are* free and creative, filled with such special substances and occasionally free from causal law, then we may wonder what entitles us to be additionally so sure that the computer programmed with Clauses 1–8 is *not*. Maybe Clauses 1–8 are all you need; the rest "emerges." Traditional dualistic claims seem, more often than not, to consist in little more than a dogmatic insistence on the fundamental difference between people and machines.

A clearer and more plausible traditional suggestion has recently been revived by Gareth Matthews (1977) (see also Ziff, 1958; Searle, 1981). Drawing on Aristotle, he submits that a necessary condition on something's being conscious is that it be *alive*. Now, this does seem to accord with many of our intuitions and explains why we balk at ascribing consciousness to the machines I have imagined, and perhaps to any machine at all. And perhaps, if something realizing Clauses 1–8 were also alive, then our reluctance to regard it as conscious would diminish. But it seems to me that several objections could be lodged against such a condition. In the first place, the very sort of worry that we raised earlier with regard to physiological conditions of emotions and of sensations could be raised here as well, for we could then ask, each in our own case, how we are so certain that *we* are alive, and not merely some artifact, like the computer that I have been imagining, that only *thinks* it is alive. Thus, as perhaps Matthews himself intends, the Cartesian Intuition would still be undermined. But one might then go on to wonder, as with these other physiological conditions, precisely *why* the condition of being alive is so important: What is the *connection* between being alive and being conscious? What is it about life processes that makes such a crucial contribution? Pending answers to such questions, it would be difficult to resist the suggestion that this condition is arbitrarily chauvinistic, as unprincipled an appeal to one's personal preferences in these matters as that of Pribram (1976), when he wrote:

> I tend to view animals, especially furry animals, as conscious—not plants, not inanimate crystals, not computers. This might be termed the "cuddliness criterion" for consciousness. My reasons are practical: it makes little difference at present whether computers are conscious or not. (p. 298)

One can imagine some one race, or the people of some one historical time (cf. Jaynes, 1977), or certainly some one *species* making similar appeals to their particular sort of cuddliness and practicality on behalf of restricting consciousness to *their* particular group. But in any case, I hope some of the considerations I have raised in my discussion here have made it clear why it does make a difference to continuing research on consciousness whether computers are conscious or not. We might, for example, want to know *what, if anything, is being researched*. Moreover, we might want to know precisely what even *in a living thing* distinguishes conscious from unconscious mental processes. Such issues are not settled merely by reflecting on one's preference for living things.

Of course, if life is *not* essential to consciousness, then perhaps one *ought* after all to regard the computer programmed with Clauses 1–8 as conscious. However, for all my faith in the mechanical duplicability of the other specific aspects of mentation that I have discussed, I must confess that I find myself quite unable to do so. I am unnerved, and I find most other people are unnerved, by the possibility of these machines and steadfastly refuse to regard them as at all conscious. It simply seems impossible to take their mental life all *that* seriously; to *care* accordingly about them; to feel morally obliged not to treat them in certain ways (not to unplug them, not to frustrate their preferences); to accord them any sorts of civil rights. It's as though they lack a certain essential "inner light," an inner light that we tend to think awakens our mindless bodies and bathes all our thoughts and feelings in such a glow as to render them immediately and incorrigibly accessible to our inner, introspective eye. We see this inner light, each of us, only in our own case; we are able only to "infer" it, however uncertainly, in the case of other human beings (and perhaps some animals); and we are unwilling to ascribe it to any machine.[4]

As I draw this familiar picture out and compare it with the details of our actual psychology that I have considered, it seems to me suddenly appallingly crude, as oversimple a conception of human psychology as the idea of karma is as an account of human misery. Just what sort of thing is this "inner light" supposed to be? What could possibly be its source? How is it "perceived," by each in her or his own case, and by

---

[4] Something very like this myth of an "inner light" is explored at some length in Rorty (1979, pp. 42–69), where he discusses what he regards as the traditional belief in "Our Glassy Essence" (he draws this term from Shakespeare and C. S. Pierce). Relying on a suggestive discussion in Matson (1966), Rorty claims that this belief and, indeed, the very notion of "conscious states" itself were not part of ancient thought but are rather something of an "invention" of Cartesian philosophy. In that book (Chapter 2) and elsewhere (Rorty, 1965, 1970), he also develops what has come to be called the view of *eliminative materialism*, or the view that mental entities do not really exist. The view I am entertaining in the present paper might be called *eliminativist* with regard to consciousness, although (ontologically) *reductionist* with regard to, for example, propositional attitudes (see Appendix, Part B).

no one in anyone else's? What is its relation to long-term and short-term memory? To attention, introspection, our ideas of others' ideas about us? To our various sorts of reasoning? To our use of language? Somehow these sorts of *detailed* questions seem inappropriate, a little like asking of a Fundamentalist, "Just how did God go about creating the world in six days? How did his saying 'Let there be light' actually cause there to be light?" Or like asking a believer in karma precisely *how* the distributions of fortune are matched to the deeds of earlier lives. Perhaps the problem is better seen the other way around: Once we *have* accounts of the various processes I have mentioned, *what is added by "consciousness"*? What further light does this "inner light" shed on our minds? Perhaps there is something. But, perhaps too, as we found in the case of karma, there is nothing *more*, and it would simply be wrongheaded to identify consciousness with any of these actual processes, singly or together. None of them really play the role that consciousness, particularly on the above picture, traditionally was supposed to play. There would seem to be no actual thing or process (or even "function"[5]) that our past usages of the term have been "getting at." In view of the claims about meaning and reference that I endorsed at the beginning of this paper, that would seem to me to afford at least *one* reason for doubting that the term refers, that is, a reason for doubting that there really is any such thing as consciousness at all.

My point is, of course, merely that the ordinary belief in consciousness *might* turn out to be problematic and mistaken in this way. And that is all that is needed to fully undermine the Cartesian intuition that anyone knows, in a way that is "absolute" and can never be refuted, that she or he is conscious. *The concept of consciousness might turn out to involve an excessively simplistic way of viewing our complicated mental lives, and that is a way that we could be mistaken in thinking of ourselves, or of anything, as conscious.*

Let us be clear about precisely what the consequences would be were we to agree that there is no such thing as consciousness. It would by no means entail any extravagant behavioristic claim that no mentalistic talk at all is scientifically respectable. I used mental terms throughout my descriptions of the capacities of people and of machines, and I doubt very much whether they could ever be reasonably eliminated. But one needn't be committed thereby to *every* piece of our prescientific mentalistic talk, or to finding for every such prescientific term some

---

[5] While appearing to advocate a view like that being entertained here, that consciousness does not exist, William James (1912, p. 4) went on to explain that he meant "only to deny that the word stands for an entity, but to insist most emphatically that it does stand for a function." But when I suggest that there may be no such thing, I mean "no such thing *whatsoever*."

postscientific equivalent. Some terms may just have to go, as *angels* did in an account of planetary motion, and as *satan, witches,* and *karma* did in our accounts of misery and misfortune.

Nor would one be committed to abandoning the term in ordinary talk. If all the term *conscious* is ordinarily meant to indicate is that a person is, say, awake and capable of intentional, attended activity, on which she or he might ordinarily be able to report, then the term is clearly harmless enough, just as the term *karma* would be, if all it were used to mean is something like "bad character." I think the term *conscious* is often used merely in this way; and it would appear to be the usage that underlies such claims as those of Moruzzi (1966) and Penfield (1975) that locate consciousness in merely the activation of the reticular formation or the "centrencephalic system." We need only notice also that, in such a usage, a computer programmed with Clauses 1–7, if my earlier arguments are correct, would seem to qualify as conscious, too.

It would seem that it is only when we begin to *theorize* about consciousness as a thing or a process that this innocuous, ordinary usage begins to slip away from us and begins to evoke the traditional picture that I have described, which can be such a source of philosophical (no less psychobiological) perplexity. Wittgenstein (1967, p. 19e) spoke of such occasions as ones on which "language went on holiday"; and perhaps no more vivid example of what he had in mind could be found than in this movement of the notion of consciousness. He wrote in immediate reply to the exclamation I quoted at the beginning of this paper:[6]

> But what can it mean to speak of "turning my attention to my own consciousness"? This is the queerest thing there could be! It was a particular act of gazing that I called doing this (for these words are not used in ordinary life). I stared fixedly in front of me—but *not* at any particular point or object. My eyes were wide open, the brows not contracted (as they mostly are when I am interested in a particular object). No such interest preceded this gazing. My glance was vacant; or again like that of someone admiring the illumination of the sky and drinking in the light. (p. 124)

"We are," he said in another place, "up against one of the great sources of philosophical bewilderment: a substantive makes us look for a thing that corresponds to it" (Wittgenstein, 1958, p. 3). But, as the vacancy of the glance Wittgenstein described above suggests, there may be *nothing* there.

Wittgenstein did make it seem, though, that it is a holiday language takes only in the company of a philosopher. I suggest that it is one that

---

[6] In the standard translation of Wittgenstein (1967), there is an apparently inadvertant omission in this passage of a parenthetical remark—"(for these words are not used in everyday life)"—that I have taken the liberty of including.

our thought tends to take whenever we begin to theorize about "the nature of consciousness" at all. It is interesting to speculate that like many of the other "natural facts" that Wittgenstein so often cited, such holidays may themselves be part of our biological—or, at any rate, our long cultural—endowment. We, like Pribram in the passage I quoted, may feel strongly disposed to treat our biological kin with a special consideration that we are not disposed to accord machines. However morally defensible this special consideration may be, we then attempt to ground it in the kind of metaphysical difference that the traditional picture of consciousness suggests, and we claim for it a certainty to which we feel introspection naturally entitles us. (On the extent to which introspection may be susceptible to this sort of imposition, see Nisbett & Wilson, 1977.) What I am proposing is that we might preserve those special considerations but abandon the attempt to provide them with any such possibly false and misleading buttressing. Maybe there is no *principled* difference between ourselves and the machines I have described, but we might *care* about ourselves a great deal more than about those machines nonetheless. In any case, we mightn't continue to demand of psychobiology that it discover for us any such buttressing, any such underlying process of consciousness that might justify these differences in our cares.[7]

But doesn't my whole line of argument defeat itself? Throughout my discussion I used intuitions about consciousness to reject one or another proposal about its nature, and then I turn around and say there may be no such thing. But this is not an unusual ploy in philosophy or, for that matter, in argument generally. Skeptics often try quite legitimately to show that there is no such thing as knowledge by taking for granted our ordinary intuitions about it and then showing that those intuitions lead us to insuperable problems and contradictions. Euclid proved that there was no greatest prime by showing the absurdity that followed from supposing that there was one. The method is *reductio ad absurdum*, and I see no reason that it isn't employable here as elsewhere.

But perhaps the traditional picture of mind and consciousness *isn't* so wrong. Perhaps there is some further psychological mechanism that I have failed to consider that would serve as a more appropriate candidate. Undoubtedly, there are defects in the (sketches of) analyses of sensation, attention, linguistic competence, and self-reference, or in

---

[7] A very similar point appears to apply to our views regarding our personal identities: philosophers have long noted the futility of searching for some underlying, unchanging personal "soul" that might serve to underwrite our concern with our personal survival (see, e.g., Hume, 1739/1965, Vol. 1, p. 6; Parfit, 1971; Rey, 1976). The possible biological sources for such a search are perhaps more evident in this case than in that of consciousness, but the comparison is, I think, instructive.

simply the notion of an intentional system that I have claimed provides the basis for the ascription of a mental life to anything. I must admit to being sorely tempted to regard much of my discussion as more a *reductio ad absurdum* of these proposed analyses than of consciousness. But of which ones? Why?

Further research, that is to say, could well support the view that there *is* such a thing as consciousness. I think that it would have to deal with some of the puzzles about it that I have raised here, with precisely what the conditions are in which a process—and in particular, a machine—might be rightly regarded as conscious. But I certainly have not produced any argument whatever that establishes that there *couldn't* be any such thing, or that a machine could *never* enjoy it. I have only been concerned to show how there *mightn't* be, and to develop at least *one* plausible reason that we could intelligibly doubt that there is. Here, as elsewhere, lingering Cartesian intuitions notwithstanding, we need to be open to the very real possibility that we are confused and mistaken.

V. Appendix

Since many readers of the present volume may be unfamiliar with some of the technical issues in philosophy and logic touched on in this paper, and since in any case these issues are of some importance in the study of mind, I offer the following brief summary of some of the basic notions. Readers interested in pursuing these topics are advised to consult almost any elementary text in modern logic (e.g., Quine, 1941/1980, supplemented by Mates, 1972, Chapters 1–4). A concise and, especially for the nonspecialist, a remarkably accessible treatment of many of the important mathematical results *about* logic can be found in Hunter (1971).

A. *Formal Logic*

Logic in general is concerned with characterizing reasonable arguments. At its core is *deductive* logic, which is concerned with so-called *valid* arguments, or arguments in which if the premises are true then the conclusion *must* be true (that is, it is *impossible* for the premises to be true and the conclusion false). For example, both of the following arguments are deductively valid:

   1. If Oedipus guesses the riddle, Thebes is freed.
      Oedipus guesses the riddle.
      Therefore, Thebes is freed.

2. Apollo is immortal.
Therefore, there exists at least one thing that is immortal.

Inductive logic is concerned with arguments in which if the premises are true, then, while the conclusion *need not* be true, it is *likely* to be, or, anyway, it is *reasonable* to think it is. Examples of inductive arguments are afforded by much of the practice of science (and, for that matter, common sense) whereby evidence is adduced for a hypothesis; for example, a sufficient number of arbitrarily selected black ravens supports the hypothesis that all ravens are black. ("Abduction," or "inference to the best explanation," or "analysis by synthesis" is a specific way of thinking about induction, e.g., as a hypothesis's being supported by the premises that it *most successfuly explains*.)

Work in deductive logic has met with the greatest success. Logicians have devised *formal languages* in which sentences are constructed according to entirely precise *syntactic* (or spelling) rules that allow for systematic and unambiguous *semantic* interpretations of them. By exploiting these syntactic rules, it is possible to determine the *truth* or the *falsity* of every sentence in a formal language relative to an interpretation of the primitives of that language (see Tarski, 1936, or, more accessibly, Mates, 1972, Chapters 3 and 4). It is then possible to specify precise *rules of inference* that apply to sentences merely in terms of their syntax and that permit the derivation of all and only the valid arguments. For example, for the Argument 1 above, there is the rule *modus ponens*: from sentences of the form "*p* only if *q*" and "*p*" (where *p* and *q* are any sentences of the language), you may derive the sentence "*q*"; and for Argument 2, there is the rule *existential generalization*: from any sentence of the form "*a* is *F*," you may derive a sentence of the form "There exists at least one thing that is *F*." Reflection on these rules should confirm that, indeed, if the initial sentences are true, then the derived sentence *must* also be true. *Modus ponens* is a standard rule of *truth-functional* logic (the logic of words like *and, or, not, only if*); *existential generalization*, of *quantification* theory (truth-functional logic plus the logic of such words as *all* and *there exists at least one*). *Modal logic* is the further logic of such words as *possibly* and *necessarily*, and reasonings about "counterfactual conditions"—what *might* have been the case even though it isn't. What the "completeness" theorems for these different areas of logic show is that there exists in each case a set of just such entirely syntactic rules that are adequate for deriving all the valid arguments in that area (for fairly readable treatments, see Hunter, 1971, Sections 29–32 and 46; Mates, 1972, Chapter 8; Hughes & Creswell, 1968, Chapter 9). And this is tantamount to saying, then, that transformations of expressions merely according to their spelling is adequate to capture deductive reasonings.

B. *Intensionality*

A claim made by many philosophers and psychologists is that the mental is "intensional" (see Brentano, 1874/1964; Chisholm, 1957; Pribram, 1976). Although a variety of things are sometimes meant by this assertion, one central idea is that "awareness is awareness *of* something, a "something" that is, moreover, no ordinary existent thing. For we seem to be able to think about *nonexistent* things (Santa Claus, Apollo, the ether), and, as will be seen below, even our thinking about existing things is subject to peculiar qualifications. (An exasperating terminological point: *intentional*—with a *t*—is often, though not always, used to refer to phenomena [systems, behavior, explanations] that involve mental idioms like *believes* and *desires*. *Intensional*—with an *s*—refers to this "*of*-ness" property, and specifically to the phenomena indicated by the logical peculiarities discussed below. So the claim of intensionality, what is sometimes called *Brentano's thesis*, is that the inten*t*ional is inten*s*ional.)

These peculiarities of the mental are most evidently demonstrated by noticing the logical failings of many mental words, specifically of the so-called verbs of propositional attitude, or those mental verbs that take a sentence complement (e.g., a "that . . ." clause) as their direct object, for example, *believes, hopes, expects,* and *prefers.* Consider again our Argument 2: from "Apollo is immortal," it follows that there exists at least one thing that is immortal; it's impossible for the first sentence to be true while the second is false. But compare it with

3. Oedipus believes that Apollo is immortal.
   Therefore there exists at least one thing that Oedipus believes is immortal.

There seems at least one natural reading in which it is certainly possible for the first sentence to be true while the second is false: after all, Apollo does not exist! Nor may any of the other things that Oedipus believes to be immortal. There may *not exist* any (real) thing that Oedipus's belief is about. Existential generalization seems to fail as a rule for deductions involving anything in the sentence complement of *believes.* (Similar problems can be raised for the other verbs of propositional attitude; e.g., from the fact that Ponce de León searched for the Fountain of Youth, it doesn't follow that there existed something for which he searched.)

Related failures involve the notion of identity (or what is more familiarly thought of as *mathematical equality*) that is standardly included as part of quantification theory (see Mates, 1972, Chapter 9, or Quine, 1941/1980, Section 45). According to a widely accepted principle known as *Leibniz's law*, if we are genuinely referring to something x, and x is identical to y, then whatever is true of x is true of y, and vice versa. We have this on Shakespeare's authority ("A rose by any other name would smell as sweet") as well as on that of Sophocles (if Oedipus marries Jocasta, and Jocasta is identical to his mother, then Oedipus marries his mother). But this principle, too, seems to fail inside the sentence complements of propositional attitudes: just because Oedipus *believes* he is marrying Jocasta, and Jocasta is identical to this mother, it doesn't follow that Oedipus *believes* he is marrying his mother; indeed, it's in a way the truth of the premises and the falsity of the conclusion that the play's all about. Put in more philosophical jargon, inside the objects of the attitudes, coreferential expressions (expressions that refer to the same object) cannot be validly substituted for one another.

This failure of substitutivity, combined with the failure of existential generalization, strongly suggests that within the object of a propositional attitude, apparently referential terms like *Jocasta*, *his mother*, and *Apollo* aren't really playing their usual referential role. Oedipus's belief is in some way not exactly about *Jocasta* (since if it were, surely it would be so "by any other name"), and his belief about Apollo is a belief about no *thing* at all. Something other than Jocasta, and certainly other than *nothing*, must be the object of his belief, something that might best be regarded as a *representation* of Jocasta or of Apollo—or, less confusingly, a Jocasta-representation or an Apollo-representation, perhaps a "Jocasta is my wife"-representation or an "Apollo is immortal"-representation. If this were so, then we could understand the observed peculiarities. After all, a "Jocasta is my wife"-representation may be very different from a "My mother is my wife"-representation, and the mere existence of an "Apollo is immortal"-representation by no means implies the existence of Apollo, or of anything immortal. Many different suggestions have been made about precisely what sorts of things these "objects of propositional attitudes" might be: ideas, "subsistent objects," sets of "possible worlds," special items called *propositions* or *intensions*. I refer the interested reader to the now vast literature on the subject, a good introduction to which may be found in many of the essays in Linsky (1971), as well as representative recent discussions in French, Uehling, and Wettstein (1977). The proposal I take up, that they ought to be regarded as *sentences encoded in the brain*, is, I should admit, controversial, but not without its adherents: see Quine (1956/1976) for the sentences, and Harman (1973) and Fodor (1975) for their being in the brain.

C. Logic and Computation

Once it became clear that logic was characterizable entirely by syntactic rules, a number of elegant results followed, some of which eventuated in the development of the modern computer.

In the first part of his celebrated "Incompleteness Proof," Kurt Gödel proved that all of these syntactic rules could be *mirrored* in elementary arithmetic: in an important sense, they could be defined as operations on numbers, not different in kind from the familiar operations of addition, multiplication, and exponentiation (such operations are called *primitive recursive functions*). He did this by devising an ingenious *coding* of the sentences of logic into the natural numbers, proceeding then to construct actual functions in arithmetic that would map, for example, code numbers of the premises of a valid argument to code numbers of its conclusion. (These code numbers are often called Gödel numbers.) For example, the rule *modus ponens* that we encountered in Example 1 could be defined in arithmetic by a function that would map code numbers of the sentences "*p* only if *q*" and "*p*" to the code number of "*q*." (The actual construction of these functions is quite beautiful, and anyone with half an interest and two free afternoons should work through at least some of the 46 of them that Gödel, 1931, provides. Those less enthusiastic can gain a great deal about the proof generally from the popular discussion in Nagel & Newman, 1958, especially Chapter 6.) Gödel also provides code numbers of the axioms of arithmetic itself—he could have provided them for any finitely axiomatizable theory—with the dizzying effect that the *theory* of arithmetic becomes thereby coded *into itself*. This has the consequence that we are then able to define in purely arithmetic terms a class of numbers that are the code numbers of sentences provable in arithmetic—or, for that matter, in any finitely axiomatizable theory. (We'll return to this important fact in Part D.)

Alan Turing (1936) was concerned with characterizing as generally as possible the computational capacities of machines. Abstracting entirely from the physical limitations of actual, physical machines, he described what has come to be called a *Turing machine*. This is a mathematical object that consists of a set of interdefined states and an infinitely long "tape" (or memory capacity). Each state consists of a specification of what the machine as a whole is to do on receipt on the tape of a particular input: in general what a machine does, after reading such an input, is to print a symbol on the same space of the tape (the "output"), move one space left or right, and proceed to a new (or perhaps the same) state. State S_1, for example, might be specified by the fact that when given as input a single stroke, it prints a dash (erasing the stroke), moves left one space, and proceeds to State S_2. S_2 might, in turn, be specified by the fact that when given a dash as input, it prints a stroke, moves right one space, and returns to State S_1. (A full discussion of the operation of such machines can be found in almost any second-year book in logic or computation theory, e.g., Kleene, 1967;

Hopcroft & Ullman, 1979.) As a result of theorems of Kleene (1936) and Turing (1936), it can be shown that all the primitive recursive functions defined by Gödel can be computed by one or another Turing machine. Indeed, according to what is widely regarded as the immensely plausible "Church–Turing thesis," all functions that are in some intuitive sense "computable" are computable by one or another Turing machine (this informal thesis about what's "intuitively" computable is distinct, however, from the *formal* theorems about the Turing computability of the primitive recursive functions). It is those results and this latter thesis that provide the mathematical foundation for the construction of actual computing machines, as well as for some of the optimism that rational thought could in principle be modeled by them. (A brief discussion of the *pessimism* in this regard, which is sometimes founded on what seems to be a misreading of Gödel's final result, I defer to the end of Part D.)

D. Self-Reference and the Rest of Gödel

Hand in hand with this increase in our understanding of the power of formal languages and computation occurred a deepening insight into their surprising limitations. Much of this insight involved the construction of often paradoxical, "self-referential" claims or properties—claims or properties that seem in one way or another to "refer to themselves," often with absurd and unacceptable consequences. A common reaction to such paradoxes is to suppose that they show that there's something illegitimate about self-reference, that there is generally something paradoxical and impossible about *anything* (a claim, a property, and particularly a mind) referring to and/or describing itself. It is worth indicating how the actual results in logic show precisely the contrary; that self-reference is a relatively trivial, and in any case a quite essential and important, feature of most interesting formal systems.

The most famous of the (seemingly) "self-referential" paradoxes is Bertrand Russell's. It concerns *sets*. It at one time seemed perfectly natural to believe—and Frege, the founder of modern logic, believed it—that there exists a set for every possible condition, namely, the set of things satisfying the condition. Thus, there is the set of elephants: the set of all those things satisfying the condition *being an elephant*; or the set of even numbers: the set of all those things satisfying the condition *being divisible by 2 without remainder*. But, asked Russell, what about the condition *not being a member of itself*? This seems to be a perfectly intelligible condition: it is certainly satisfied by every elephant individually, since an elephant, not being a set, can hardly be said to have *any* members, least of all itself. And it is also satisfied by the *set* of elephants, since that set, not being an elephant, is clearly not a member of itself. Moreover, there are things that *do not* satisfy the condition. Take, for example, the set of all sets with more than one member: there are surely at least *two* sets like that (all the sets we've mentioned so far will do); so *that* set *is* a member of itself and so fails the condition. So the condition seems perfectly clear. But is there a set corresponding to *it*? Well, suppose there were. Now, either *it* is a member of itself or it isn't. If it *is* a member of itself, then it fails the corresponding condition and so *cannot* be a member of itself. And if it's *not* a member of itself, then it satisfies the corresponding condition and so *is* a member of itself. We arrive at a contradiction in either case. Consequently, there can be no such set. The intuitively plausible axiom, that there's a set for every condition, must be false. The problem for set theory was then to determine precisely what sets *could* be said to exist.

To be sure, *one* response to this problem—Russell's own, in his "theory of types"—is to rule out of set theory any sentence that asserts or denies self-membership (there are less drastic measures, e.g., von Neumann's; see, e.g., Quine, 1941/1980, Section 48). But at worst, this is merely a restriction on *set theory*. For the rest of things, there's still *suicide, self-love,* and *self-aggrandizement,* to say nothing of *self-identity,* so essential to almost any formalized theory. Indeed, Russell's paradox is only an instance of a very general, slightly surprising logical truth: for any two-place relation R, nothing Rs all and only those things that do not R themselves (thus, nothing shaves, loves, hates, helps, or has as members all and only those things that do not do those things to themselves; for if something did, it would do it to itself if and only if it didn't). This logical truth obviously presupposes, and therefore does not refute, the possibility of a reflexive relation—of, if you like, this sort of "self-reference."

But more to the point, it was another of Gödel's achievements to show that self-reference even within a sentence could be rendered as legitimate as elementary arithmetic. Exploiting the same ingenious coding of the sentences of arithmetic into numbers that we discussed in the previous section, he was able to construct a sentence of elementary arithmetic whose code number was, say, g and that said (in rough English translation) "g is not the code number of a sentence provable in arithmetic." That is, *through the code,* the sentence manages to refer to itself, and to say of itself that it is not provable. Suppose that this sentence is false. Then the sentence with code number g—namely, that very sentence itself—must, in fact, be *provable.* But if a falsehood of arithmetic is provable in it, that is tantamount to arithmetic's being *inconsistent.* So, suppose instead that the sentence is true. But if it's true, then, as it says, it's *not* provable. But if there's a truth in a theory that's not provable in that theory, then that theory is (by definition) *incomplete*. Now, either this sentence of Gödel's is false or it's true. Therefore (to state Gödel's famous conclusion), *either arithmetic is inconsistent or it is incomplete*. Again, as in the Russell case, but even more pointedly, this result depends on and therefore does not refute the possibility of self-reference, even in a sentence. (For an extremely elegant discussion of just how weak a language can be in order to permit effective self-reference, see Smullyan, 1957/1969, in particular Theorem 2.1.)

Many writers have sought in these results, especially Gödel's, some way of refuting the hypothesis presumed in the present paper that the mind is a kind of machine (see Lucas, 1961; Nagel & Newman, 1958; and perhaps Globus, 1976). For it would appear that for any given machine that purports to replicate someone's psychology, there would be at least one sentence—namely, the appropriate Gödel sentence, as constructed above—that the person could know to be true but the machine couldn't, since the machine couldn't prove it. The arguments get a little more intricate than can be adequately summarized here. Suffice it to say that received opinion among most philosophers and logicians who have discussed the matter is that the theorem proves no such thing. Most frequently, what is ignored in such arguments is the essentially *disjunctive* character of Gödel's conclusion: *either* arithmetic is inconsistent *or* it is incomplete. There is a sentence that a person could know to be true that a given machine couldn't prove *only if* that person could also know that the theory that he/she is using to know it is itself consistent. Now, in order to stand a chance of knowing it, it would seem that she/he would have to be using some theory at least as strong as arithmetic. But by Gödel's second theorem—a corollary of the one above, and proved in the same paper—*no theory strong enough to express arithmetic can prove its own consistency*. Indeed, any system that *did* prove its own consistency would do so only by *being inconsistent*! And in an inconsistent system, *anything* can be proved—small comfort for those claiming that a person could prove something that a (presumably consistent) machine couldn't. But how else is someone to know that her/his own theory is consistent? Perhaps by some pure intuition? After all, arithmetic surely *seems* consistent. But if results like Russell's have shown us anything, it's that contradictions can pop up as consequences of the most *intuitively plausible*-seeming assumptions (who would have thought there wasn't a set for every condition?). So, pending some way for a person to establish her/his own consistency without at the same violating it, it is not at all a consequence of Gödel's proof that there's something a person could know that a given replicating machine couldn't prove. There are certainly things that no machine can do (for example, prove all the truths of arithmetic *without contradicting itself*) but it remains to be shown that any person can do them either. (Readers eager to pursue this topic further should consult Webb, 1980; and Albert, 1981.)

ACKNOWLEDGMENTS

This paper originated as an invited address to a meeting of the Eastern Association of Electroencephalographers, Mont Gabriel, Quebec, March 1979. I am grateful to the organizer of that conference, Dr. Roger Broughton, for that occasion to address the present topic, as well as to the audience there for their reactions. I subsequently worked on the manuscript in a seminar sponsored by the National Endowment for the Humanities in the summer of 1980 and would like to thank the Endowment for its financial support during that time, but particularly the leader of that seminar, Gareth Matthews, for his extraordinarily generous and acute remarks. Ned Block, Richard Davidson, and Eleanor Saunders also voiced their advice from time to time, and I'm grateful to all of them, even for those portions of their advice that, as they might have expected, I didn't heed.

REFERENCES

ALBERT, K. *Mechanism and metamathematics*. Unpublished senior thesis(on file in library), State University of New York, College at Purchase, 1981.
ALSTON, W. Varieties of privelaged access. *American Philosophical Quarterly*, 1971, *8*, 223–241.
BERLINER, H. Computer backgammon. *Scientific American*, 1980, 242(6), 64–85.
BLOCK, N. Troubles with functionalism. In N. BLOCK (Ed.), *Readings in philosophy of psychology* (Vol. 1). Cambridge, Mass.: Harvard University Press, 1980.
BRENTANO, F. Psychology from an empirical standpoint. In G. VESEY (Ed.), *Body and mind*. London: Allen and Unwin, 1964. (Originally published in 1874.)
BROWN, G. The believer system (Technical Report RUCBM-TR-34), July 1974. Department of Computer Science, Rutgers University.
CASTENEDA, H. On the logic of attributions of self-knowledge to others. *Journal of Philosophy*, 1968, *65*, 439–456.
CHISHOLM, R. *Perceiving*. Ithaca, New York: Cornell University Press, 1957.
CHOMSKY, N. *Language and mind* (Enlarged edition). New York: Harcourt Brace Jovanovich, 1972.
CHOMSKY, N. *Reflections on language*. New York: Random House, 1976.
DAVIDSON, R. Consciousness and information processing: A biocognitive perspective. In J. DAVIDSON & R. DAVIDSON (Eds.), *The psychobiology of consciousness*. New York: Plenum Press, 1980.
DENNETT, D. *Content and consciousness*. London: Routledge and Kegan Paul, 1968.
DENNETT D. Intentional systems. *Journal of Philosophy*, 1971, *68*, 87–106.

DENNETT, D. Conditions of personhood. In A. RORTY (Ed.), *The identities of persons*. Berkeley: University of California Press, 1976.

DENNETT, D. Towards a cognitive theory of consciousness. In D. DENNETT, *Brainstorms: Philosophical essays on mind and psychology*. Cambridge, Mass.: Bradford, 1978.

DESCARTES, R. *Meditations on first philosophy (with replies to objections)*. Reprinted in *The Philosophical Works of Descartes*, ed. by E. S. HALDENE and G. R. T. ROSS. London: Cambridge University Press, 1911. (First published 1641.)

DEVITT, M. *Designation*. New York: Columbia University Press, 1981.

ECCLES, J. Conscious experience and memory. In J. ECCLES (Ed.), *Brain and conscious experience*. Berlin: Springer-Verlag, 1966.

FODOR, J. *The language of thought*. New York: Crowell, 1975.

FODOR, J. Methodological solipsism as a research strategy in cognitive psychology. *Brain and Behavioral Science*, 1980, *3*, 63–73.

FRENCH, P., UEHLING, T., & WETTSTEIN, H. *Contemporary studies in the philosophy of language*. Minneapolis: University of Minnesota Press, 1977.

GLOBUS, G. Mind, structure, and contradiction. In G. GLOBUS, G. MAXWELL, & I. SAVODNIK (Eds.), *Consciousness and the brain*. New York: Plenum Press, 1976.

GÖDEL, K. On formally undecidable propositions of *Principia Mathematica* and related systems I. In J. VAN HEIJENOORT (Ed.), *From Frege to Gödel: A Source Book in Mathematical Logic, 1879–1931*. Cambridge, Mass.: Harvard University Press, 1967. (Originally published in 1931.)

GOODMAN, N. *Fact, fiction, and forecast*. Indianapolis: Bobbs-Merrill, 1963.

GRICE, H. Meaning. *Philosophical Review*, 1957, *66*, 377–388.

HARMAN, G. Inference to the best explanation. *Philosophical Review*, 1965, *74*, 88–95.

HARMAN, G. *Thought*. Princeton, N.J.: Princeton University Press, 1973.

HEMPEL, C. *Aspects of scientific explanation*. New York: Free Press, 1965.

HENKIN, L. The completeness of the first-order functional calculus. In J. HINTIKKA (Ed.), *Philosophy of Mathematics*. New York: Oxford University Press, 1969. (Originally published 1949.)

HINTIKKA, J. *Philosophy of mathematics*. New York: Oxford University Press, 1969.

HIRIYANI, M. *Essentials of Indian philosophy*. London: Unwin, 1978.

HOPCROFT, J., & ULLMAN, J. *Introduction to automata theory, languages, and computation*. Reading, Mass.: Addison-Wesley, 1979.

HUGHES, G. & CRESSWELL, M. *An introduction to modal logic*. London: Metheun, 1968.

HUME, D. *A Treatise of Human Nature* (Ed. by L. A. SELBY-BIGGE). Oxford: Clarendon Press, 1888 (reprinted 1965). (Originally published in 1739.)

HUNTER, G. *Metalogic: An introduction to the metatheory of standard first order logic*. Berkeley: University of California Press, 1971.

JAMES, W. Does consciousness exist? In R. B. PERRY (Ed.), *Essays in radical empiricism and a pluralistic universe*. New York: Dutton, 1912.

JAYNES, J. *The origin of consciousness in the breakdown of the bicameral mind*. New York: Houghton-Mifflin, 1977.

JOHN, E. R. "A model of consciousness." In G. E. SCHWARTZ & D. SHAPIRO (Eds.), *Consciousness and self-regulation* (Vol. 1). New York: Plenum Press, 1976.

KAHNEMAN, D. *Attention and effort*. Englewood Cliffs, N.J.: Prentice Hall, 1973.

KLEENE, S. General recursive functions of natural numbers. *Mathematical Annual*, 1936, *112*, 727–742.

KLEENE S. *Mathematical logic*. New York: Wiley, 1967.

KNAPP, P. The mysterious "Split": A clinical inquiry into problems of consciousness and brain. In G. GLOBUS, G. MAXWELL, & I. SAVODNIK (Eds.), *Consciousness and the brain*. New York: Plenum Press, 1976.

KRIPKE, S. A completeness proof for modal logic. *Journal of Symbolic Logic*, 1959, *24*, 1–14.

KRIPKE S. *Naming and necessity*. Cambridge, Mass.: Harvard University Press, 1980. (Originally published 1972.)

LACKNER, J. R., & GARRETT, M. Resolving ambiguity: Effects of biasing context in the unattended ear. *Cognition*, 1973, *1*, 359–372.

LAING, R., Phillipson, H., & Lee, A. *Interpersonal perception: A theory and method of research.* London: Tavistock, 1966.

LEWIS, D. Lucas against mechanism II. *Canadian Journal of Philosophy*, 1979, *9*, 373–376.

LINSKY, L. *Reference and modality*. New York: Oxford University Press, 1971.

LOCKE, J. *An essay concerning human understanding*. New York: Dutton, 1961. (Originally published 1690.)

LUCAS, J. Minds, machines, and Gödel. *Philosophy*, 1961, *36*, 112–127.

LUCAS, J. Satan stultified: A rejoinder to Paul Beneceraff. *Monist*, 1968, *52*, 45–48.

LURIA, A. R. The human brain and conscious activity. In G. E. SCHWARTZ & D. SHAPIRO (Eds.), *Consciousness and self-regulation* (Vol. 2). New York: Plenum Press, 1978.

LYCAN, W. Form, function, and feel. *Journal of Philosophy*, 1981, *78*(1), 24–50.

MACKAY, D. Mind-like behavior in artifacts. *British Journal for the Philosophy of Science*, 1951, *2*, 105–121.

MATES, B. *Elementary logic* (2nd ed.). New York: Oxford University Press, 1972.

MATSON, W. Why isn't the mind/body problem ancient?" In P. FEYERABEND & G. MAXWELL (Eds.), *Mind, matter, and method: Essays in philosophy of science in honor of Herbert Feigl.* Minneapolis: University of Minnesota Press, 1966.

MATTHEWS, G. Consciousness and life. *Philosophy*, 1977, *52*, 13–26.

MILLER, G. The magic number seven plus or minus two: Some limits on our capacity for processing information. *Psychological Review*, 1956, *63*, 81–97.

MORUZZI, G. Functional significance of sleep with particular regard to the brain mechanisms underlying consciousness. In J. C. ECCLES (Ed.), *Brain and consciousness experience*. New York: Springer, 1966.

NAGEL, E., & NEWMAN, J. *Gödel's proof*. New York: New York University Press, 1958.

NATSOULAS, T. Consciousness. *American Psychologist*, 1978, *12*, 906–914.

NISBETT, R., & WILSON, T. Telling more than we can know. Verbal reports on mental processes. *Psychological Review*, 1977, *84*(3), 231–259.

Oxford English Dictionary. Oxford: Oxford University Press, 1933.

PARFIT, D. Personal identity. *Philosophical Review*, 1971, *80*(1), 3–28.

PENFIELD, W. *The mystery of the mind*. Princeton, N. J.: Princeton University Press, 1975.

PERRY, J. The problem of the essential indexical. *Nous*, 1979, *13*, 3–21.

PIAGET, J. *The child and reality: Problems of genetic epistemology*. New York: Penguin, 1976.

POPPER, K., & ECCLES, J. *The self and its brain*. New York: Springer International, 1979.

PRIBRAM, K. Problems concerning the structure of consciousness. In G. GLOBUS, G. MAXWELL, & I. SAVODNIK (Eds.), *Consciousness and the brain*. New York: Plenum Press, 1976.

PUTNAM, H. The analytic and the synthetic. In H. PUTNAM (Ed.), *Mind, language and reality*. Cambridge: Cambridge University Press, 1975. (a)

PUTNAM, H. Is semantics possible. In H. PUTNAM (Ed.), *Mind, language and reality*. Cambridge: Cambridge University Press, 1975. (b)

PUTNAM, H. (Ed.). *Mind, language and reality* (Philosophical papers, Vol. 2). Cambridge: Cambridge University Press, 1975. (c)

PUTNAM, H. The meaning of meaning. In H. PUTNAM (Ed.), *Mind, language and reality*. Cambridge: Cambridge University Press, 1975. (d)

QUINE, W. *From a logical point of view and other essays*. Cambridge: Harvard University Press, 1980. (Originally published 1951.)

QUINE, W. *Ways of paradox*. Cambridge, Mass.: Harvard University Press, 1976.

QUINE, W. *Elementary logic* (rev. ed.). Cambridge, Mass.: Harvard University Press, 1980. (First edition published in 1941.)

REY, G. Survival. In A. RORTY (Ed.), *The identities of persons*. Berkeley: University of California Press, 1976.

REY, G. Functionalism and the emotions. In A. O. RORTY (Ed.), *Explaining emotions*. Berkeley: University of California Press, 1980.

RORTY, R. Mind-body identity, privacy, and categories. *Review of Metaphysics*, 1965, *14*(1), 24–54.

RORTY, R. In defense of eliminative materialism. *Review of Metaphysics*, 1970, 24(1), 112–121.

RORTY, R. *Philosophy and the mirror of nature*. Princeton, N.J.: Princeton University Press, 1979.

RYLE, G. *The concept of mind*. London: Hutchinson, 1949.

SCHIFFER, S. *Meaning*. London: Oxford University Press, 1972.

SCHMIDT, C., & D'ADDAMI, G. A model of the common sense theory of intention and personal causation. *Proceedings of 3rd International Joint Conference on Artificial Intelligence*. Stanford, Calif.: Stanford University Press, 1973.

SCHWARTZ, S. *Naming, necessity, and natural kinds*. Ithaca, N.Y.: Cornell University Press, 1977.

SEARLE, J. Analytic philosophy and mental phenomena. In P. FRENCH, T. UEHLING, & H. WETTSTEIN (Eds.), *Midwest Studies in Philosophy* (Vol. 6). Minneapolis: University of Minnesota Press, 1981.

SELLARS, W. *Science, perception, and reality*. London: Routledge and Kegan-Paul, 1963. (First published 1956.)

SMART, N. Karma. In *Encyclopedia of Philosophy* (Vol. 4). New York: Macmillan, 1967.

SMULLYAN, R. Languages in which self-reference is possible. In J. HINTIKKA (Ed.), *Philosophy of mathematics*. New York: Oxford University Press, 1969. (First published in 1957.)

TURING, A. On computable numbers with an application to the *Entscheidungsproblem*. *Proceedings of London Mathematical Society*, 2:42, 230–265.

VESEY, G. (Ed.). *Body and mind*. London: Allen and Unwin, 1964.

WEBB, J. *Mechanism, mentalism, and metamathematics*. Hingam, Mass.: D. Reidel, 1980.

WEBER, M. The nature of social action. In W. G. RUNCIMAN (Ed.), *Weber: Selections in translation*. Cambridge: Cambridge University Press, 1980. (Originally published 1922.)

WEIZENBAUM, J. ELIZA—A computer program for the study of natural language communication between man and machine. *Communication of the association for computing machinery*, 1965, 9(1), 36–45.

WIENER, N. *The human use of human beings*. Garden City, N.Y.: Doubleday, 1954.

WILLIAMS, B. *Descartes*. London: Penguin, 1978.

WINOGRAD, T. *Understanding natural language*. New York: Academic Press, 1972.

WITTGENSTEIN, L. *The blue and brown books*. New York: Harper & Row, 1958.

WITTGENSTEIN, L. *Philosophical investigations* (Trans. by G. E. M. ANSCOMBE). Oxford: Blackwell, 1967.

ZIFF, P. The feelings of robots. *Analysis*, 1959, *19*, 64–68.

2   *Conscious Contents Provide the Nervous System with Coherent, Global Information*

BERNARD J. BAARS

Consciousness is what we might expect in an
organ, added for the sake of steering a nervous
system too complex to handle itself.
William James (1890)

I. BRIEF OVERVIEW

Renewed interest in consciousness is evident in contemporary cognitive psychology. While there is reasonable agreement on the empirical constraints on a theory of consciousness, there is less consensus on the shape of a theory. This paper specifies a number of empirical constraints, stated as pairs of *conscious-unconscious contrasts*, and suggests a rather small set of principles that can organize these constraints in a rather straightforward way. These principles include the following:

First, the nervous system is viewed as a "distributed" information processing system, in which highly complex and efficient processing is performed by specialized processors in a relatively independent way. These processors may be "data driven"—i.e., they may decide by their own criteria what is worth processing, so that a central mechanism is not needed to exercise executive power over the specialized processors. However, these specialists do require a "central information exchange" in order to interact with each other. This central interchange has been

BERNARD J. BAARS • Department of Psychology, State University of New York, Stony Brook, New York.
The development of this paper was supported by the Cognitive Science Program, UCSD Center for Human Information Processing, supported by the Alfred P. Sloan Foundation, and by USPHS Biomedical Research Support Grant 5 S07 RR 07067-12 to the State University of New York at Stony Brook.

41

called a global data base. In operation, a global data base bears a striking resemblance to "working memory."

Conscious contents are thought to reflect a special operating mode of a global data base, namely one in which there is a stable and coherent *global representation* that provides *information* to the nervous system as a whole. This implies that any specialized processor in the nervous system can receive the global information, depending upon its own internal criteria. If the global information is relevant to some specialized processor, it will make predictions regarding it, and if the predictions fail, it will work to reduce the mismatch. That is, it will tend to *adapt* to the global information. Each specialist can also engage in *local* information processing without the benefit of the global data base.

A group of specialists can specify a global representation by co-operating or competing with each other until a consistent representation emerges. Those components of a global representation that are entirely stable can be called a *context* because they will influence other components to organize themselves in a way that fits their constraints. Contexts are not necessarily complete. They can leave a number of degrees of freedom to be filled in. If there are processors in the system that are able to complete a set of stable global constraints (a context), they will tend to do so. This provides a mechanism whereby a global context will be able to pose a problem to the system as a whole, such that distributed processors will act to provide a solution to the problem.

Two sets of empirical constraints fit this analysis. First a set of *capability constraints* are used to support the idea that consciousness reflects an operating mode of a global data base. Secondly, a set of *boundary constraints* show the limits of our experience of some conscious content. Together, these empirical constraints place strong limits on any possible theory.

The theoretical discussion precedes the empirical analysis. Some readers may wish to read the empirical sections (III and IV) before the theory section (II).

II. INTRODUCTION

In recent years, psychologists have begun to approach the issue of consciousness quite pragmatically, largely free from the theoretical obstacles that restricted the scope of earlier attempts. Recent authors agree reasonably well on the phenomena that a theory of consciousness must explain, and it appears that some theoretical consensus is beginning to emerge as well. For example, authors like Posner and Warren (1972), Mandler (1975a,b), and Straight (1979) agree that consciousness is closely

autonomous specialized processor. This kind of flexibility may discomfit a builder of neat minitheories, who would like to have building bricks that remain stable in all circumstances. But the nervous system probably profits by this potential for flexibility.

As we noted above, global representations are distributed to specialized processors much as a television program is distributed to a large number of viewers. Each viewer has the option of processing or not processing the television program. If the viewer already knows the information, or if it is irrelevant, it may be ignored. If a global representation is neither redundant nor irrelevant to some specialist, it will attempt to *adapt* to the global information. Adaptation is defined as an attempt by the specialized processor to match the global information in its domain, to *reduce the mismatch* that triggered it in the first place. At a physiological level, there is extensive evidence for processes like this: both neurons and systems of neurons *habituate selectively* to input, ceasing to fire when the input is absorbed. But if a change occurs in the habituated pattern (that is, in conditions of mismatch with the previous adaptation), these systems activate again until the new input has become redundant, equilibrium is restored, and they cease firing (Sokolov, 1963; Asratyan, 1965). Note that selective habituation to current input is, in fact, a way in which neurons can store information about any current state of the input. (See Figure 2.)

Any global representation that triggers widespread adaptation can

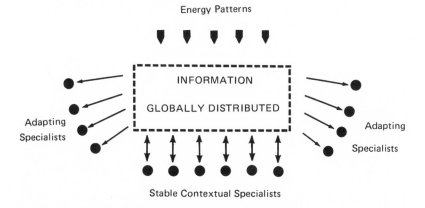

FIGURE 2. A somewhat more complete diagram, showing that the global information is, in fact, the result of an interaction between incoming energy patterns and a stable set of specialized systems, which provide a context. The resulting global representation, when it has become stable, triggers adaptation in the remaining specialists in the system. Each of the specialists attempts to reduce mismatch between global information in its specialized domain and its own model of the input. Since the global data base exists in a "distributed" system, the processing initiative is left to the specialists themselves.

be said to provide *global information* (MacKay, 1969). Neurophysiological evidence on this point is quite good: new events in the environment, those that are psychologically most likely to be conscious, cause extensive neural activity, far beyond the anatomical pathways of the sensory modality involved (John, 1976). But when this same input is presented repeatedly, the pattern of activity becomes much more localized and limited to special pathways. Redundant input ceases to be global.

Thus, global information is defined as being information to the system as a whole—and here again, one may use the television analogy. If everyone in a country tuned in to a television news program at the same time, one might similarly speak of the content of the news program as providing *global* information to the country *as a whole*. Global information is to be distinguished from *local* information, which is information that is processed within a single specialist without the benefit of the global data base.

B. The System in Operation

A number of different processors may cooperate or compete in sending hypotheses to the global data base by acting to confirm or disconfirm global hypotheses until all competition is resolved. If some global hypothesis proposed by one specialized processor is immediately contradicted by another, the hypothesis will have only a transient existence. In order to establish a *stable* global representation, a number of processors must cooperate; that is, they must create a *context*.[1] A context is defined as being a set of stable constraints on a global representation,

---

[1] The word *context* is often rightly criticized for being theoretically and empirically empty. In this paper, however, it has a number of very specific implications. Theoretically, it is defined as a set of stable, global constraints, which serve to guide and define inputs to the global data base. Empirically, contextual factors are defined as being those factors that can change conscious contents without themselves being conscious. Thus, in any experimental situation, it is clear what factors are and are not part of context, though, of course, this definition does not tell us ahead of time which factors will be contextual in any particular case. Nevertheless, it is quite possible to make some rather strong empirical claims, which include the following: Any conscious content can become a contextual constraint when the system is globally habituated to it. As such, the formerly conscious content will constrain the interpretation of future conscious contents. Components of a context must always be mutually consistent, otherwise competition would occur between them. Incomplete contexts serve to mobilize processors able to complete them, and whenever any component of a context is strongly violated, it will tend to become conscious. All these predictions can be tested in appropriate experimental situations. Thus, the word *context*, as used here, is nonempty both theoretically and empirically.

provided by a set of cooperating processors. That definition implies, of course, that these constraints are consistent with each other; if this were not so, the processors providing the constraints would begin to compete, and the global representation would lose stability. One can view a context as consisting of the set of constraints that is relevant to some particular process to which the system as a whole has *already* adapted.

A set of stable global constraints (a context) is not necessarily complete; there may be many degrees of freedom left, so further constraints can be added to the context. Indeed, some of the constraints that define a context may be changed by incoming information. Finally, incoming information may be able to fill in certain parameter values in dimensions that are specified by the context. Thus, the existence of a stable, coherent set of contextual constraints is not incompatible with the acquisition of new information.

So far, all these definitions have been purely conceptual. Our psychological argument will be that in the nervous system, a stable, global representation becomes conscious *if it provides global information* (Section IV). Conscious representations provide information to the system as a whole, or alternatively, one may say that they trigger adaptation in the system as a whole. Thus, any specialized processor can respond to conscious information relevant to its domain.

It is important to be aware that a global data base is not an executive, though it may be *used by* systems acting in an executive capacity. Indeed, the power and usefulness of distributed information-processing derives from its decentralized organization (Greene, 1972; Turvey, 1977). Again, it is more accurate to compare the global data base with a broadcasting station, which can send information to a vast number of processors, and which can, in turn, be controlled by some processors. In much the same way, a government can control a broadcasting station—but it is the government that acts as an executive, while the broadcasting facility is merely a medium. Consciousness is viewed in this paper as a certain operating mode of this medium, and consciousness can likewise be *used by* processors acting as executives, without itself being an executive.

In many ways, this approach is not new. The global data base has been used by a number of researchers in artificial intelligence (Kaplan, 1973; Erman & Lesser, 1975), and it has a clear similarity to the idea of working memory. Mandler (1975b) has pointed out the close relation of consciousness to short-term memory. Furthermore, Shallice (1972, 1978) has proposed that action systems may dominate the limited-capacity system in much the way that this chapter suggests that consistent sets of processors may dominate the global data base. Others have discussed this kind of a system in a number of different contexts (Lindsay & Norman, 1976; Arbib, 1982; Tart, 1975; Hilgard, 1977; Baars & Kramer,

1982). Nonetheless, the present approach does suggest new ways of viewing the psychological implications of such a system.

Given this perspective, a large amount of evidence falls into line. In Section III, detailed evidence is discussed for associating consciousness with the psychological equivalent of a global data base, and Section IV presents evidence concerning the boundaries of conscious contents.

C. *Advantages of the Global Data Base*

The special advantages and disadvantages of global data bases can be enumerated. First, the advantages:

1. Global information is distributed to all relevant processors, so that if there exists some specialist able to handle it in a fast, efficient way, it can be found immediately.

2. In a problem space that is uncertain or badly understood, a global data base can unite information from many incomplete sources to produce greater certainty than any individual specialist could produce by itself (Erman & Lesser, 1975).

3. A distributed processing system with a global data base would seem to be an ideal learning device. In our version, it is inherently an adapting system since global information is displayed to many different specialists, which are assumed to adapt to those new aspects of the global display that are within their purview. Indeed, we argue in Section IV that we have an *experience* of some event whenever the system as a whole is adapting to a stable, global representation of the event.

4. A global data base can optimize the fundamental trade-off between structure and flexibility. This is a general problem for large systems: on the one hand, it is vital to have specialized, structured solutions available for standard problems, and on the other hand, such structured solutions can be a drawback when the system is faced with really new conditions. In new situations, *flexibility* is at a premium. A global data base permits one to change from a highly structured approach to a highly flexible one. One can have the advantage of structure if the problem is in the province of specialization of a particular processor, along with the advantage of flexibility in choosing between alternative processors, and in the possibility of having a number of specialized processors cooperate in solving some problem.

5. Though a global data base is not an executive, it can be *used by* executive systems. Executive systems can use the global data base to distribute information to control other systems, and to receive feedback from subordinate systems.

6. New processors can be added in a modular fashion. The system can grow without serious disruption, since specialized processors can be added without having to change the previous set of processors. Indeed, the entire configuration may be used to *develop* new specialized processors: as joint information from partial knowledge sources becomes more and more determinate, a new rule-set is defined. This new rule-set may become autonomous and may begin to behave as a specialized processor in its own right. Karmiloff-Smith (1979) has observed a process very much like this in the acquisition of language and other representational systems by children.

7. The same processor may be used in different tasks. For instance, speech perception and speech production have many components in common; thus, it may be that speaking and listening, in fact, involve many of the same processors, which are merely organized differently for speech input and output. Along these lines, Geschwind (1979) claimed that "the primary motor and sensory areas are specialized in the sense that each one is dedicated to a specific function, but the functions themselves are of general utility, and the areas are called on in a great variety of activities."

8. In terms of *content addressability*, one does not need to call any particular processor from a global data base: it is necessary only to present the conditions that the processor finds unambiguously informative. The "name" of any processor is, in a real sense, the information to which it is responsive. This property has considerable advantages and corresponds well to what is known about human cognition (e.g., Norman, 1976).

9. A global data base can solve the need for a mental *lingua franca* (Dennett, 1978). In Western thought, the idea that there must be a common mental code so that one sense modality can communicate with the others goes back to Aristotle's notion of a "common sense." The problem is, of course, that visual information is to some extent unique and different from auditory information, which differs, in turn, from the motor code that controls speech articulation (e.g., Norman, 1976). The unique properties associated with the efficient control of speech are simply not directly translatable into a visual code. Thus, on the one hand, a *lingua franca* is desirable; on the other, it would vitiate the advantages of specialized languages.

A global data base operating in a distributed system obviates this need for a *lingua franca*. Only those systems will respond to a global representation that already "speak the language" of the global representation. Other systems simply don't look at this information, because they do not speak the language. This is perhaps a poor metaphor because the system has not an arbitrary code like natural language, but a content-addressable code more like a semantic network. If the content of the global data base changes, or if in the process of adaptation the specialists change so that they become sensitive to new dimensions of the global information, one might say that they are "learning to speak" the language of the global representation.

There may be one common code able to access all processors, and that is temporal simultaneity. Work on evoked potentials (John, 1976) shows that for a brief time, a prominent new event in any sensory modality reverberates widely throughout the nervous system, far beyond the special anatomical areas and pathways associated with the sensory input. Further, we know from biofeedback research (Schwartz, 1975) that an enormous variety of specialized processors can respond intelligently to those widespread events that affect the whole nervous system simultaneously for a short period of time. It is well established that conscious feedback can be associated with remarkably specific events in the nervous system, events that are presumably controlled by specialized processors. Note that we are not claiming that these events—EEG rhythms, autonomic functions, or single motor neurons—are controlled consciously. In fact, we do not control anything consciously in the literal sense of knowing precisely how we do things (Baars & Mattson, 1981). Rather, the idea is that in biofeedback, specialized systems that control EEG rhythms, or single motor units can independently decide to respond and adapt to widely broadcast information if there is effective temporal simultaneity.

10. A final advantage of this kind of system has been pointed out by Hayes-Roth and Lesser (1976): it consists of flexibility of access to the global data base. Given the same set of specialists, it is possible to experiment with various strategies to control access to the global data base. Certain specialized processors may be given a higher priority than others. This "focus-of-attention" problem has intriguing parallels to the psychological issue of attention. Furthermore, it provides a theoretical mechanism whereby certain potential conscious contents can be avoided, so that in principle, one could incorporate ideas of repression and the dynamic unconscious.

D. Disadvantages of the Global Data Base

No system design is without drawbacks, and the global data base has some obvious ones. For one, it uses a large number of processing resources because all specialists must continually monitor the central information relevant to their domain. Further, global problem-solving is relatively slow, certainly when compared with the fast and efficient action of a specialist that knows how to solve a specific problem. Many different processors must learn to cooperate in order to produce a solution to the global problem. Whenever possible, the global data base should relegate some problem to a specialist (i.e., as soon as a determinate solution is found).

As we point out below (Section IIIA), all these disadvantages have parallels in the "computational inefficiencies" of consciousness: consciousness, too, seems to demand a very great number of resources; it, too, is slow compared with unconscious information-processing. When a conscious solution to a problem is discovered, it is also quickly relegated to unconscious processors: it becomes habituated or automatic.

This paper does *not* claim that consciousness is identical to the operation of a global data base in the nervous system. Rather, it seems that we are conscious of some content when there exists an internal representation that meets three criteria: it must be global, stable, and informative (Section IV).

We turn now to a set of arguments to show that conscious processes are closely associated with a system that acts very much like a distributed system with a global data base.

III. Capability Constraints: Arguments for Associating Consciousness with a Global Data Base

How do we know when someone is conscious of something? Most obviously we are willing to infer that someone is conscious of an object if the observer can describe it. But consciousness cannot be limited to verbal description—first, because that would confound the construct of consciousness with the evidence that is used to infer it, and second, because that would include talking parrots and computers while excluding babies, aphasics, and ourselves when we are not talking! Adequate measures for any construct *result* as much *from* good theory as they *lead to* it. Thus, any initial definition may need to be changed as the theory is developed. But as a first approximation, we may say that we are willing to infer consciousness when someone can potentially *act discriminatively* toward some internal representation, especially when the internal representation is nonroutine. This inference would include babies, aphasics, at least some animals, and ourselves in our more silent moments; it would exclude even ourselves if we were engaged in extremely routine tasks or were processing very routine representations of things. It would include the objects of perception, which can reasonably be thought of as represented in the nervous system because one can do sensitive memory tests afterwards, for example, and find quite remarkable recognition memory for these perceptions. Also, it would include images among conscious experiences, since all cognitive measures of imagery ask the subject to behave discriminatively toward the image (e.g., Paivio, 1975). Note that a subject does not have to act discriminatively at all times toward some internal representation to be considered conscious of the object. As long as the subject can *potentially* do this, we may consider him or her to be conscious because of this potential.

In practice, we capitalize on the fact that people can consistently answer questions like, "Are you conscious of the words in front of you?" "Before you read this question, were you conscious of the feel of your chair, of the presuppositions of this question, of the breakfast you ate yesterday?" Such questions are answered so consistently by so many people that when it comes to collecting empirical constraints on a theory of consciousness (Tables 1 and 2), no practical obstacles arise.

An initial definition like this may not help us to decide on difficult cases like trance states, automatic writing, cases of multiple personality (e.g., Hilgard, 1976, 1977), or reports of "consciousness without content" (e.g., Naranjo & Ornstein, 1971; Globus & Franklin, 1980). Further, it is possible that people can be conscious of some things so fleetingly as to be unable to answer these questions accurately, as suggested, for example, by the well-known Sperling (1960) phenomenon. But in theory building, as in law, hard cases make bad laws. The great bulk of phenomena we wish to capture can be incorporated in the definition. Perhaps further insight can be gained by considering the more typical phenomena first so that we can then approach these other fascinating questions more intelligently.

Table 1 compares the capabilities and limits of conscious and unconscious processes. These comparisons are purely relative. For example, when we claim that entirely conscious processes are computationally inefficient, this is only in comparison to the evident efficiency

TABLE 1
Capability Constraints on a Theory of Consciousness[a]

Conscious processes	Unconscious processors
1. Computationally inefficient.	Highly efficient in special tasks.
2. Great range and relational capacity.	Limited domains and relative autonomy.
3. Apparent unity, seriality, and limited capacity.	Highly diverse, can operate in parallel, and together have great capacity.

[a] The capability constraints provide one set of conscious-unconscious contrasts that is quite well established and uncontroversial. Yet, these constraints place considerable limits on possible theories.

of unconscious processors. Note, by the way, that the first column refers to unitary conscious process*es*, while the second column refers to multiple unconscious process*ors*. This is itself, of course, a theoretical claim that is supported by some of the arguments made below.

In this section, we discuss each of these points in detail and show how, together, the capability constraints lead to the notion that consciousness reflects the functioning of a global data base in a distributed processing system.

A. Computational Inefficiency

If by *computational efficiency* we mean the ability to compute some standard algorithm quickly and without error, then it is clear that conscious processes lack computational efficiency, while unconscious processors are often remarkably efficient.

1. Some Limitations of Conscious Phenomena

Virtually all authors have noted that the vast preponderance of truly effective human information processing is *not* normally open to awareness (e.g., Miller, 1962; Mandler, 1975a,b; Shallice, 1972, 1978; Straight, 1979). In recent years, we have grown increasingly aware of the awesome complexity of processes needed in the comprehension of even a single sentence, the analysis of a visual scene, or the control of a single motor gesture. People can point to correct and incorrect instances of these events, but they cannot specify the rules involved or explain how they work. This lack of awareness of processing details is universal: it applies to perception and memory retrieval, to most of problem solving, to the control of speech and action, and so on. Where we *are* able to carry out some mental algorithm in a largely conscious way (as in mental arithmetic), the process is often slow and prone to error. Indeed, as conscious processes become more and more proficient, they also become less and less consciously available.

Some people may be tempted to conclude from these observations that consciousness is unimportant or even "epiphenomenal", that is, that it has no *functional* role to play in the nervous system. That is not the solution advanced here. However, it is clear that a functional role for consciousness cannot be found in its computational efficiency.

2. Comparison with Unconscious Processors

The claim that unconscious processors are *highly efficient and specialized for routine tasks* is clearly inferential, but not unreasonable. We may be aware of the sound of a sentence, and of the words, but we are certainly not aware of the fast, complex, and generally error-free processes that mediate between the awareness of sound and the awareness of words. We get some inkling of this complexity when we first acquire some knowledge or skill, but once the new ability is learned to the point of proficiency, it drops out of consciousness. It is then no less complex than before, and it is processed a good deal more efficiently than when it was first acquired—yet, it *seems* easier, presumably because the processing is handled by specialized systems that make little demand on our conscious processing capacity.

There is well-known physiological evidence for independent special-purpose processors in speech, spatial analysis, emotion, metabolic control, and even music (e.g., Geschwind, 1979). On the other hand, there is also a large amount of well-established evidence to show that neural activity in response to new or significant information is extremely widespread, going far beyond the classical neuroanatomical pathways of each sensory modality (John, 1976). (Notice that consciousness of some content is also associated with new or significant events; see Table 2.) But there is no contradiction between localized, dedicated processors and global activities: the tasks performed by the brain require both specialization and global coordination.

It makes sense to suppose that all the truly efficient processors are specialized. The rule systems for spatial analysis are different from those involved in moral judgments, which, in turn, differ from the rules of syntax. Different, yes, but not absolutely autonomous. If we want to understand property law, we must understand how spatial relationships such as boundaries, thoroughfares, and surface features interact with considerations of morality; and, of course, the law has its own syntactic devices to make these considerations explicit. Thus, these three highly cohesive rule systems—morality, spatial relations, and syntax—must

TABLE 2
Boundary Constraints on the Contents of Consciousness[a]

Conscious events	Events that do not become conscious
Synchronic phenomena:	
1. Percepts.	Context required to organize percepts.
2. Input consistent with context.	Input inconsistent with context.
Diachronic phenomena:	
3. Percepts.	Preperceptual processes.
4. Any change in a habituated stimulus.	Habituated percepts.

[a] The boundary constraints suggest that conscious contents are coherent (and hence stable) and also informative.

interact in some cases. More generally, one can claim that for any two apparently separate and internally cohesive rule-systems one can discover a context in which they must interact. Consciousness is presumably involved in facilitating the interaction between such rule systems, until their interaction becomes routine. Once it has become routine, one could speak of a single moral–spatial–syntactic processor with a considerable degree of internal coherence.

3. Relevance of These Points

All of these points are consistent with the view that consciousness is associated with a global data base in a distributed processing system. In such a system, purely global processes would be slow and inefficient, because they require the cooperation of a number of otherwise separate processors. By comparison, once some specialist is able to compute a standard algorithm for some known problem, it can do so with very great speed and efficiency.

B. Some Advantages of Conscious Processes

While completely conscious processes are computationally inefficient, the contents of consciousness have extraordinary *range, relational capacity*, and *context sensitivity*. By contrast, unconscious processors by themselves have *limited domains* and are *relatively autonomous* (Table 1).

1. Conscious Phenomena

(a) *Range.* Consciousness seems to participate in all known mental processes at some time. This extraordinary range of conscious contents is one of those "obvious" facts that become puzzling only on further examination. If, for instance, perceptual experience were merely the result of energy transduction, we might explain the vast variety of conscious percepts quite simply: we need only suppose that many different kinds of energy are transduced into some common electrochemical form. But sensation and perception seem to require highly intelligent algorithms, which are probably so complex that each different form of perception demands a specialized set of processors. And if perceiving one kind of object or event demands a specialized processor, how many processors do we need to account for the vast range of percepts, thoughts, feelings, and intentions to which we have conscious access?

Indeed, we seem to have access to an astonishing variety of events in the nervous system. Under optimal conditions, sensory sensitivity approaches the theoretical minimum in which a single retinal receptor may be stimulated by a single photon, or (in the case of hearing) a hair cell may be stimulated by the Brownian motion of molecules in the ear canal. Electrical stimulation of cortical neurons can sometimes be experienced, and by means of conscious feedback, the firing patterns of a single spinal motor unit can come under voluntary control (Schwartz, 1975). This does not mean that the biofeedback subject is conscious of what she or he is doing; rather, it means that the system controlling the motor unit behaves as a specialized distributed processor, able to look at global information. The conscious feedback signal presumably represents such global information. Further, stimulation to which we have become habituated can become conscious (as when we are reminded of background noise, of the effects of gravity, of the feel of a chair, and so on). The unconscious presuppositions of perception, comprehension, and action can become conscious when they are strongly violated (e.g., Offir, 1973; Hornby, 1974). And memories we had long thought lost can reappear in a variety of circumstances (Williams & Hollan, 1981; Hilgard, 1977).

Contrary to widespread opinion, the contents of consciousness are not limited to the so-called higher mental functions. Indeed, there is a striking ability to range far and wide between the most abstract conceptual representations and supposedly more "concrete" sensory-perceptual elements.

What kind of a system could model this extraordinary range of contents? Certainly, a single task-specific processor could not do it. Insofar as a processor is good at some particular task, it is likely to be limited in doing other tasks. No such limitation appears for consciousness.

(b) Relational Capacity. We can relate the contents of consciousness to each other almost without limit. Many decades of research on conditioning indicate that people and even animals have a remarkable capacity for learning arbitrary relationships between different stimuli and between stimuli and responses, though it is easier, of course, to learn nonarbitrary relations.

Although there seems to be evidence that humans can sometimes absorb input without awareness (Dixon, 1971), there is little or no evidence that we can acquire new relationships between inputs without awareness (Brewer, 1974). Indeed, several decades of experimental attempts have shown how difficult it is to demonstrate this. Clearly, the acquisition of new relationships generally involves awareness. Indeed, Smith (1969) has proposed that the capacity to arbitrarily relate any stimulus to any other, or to any response, *is* the criterion-like property of consciousness.

In humans, there is one relational capacity that is of special importance, and that is, of course, our ability to operate on conscious contents with highly specialized linguistic processors. It is important to note again that the existence of some conscious content does not depend on our capacity to express it in words. Verbal report is usually good evidence of some conscious content, but it is not the same as the conscious content.

(c) Context Sensitivity. This is a special kind of relational capacity, and it is of fundamental importance to the present discussion. It differs from the kind of relational capacity that is shown in cases like conditioning. During classical conditioning, for example, we learn that a tone signals the coming of a shock; both of these events are experienced *as* events. They each "stand out as figure from ground." But when we speak of context sensitivity in this chapter, we mean that an experience is affected by factors that do not stand out in this manner. It is a truism that experimental tasks are always affected by a host of variables of which the subjects are not aware. Many of these variables may have been conscious at one time, but they often have their effect long after they have become unconscious. This kind of context sensitivity is basic to the arguments made in this chapter (see Section IV).

While context sensitivity implies that conscious contents are affected by a variety of unconscious factors, one can equally well make the complementary point that conscious contents have widespread *effects* that are themselves not conscious. Both of these observations make sense if we think of consciousness as an operating mode of a global data base in a distributed processing system. Specialized processors sensitive to contextual factors can affect conscious representations, and, in turn, the conscious representations can have a widespread effect throughout the system.

2. Corresponding Unconscious Phenomena

Compare the wide range, the relational capacity, and the context sensitivity of conscious events to what we claim to be the relatively *limited domain of unconscious processors and their relative autonomy.* What is the evidence for these claims?

In this view, unconscious processors *by themselves* (i.e., without the intervention of the global data base) are relatively limited and autonomous. The only problem with this claim is that the people we study are generally conscious, so that the limitations of unconscious processors are seldom exhibited overtly. But in the case of involuntary slips of speech or action, we are privileged to see some unconscious processors in a relatively uncontrolled way. Involuntary slips can apparently violate any level of linguistic control (Fromkin, 1973, 1981), and the same observation applies to slips of complex action (Norman, 1981). We can define involuntary slips as those actions that are surprising to the actor: they are not consistent with his or her own previous plans. In extreme cases, slips like this can violate rules that the actor is highly motivated to follow. But in all cases, one can argue that *some specialized rule system, which should have anticipated and prevented the slip, was momentarily decoupled*. Since slips can violate *any* kind of rule system, it follows that any particular system can be momentarily decoupled from the others.

Presumably, if the actor had only a little more time to think about the action, or if his or her attention had been drawn to the relevant dimension, he or she would have anticipated the problem and prevented it (e.g., Baars, Motley, & MacKay, 1975). People are invariably surprised at having made a slip *when they become aware of it*; but this surprise implies that after the slip has been committed, the straying processor must have become coupled again (otherwise the slip would not be recognized as a slip). Indeed, it seems that the process of becoming conscious of an action has the effect of relating the action to its proper context. This again makes sense from the viewpoint of a global data base: if some representation is globally distributed, all the relevant factors can operate on it and respond to it. Conversely, as long as a processor is isolated from the global data base, it can violate rules imposed by other specialized processors.

That unconscious rule systems are relatively autonomous also follows from our frequent inability to exert lasting voluntary control over undesired habits. Most people seem to have automatisms that they would like to eliminate but that seem to be quite autonomous and resistant to external considerations. The more overlearned they are, the less they are conscious, and the harder it may be to exert voluntary control over them. They seem to appear especially when we are consciously distracted or overloaded.

For another example, consider the apparent autonomy of inputs to which we have become habituated. Suppose we have an air conditioner that emits a constant hum of which we rapidly lose awareness. If we need to leave the house and want to shut off the air conditioner (i.e., if the context changes so that we need to operate on the source of the habituated stimulus), we need to *become aware* of the fact that the air conditioner is on. If we fail to bring this fact to awareness, we are likely to leave the air conditioner on, because the habituated representation of this information is not sensitive to changes in context (i.e., to the fact that we are leaving the house).

3. Relevance of These Points

Like consciousness, a global data base in a distributed processing system has enormous range, relational capacity, and context sensitivity. By comparison, each specialized processor has a relatively limited domain and is relatively autonomous.

C. Apparent Unity, Seriality, and Limited Capacity

1. Conscious Phenomena

The impressive relational capacity and context sensitivity of conscious contents should not suggest that there are no limits on our conscious relational ability. However, these limits are of a very interesting kind and seem to depend exclusively on the mutual *informational* compatibility of the mental contents. There are many well-known demonstrations suggesting that we cannot simultaneously experience two mutually exclusive organizations of input (Gregory, 1966; Bransford & Johnson, 1973; Bransford & McCarrell, 1974).

Along very similar lines, there is an extensive lore in the history of science regarding the inability of scientists working within one paradigm to understand a competing paradigm (Kuhn, 1970). Comparable demonstrations of "fixedness' in problem solving go back to Luchins (1942) and Duncker (1945), illustrating the very general fact that a problem cannot be solved if approached within a framework that resists the correct solution. Similarly, Levine (1971) has demonstrated that an extremely simple discrimination task cannot be solved, even under "ideal S-R reinforcement contingencies," if subjects approach it with the wrong set. In the area of conditioning, Dawson and Furedy (1976) have shown that human galvanic skin response (GSR) conditioning will not take place if people are given an explanation of the conditioned-stimulus–unconditioned-stimulus relation that "masks" the contingency between these events. Similar conclusions emerge from work on ambiguous stimuli (e.g., MacKay, 1970) and on brain damage (e.g., Gazzaniga & LeDoux, 1978). If one can safely generalize over a large literature involving such disparate experimental techniques, one might say that any two pieces of information can be consciously related to each other, provided that they can coexist within a single, coherent framework. Facts like the above suggest that conscious organization demands unity, even if the unity is spurious.

The "unity of consciousness" fits quite well with the global-data-base notion. Any global representation that is not consistent with some processor will quickly encounter competition, so that it will be very unstable. Stable global representations must be coherent at any one time, though they may be contradicted at some later time by another stable global representation.

If the contents of consciousness must be coherent, this requirement also implies that incompatible contents must become conscious *serially*, and that there is a *limited capacity* for competing contents. Thus, the apparent unity, seriality, and limited capacity of conscious contents seem to belong together as a set of related phenomena.

Shaffer (1976) has pointed out that people can do a number of tasks (such as conversing and playing the piano) simultaneously, though we would ordinarily consider them contradictory. It is to be noted that Shaffer's subject is extremely well practiced at these tasks, so that her *conscious* capacity is not likely to be taxed. In general, it appears that tasks that compete when they are new stop competing after enough practice has been gained (i.e., after the tasks are taken over by efficient and relatively autonomous specialized processors). Thus, it may well be that two otherwise "incompatible" tasks can go on in the nervous system, provided that they are not conscious at the same time. Hilgard (1977) provided some spectacular examples of such apparently incompatible processes.

2. Comparison with Unconscious Processes

Compared with the unity, seriality, and apparent limited capacity of conscious processes, it appears that unconscious processors are *highly diverse*, that they can operate *in parallel* (unless they need to interact in some way), and that together, the set of specialized unconscious processors has a very great processing capacity. What is the evidence for these claims?

The diversity of processors follows immediately from the idea that they are highly specialized, combined with the incontestable observation that the nervous systems does an enormous number of different things. Parallelism and the idea of a very large unconscious processing-capacity can be viewed in the following way.

(a) *Capacity*. Consider the physiological facts. There are some 10^{10} neurons in the cerebral cortex alone, firing at an average rate of perhaps 40 Hz (Eccles, 1973). Thus we have about 40×10^{10} events taking place each second, or roughly one-half trillion. This certainly seems like a system with very great capacity—yet we know that conscious capacity seems extraordinarily limited. We can store only 7 plus or minus 2 isolated items even with conscious rehearsal, we can process only one stream of speech at a time, and it takes us at least 100 msec to react to a conscious stimulus. Unless we assume that most neurons are firing away "epiphenomenally," so that their activity has little effect on psychologically interesting variables, we must somehow reconcile this picture of frenetic activity and relatively ponderous conscious processing. The idea of a global data base appears to reconcile this apparent conflict. As a distributed system, it is no surprise that the great amount of processing activity is not global but is relegated to dedicated processors. Because a global representation requires the cooperation of a number of specialists, it must change much more slowly than any single specialist. This view helps to resolve what seems to be a contradiction between the limited capacity of consciousness and the enormous amount of processing activity that we observe at the same time.

(b) *Parallel Processing.* The neurophysiology also suggests that "the organization of the brain implies parallel processing" (Thompson, 1976; Anderson, Silverstein, Ritz, & Jones, 1974). However, we well know that conscious processes seem to be quite serial (e.g., Newell & Simon, 1972). How can these different impressions be reconciled?

Consider some of the general properties of parallel information processing. Superficially, it would seem that one could get much more accomplished by parallel than by serial processing. However, parallel processors are restricted if there is some contingency between one process and another—and intelligent processes often involve a series of contingent decisions. In particular, if processors operating in parallel need to interact, there exists a contingency between otherwise independent systems. The result is a bottleneck, which behaves in an apparently serial fashion. These considerations are especially relevant to this discussion, because *a global data base can be viewed precisely as a device that facilitates interaction between otherwise independent, parallel systems.* Marslen-Wilson and Welsh (1978) have provided evidence that some components of speech perception are, in fact, mediated by a parallel-interactive system of this kind.

3. Summary: How the Global Data Base Fits the Capability Constraints of Table 1

The relevance of this theoretical metaphor for consciousness is now beginning to emerge. A global data base is not itself an efficient computational device; rather, it permits a multitude of efficient processors to communicate in some commensurable way. Hence, it must be able to display an enormous range of representations, and to relate any two arbitrary representations to each other, so that distributed processors can help to specify the relationship between any two global representations. At any one time, the global data base can display only a single *coherent* content; incoherent representations will swiftly decay because of internal competition. Indeed, a *context* has previously been defined as a stable, coherent set of constraints on a global representation. This need for unity at any one time will make it appear that the global data base has a very limited capacity, and for this reason, competing contents must appear serially. In short, all of the capability constraints of Table 1 very naturally "fall out of" the concept of a global data base.

By contrast, the specialized processors in a distributed system are highly efficient in their special tasks; necessarily, their domains of specialization are also limited and relatively autonomous. They are highly diverse, they can operate in parallel (provided they do not need to interact), and together, they possess great processing capacity.

Thus, there is a close association between consciousness and the kind of systems configuration discussed here, but not an identity. In the following section, arguments are given that conscious representations must be global, and also stable and informative.

IV. THE BOUNDARIES OF CONSCIOUS CONTENTS

What does it mean to experience something? What are the boundary conditions of *conscious contents*? More is known about perception than about any other kind of conscious content, and most detailed examples will be perceptual. However, the conclusions to be drawn from these examples should suggest an approach to such conscious contents as images, which are not dependent on external input. The arguments given here depend on a detailed consideration of the boundary constraints (Table 2, p. 56) which show under what conditions conscious events become unconscious, and vice versa. Following is a short summary of the arguments, followed by more detailed considerations.

Two kinds of boundary conditions may be called synchronic, since they exist at the same time as any conscious experience, though they are not themselves conscious. First, we know that there must be internal representations of the context within which a percept is defined, but that this contextual representation is *not* conscious. In Section II, a *context* was defined as a stable set of constraints on any global representation. Thus, the claim is made that those properties of a global representation that are *entirely constrained* are not conscious. Until we encounter an Ames trapezoidal room, we are not conscious of the fact that we interpret trapezoidal shapes as rectangles in our carpentered world, and until we encounter someone of a different ancestry and culture, we are not conscious of the fact that we have certain assumptions about people's appearance, dress, and mannerisms. These contextual assumptions are clearly used constantly to make sense of the world, but they are not conscious. Second, it is also the case that sensory input that is *not interpretable within the current context* is not conscious. When we hear a word in a meaningful sentence, we are typically conscious of only one meaning, even though a glance at a dictionary should convince anyone that all words have more than one meaning. We are not conscious of any other meaning until we are in the right context. When we are confronted with a foreign language, especially one with a very different phonology, the sounds of the language do not become conscious until the phonology is spelled out, or until we practice it, or until we hear minimally contrastive pairs of words. We can listen to rock music many times without understanding the words, until someone tells them to us; after that, the words seem limpidly clear. The examples can be multiplied indefinitely. All the phenomena discussed under the heading of "Apparent Unity, Seriality, and Limited Capacity" (Section IIIC), represent cases where some input is perfectly interpretable within one context, but incoherent in another one.

These two points can be summed up as follows: Context, taken by itself, is unconscious, and input, taken by itself and in the absence of the appropriate context, is also unconscious. Only when *both* of these conditions exist—that is, when there is input that can be organized within a current context—are we conscious of some percept.

Next, there are two kinds of unconscious representation that exist diachronically, before and after a conscious representation. The first of these diachronic representations involves *preperceptual* processes, which are clearly representational in nature but not conscious. Second, and of very great importance to the present argument, conscious percepts *habituate* rather quickly, if the input remains predictable. Habituation in all its forms is something of a stepchild in the psychological literature on learning and memory. It is often treated as a rudimentary kind of learning, but one that is not very interesting because it is not associative. Perhaps it is a result of "neural fatigue," etc. In any case, habituation is viewed as something of a by-product, of limited interest.

But in the present approach, habituation is thought to be an intelligent matching of input by any neural system—perhaps the fundamental form of learning, therefore. Neural systems stop working when they complete an internal match of the input, as suggested by Sokolov (1963), and this decrement of responding may resemble a kind of fatigue from the outside. But the decrement simply reflects the fact that after the system actively matches the input, the input becomes redundant with respect to the system. Habituation of *consciousness* of some object is treated in this chapter as *global redundancy*, indicating that the system as a whole has adapted to some stable global representation (see also

Nadel, 1981). In the same sense, actions that have become automatic can be considered globally redundant, though they do require *local* information processing (see Section II). The notion of global redundancy emerges most clearly from a consideration of habituation of awareness, but once established, it can be seen in a number of other cognitive phenomena.

What follows now is a detailed presentation of these arguments.

A. Contexts

It is a very general fact that the perception of some object or event requires a stable context or framework (e.g., Minsky, 1975; Asratyan, 1965) and, indeed, that without this stable context a percept cannot be established. A change in the relevant context will produce a different experience or render the input pattern incoherent. This is true whether we speak of linguistic presuppositions, of assumptions made about space in order to process the visual world, or of the set of assumptions that produce fixedness in problem solving.

Contextual constraints of any experience must be represented with great precision, *yet they are invariably unconscious*. That does not mean that we cannot become aware of some contextual assumption, but that as we become aware of it, it ceases to be context and requires some other unconscious assumptions to be comprehended. The context *as* context always escapes our awareness.

One way to bring a contextual constraint to awareness is by violating it strongly (e.g., Offir, 1973; Hornby, 1974). In the Ames trapezoidal room, such a violation occurs when the observer tosses a ball against the wall, and the ball bounces back in an unexpected way. As the observer becomes aware of the trapezoidal shape of the room, his or her contextual assumptions—the stable constraints on his or her conscious representation of the room—go through a transformation. Indeed, one may argue that contextual factors can become conscious *only* when they are challenged.

Cognitive psychologists can often avoid dealing with stable contextual factors by operating *within* a given experimental situation. In other disciplines, such as anthropology, developmental psychology, or the history of ideas, this is not possible. As a result, scholars in these fields are often acutely aware of the effects of changes of context. But it seems that in any situation, the invisible context contains the most powerful factors in the situation, so that this contextual frame is well worth the attention of cognitive psychologists.

Are we defining *context* circularly? Ultimately, we need to work with well-defined theories that make explicit exactly the content of contextual frameworks. Fortunately, over the past 20 years, workers in artificial intelligence have made great strides in the direction of specifying the knowledge needed to understand everyday situations. It seems likely that over the next few decades, this work will yield theories rich enough, and explicit enough, so that we can follow someone around a supermarket, perhaps, talking about being conscious of this and that while taking for granted active but unconscious contextual knowledge.

B. *Undefined Inputs*

There is a second synchronic boundary to a conscious experience, which becomes especially clear in the case of perceptual input. Consider a perceptual demonstration of a hidden figure, such as the well-known "Dalmatian in the park," which shows a spotted Dalmatian in a shadow-flecked park. Since the entire picture is in black and white, it is initially very difficult to spot the hidden figure. Until the right organization is discovered, it does not become conscious. (It is noteworthy that contextual factors, in the sense defined before, can suggest the correct organization.) However, once proficiency is gained in spotting the hidden figure, the process of spotting the figure becomes fast and efficient to the point where it becomes very difficult to *avoid* seeing the dog. Now the situation is reversed: it becomes difficult to see the spots *as* spots, unless the image of the dog is further obscured (for instance, by turning the picture upside down). Thus the hidden figure is bistable, much like an ambiguous stimulus, but it is nonreversible; once the hidden dog is discovered, the newer, more coherent representation tends to prevail.

This example is really a paradigm case for much of this discussion. The idea of a "hidden pattern" may be generalized to cover a multitude of psychological tasks. For example, in word perception, there is, in a reasonable sense, a "hidden figure" in the pattern of sound. Before one makes a scientific discovery, there is, so to speak, a hidden pattern in the evidence. The reader can no doubt supply further examples of the search for hidden patterns. The analysis of this example may be applied to many similar cases.

The input pattern specifying the Dalmation is unconscious *until* we find the right context—the right set of stable constraints—within which to interpret the input. Thus, we can now state a second very general boundary condition on consciousness of input: available energy patterns are unconscious if they are not defined coherently within the current context. The problem of organizing a pattern in the right way is the problem of finding the right set of stable contextual constraints for that pattern.

The first and second boundary conditions are really different sides of the same coin. The first claims that, to be conscious, any input demands some contextual constraints that are themselves unconscious. The second one states that any pattern is unconscious unless the right framework is available to organize it in a coherent fashion. In the absence of the right context, any input pattern is unconscious. *Thus, context alone is unconscious and input alone is unconscious.* Only when these two unconscious components interact in the right way are we conscious of some event. This is a fundamental claim.

The third and fourth boundary conditions on conscious contents add another requirement. Not only must a conscious representation be coherent and stable, but it must also provide *global information*; that is, it must make a difference to the system as a whole. Arguments for this requirement are discussed next.

C. *Global Information and Global Redundancy*

Consider the very general phenomenon of habituation of awareness, the third boundary condition. When some stimulus is repeated or continued past a certain point, it is no longer experienced. This effect is as general as perception itself: it occurs in all sensory modalities, with any kind of stimulation.[2] Indeed, at any time, there are a large number

---

[2] It may be objected that one can have the "same" experience many times without losing awareness of it. For example, one may travel the same road to work each day without a complete loss of awareness of the road. There are a number of answers to this objection. First, we lose complete awareness only of stimuli that are entirely predictable and, in particular, of stimuli with entirely predictable temporal properties. Very often, we do not adapt completely to some conscious content; we simply shift to a different content. Nevertheless, it is easily conceivable that we shift away if some particular dimension of the content has been absorbed, especially if that dimension is relevant to a current task. Second, we are not merely exposed to the same road each day; we interact with it, so that often we can voluntarily override the tendency to lose awareness of the information. Third, whenever some change takes place in a well-known environment to which we have become habituated, the change must be integrated into a larger set of events. If someone is exposed to a regularly repeated burst of noise, for instance, and we change only one aspect of the noise burst, all the other properties of the stimulus must be reevaluated. Thus, if the onset ramp of the habituated noise is changed, the subject will not become aware of the onset ramp *in abstracto* but will become aware of the whole noise burst. Similarly, if one aspect of the road to work changes, other aspects must become conscious as well. In sum, our continued awareness of routine events does not constitute a counterexample to the claim made here.

of predictable energy patterns impinging on us, from gravity to the ambient light, sound, and temperature, to the pressure of our clothing. All these energy patterns are typically unconscious. It may be that the visual system is especially protected against premature habituation to constant inputs by means of physiological nystagmus (the constant high-frequency tremor of the eyes), which causes light edges in the visual field to fall always on a slightly different part of the retina. Without this feature, awareness of the visual input is lost within seconds. Clearly in all other sensory modalities, awareness of some redundant input tends to habituate quite rapidly.

Habituation of neural structures occurs at all levels, from single cells to complex structures. As we noted above, habituation has not been thought to be a full-fledged kind of learning in the literature on learning and memory, even though, as Sokolov (1963) pointed out, habituation cannot be a form of fatigue because it is stimulus-specific, and because habituated animals will dishabituate to the *absence* of the repeated stimulus. That is, dishabituation is a response not to energy input but to new information. And if dishabituation (orienting, etc.) is a response to information, it is not too great a leap to suppose that habituation is a response to redundancy (Asratyan, 1965; Nadel, 1981). In the present perspective, it is assumed that all specialized processors attempt to model global input that is relevant to them, and that having done so, they cease responding to this input. Thus, habituation for these processors is a sign that learning has occurred; that is, the input matches the local representation sufficiently so that no further adaptation is required. In this view, *habituation of awareness* means that the system as a whole has adapted to the input, so that the input no longer provides global information. (Recall that *global information* has been defined as a global representation that triggers adaptation in the system as a whole, so that any relevant processor can adapt to it.) Thus, habituation of awareness to any input may be considered a sign of global redundancy, which is simply the absence of global information.

But now we can go one important step further. By definition (see Section II), a context is a set of stable, global constraints—constraints to

---

What about the impact of significant stimuli on habituation? It seems obvious that awareness of significant events is lost more slowly than awareness of insignificant ones. In some cases, like chronic pain, one could indeed maintain that awareness is never permanently lost. It seems useful to treat the effect of significance in informational terms. It is highly plausible to think that significant events require more adaptation throughout the system; thus, in a very strict sense, significant events are more "informative" than other events. Significant changes must propagate more widely throughout the system before adaptation can take place. Presumably significant events also demand more problem solving (Baars & Kramer, 1982) before the system achieves complete adaptation.

which the system as a whole has adapted. But this is, of course, equivalent to saying that these constraints are globally redundant. Anything that is globally redundant can therefore become part of a new context, able to affect the way relevant new stimuli will be experienced. We may say, then, that conscious representations that are lost from awareness because of habituation do not disappear: they continue to provide a context within which future related representations are defined.

This is not surprising if we consider well-established facts on gross perceptual readaptation (e.g., Köhler, 1962). Consider an everyday example. When we first step onto a small sailboat, we are very much aware of the movements of the boat, but most of us adapt fairly rapidly, so that the movements of the boat become highly predictable and are lost from awareness. They become globally redundant, in the sense suggested above. What previously constituted information has habituated and is now a part of the context. It is easy to show that this habituated information is not completely lost; it merely becomes the framework within which new information is defined. Thus, on returning to dry land, what is usually in the background now becomes information. That is to say, it now seems as if the *world* is reeling drunkenly: we make false predictions regarding our orientation to gravity and attribute the source of this information not to ourselves but to the world. What was globally redundant (and unconscious) at sea now becomes globally informative and hence conscious, until we once again adapt to land, and the spatial context once again fades into the background.

Thus, habituation of conscious contents can create new contextual constraints that can affect the way conscious information is structured. This is true not only of relatively gross properties, such as our orientation to gravity. Rather subtle properties of our perceptual experience can also be affected by a habituation phenomenon like selective adaptation (e.g., Eimas & Corbit, 1973). In the remainder of this chapter, the idea that habituated conscious contents can create the context for future conscious contents will be considered a general and very important property of the system.

Note that even though a certain process may be globally redundant, it can still require some *local* information-processing. Consider automaticity, which is the counterpart of habituation in the case of a proficient skill (LaBerge, 1974). As we walk around the world, we are largely unaware of the fast, complex, and subtle details of balancing and moving. That is, the action of walking is largely globally redundant, in the sense defined above. Yet we cannot claim that these fast-moving details of walking are nowhere computed; rather, we may say that they do not require global information-processing, because they are essentially routine and predictable at a global level. This is presumably not true for babies just beginning to walk, nor is it true for bed-ridden individuals who are readapting to walking, nor for people just stepping off a small sailboat. For all these individuals, walking requires global information-processing.

Again, the question may be raised whether we are defining *information* and *redundancy* in a circular way, by reference to the phenomena they are supposed to explain. We know that when we can control stimulation, we can repeat a stimulus over and over again, and it will disappear from consciousness. Further, we know that if we change only one dimension of the stimulus—its amplitude, energy envelope, quality, or temporal parameters—the stimulus will become conscious again. These are not circular claims if we have experimental control. But this explanation is still far from satisfactory. We cannot predict the informativeness of a new stimulus in many situations, and until we have adequate theoretical representations of these situations, we will not be able to specify what is informative and what is not. Work in artificial intelligence does seem to be moving rapidly in the direction of such explicit representations for everyday situations.

So far, the argument applies to entirely predictable inputs, such as the ambient light or temperature. However, the notion of global redundancy can also apply to highly predictable *components* of input. For example, when we hear a series of paraphrases of a single sentence, there is little doubt that we will begin to ignore the meaning rather quickly, even though the physical input is continuously changing. Indeed, it will be difficult to attend to the meaning at all: it has become globally redundant. More generally, it seems likely that as soon as we fully understand the meaning of any sentence, any repetition of the meaning will be globally redundant. One may interpret the "click" of comprehension as that moment in which the meaning of a sentence becomes globally redundant, so that now it can be used to interpret new, incoming information. Thus, the notion of global redundancy can be extended beyond the pure case of completely predictable input.

The idea that globally redundant constraints are not conscious adds a very important qualification to the discussion so far. Such things as predictable stimuli and automatic skills must be represented in the nervous system in a coherent fashion, but of course they are not conscious. But this means that the coherence of a representation is a necessary but not a sufficient condition for the representation to be conscious. A conscious representation must be new or *globally informative* as well as coherent. We can now add this to the set of boundary conditions specified so far and claim that *conscious experience of some content involves an inter-*

action between an energy pattern and contextual constraints, resulting in a
coherent representation that provides global information to the system. This is
one of the major conclusions of this chapter.

We now have three sets of constraints along with a reasonable
theoretical interpretation. Conscious contents always seem to involve
an interaction between some energy pattern and a set of contextual
assumptions, so that the interaction results in a coherent representation.
But if this coherent representation provides no news, if it is not informative in some sense, it is not conscious. This observation suggests that
after habituation of awareness, contextual processors have adapted to
the representation so that the news has been absorbed and has indeed
become a part of the system itself.

D. Preperceptual Processing

Consider now the fourth boundary condition of perception. The
idea is widely accepted that input information is preprocessed for a few
tenths of a second before it becomes conscious (e.g., Neisser, 1967).
Preperceptual processing is usually viewed as a kind of hypothesis testing, in which many different hypotheses are brought to bear on the
problem of representing the input. Hypotheses are representations, of
course, and we must explain why this kind of input representation is
not conscious. This is the fourth boundary condition for conscious experience, and it is "diachronic" because it refers to a stage of stimulus
representation that comes before the conscious experience.

Indeed, in practice, the global-data-base configuration has been
used primarily for the kind of hypothesis testing that presumably takes
place before the establishment of a percept (Erman & Lesser, 1975). The
global data base is useful when the processors needed to analyze the
input are unknown, so that *any* relevant processor can be brought to
bear on any global hypothesis. Because the global data base is very
useful in broadcasting information to relevant but unpredictable processors, it seems plausible to assume that the nervous system makes
use of something like a global data base during prepreceptual processing. But this means that there must be global hypotheses that are
not conscious. Now explain the difference between conscious hypothesis-
testing and the unconscious hypothesis-testing that presumably takes
place before perception?

That explanation is really already available. It was previously shown
that input patterns not defined within the current context are not conscious. But preperceptual processes involve precisely a set of hypotheses
that are undefined within the current context, because they are unstable

and mutually competitive. By the time they cooperate sufficiently to establish a coherent context, they become conscious. It is therefore not surprising that the preprocessing of input is not conscious.

If we look at the hidden-figure example again, we can observe this process in slow motion. In the beginning, it is difficult to find the Dalmatian at all, but given the right context (which can be induced by external hints, etc.), the input can be interpreted in the right way. On repeated exposure, it is indeed difficult to avoid seeing the dog, to access the less-coherent interpretation of the input. But even when the pattern is analyzed quite efficiently, we can presume that preprocessing still takes place. It is then no longer conscious, presumably because the processing has speeded up and the lower-level hypotheses are fleeting and unstable.

This point is further supported by a set of examples that show the opposite effect. That is to say, what would happen if we were to *slow down* preperceptual processing? Would the previously unconscious process of hypothesis testing become conscious? This has in fact been tried (Norman, 1976; Kolers, 1978; Bruner & Potter, 1964). For instance, when we read a sentence such as this one, fast and efficient unconscious processes take care of letter and word recognition. But try reading a sentence upside down: suddenly we begin to test *conscious* hypotheses about letters and words. Similarly, when we see an unfocused slide that is gradually brought into focus, we begin "spontaneously" to generate conscious hypotheses. These conscious hypotheses are probably very similar to the unconscious ones that occur preperceptually, although they may be more coherent than the unconscious hypotheses.

There is thus a rather thin dividing line between unconscious hypothesis-testing and conscious hypothesis-testing. It is not clear whether the global representation becomes conscious because it is coherent or because it is stable, because stability and coherence tend to covary perfectly. Certainly, in the model developed so far, specialists that compete with each other can display a global hypothesis for only a very short time before it is contradicted. Therefore, any hypothesis that is coherent will also be stable, and vice versa. Thus, it is safer to restate the conclusion reached above as follows: "Conscious experience of some event always involves an interaction between some energy pattern and a contextual framework that results in a coherent *and stable* representation that provides global information to the system."

This is the fundamental perspective on conscious contents that is advanced here. It seems to account for the empirical constraints in an economical fashion. The model is still a thinking tool—not a permanent position to cling to. But it appears to be both adequate and economical. For instance, it is theoretically pleasing to see that the four general boundary conditions actually reduce to only two properties of conscious contents. First, preprocessing and undefined input turn out to be unconscious for the same reason. Preperceptual processes are unconscious because they lack a stable and coherent context, and similarly, undefined inputs lack such a context. Further, context and highly predictable input patterns are both unconscious because they both involve stable, global representations to which the system as a whole has *already adapted*. Thus, four classes of phenomena reduce to two theoretical terms: events are unconscious if they are undefined in the current context, or if they are so stable as to be part of the context. This theoretical economy is encouraging and suggests that the analysis is on the right track.

V. SUMMARY AND CONCLUSIONS

The metaphor of a global "information exchange" in a distributed processing system helps to explain a number of psychological phenomena. It appears that we are conscious of something when there is an interaction between input and context, resulting in a stable and coherent global representation that provides information to the nervous system as a whole. this description fits the empirical constraints of Tables 1 and 2 and makes a good deal of functional sense as well. When we are conscious of something, we are adapting to it in a global way.

A. Extensions of the Theory

Because of limitations of space, we can only suggest several extensions of this theoretical framework to incorporate further empirical constraints (Baars, 1980; Baars & Mattson, 1981). For example, the theory can incorporate the classic "insight" phenomena in problem solving, and it suggests a role for the conscious components of intentional action. These points are briefly summarized.

In both spontaneous problem-solving and intentional action, a global context serves to guide specialized processors able to complete the context. Although we are not directly conscious of this global context, any of its components can become conscious when contradicted in some way, by either internal or external influences. In problem solving, one accumulates a set of constraints that are at first fully conscious, and as the system adapts to these constraints, they become components of the problem context. As part of a context, these constraints are, of course, not conscious unless they are violated in some way.

An *intention* may be considered a special kind of problem context, one that serves as a global goal to mobilize and organize a large, diverse set of action specialists to prepare and execute an action. Further, the intention has a timing component that permits the action to run off when it is ready.

When there is a conflict between different intentions, or when some action violates a component of its intention, the appropriate component of the intention seems to become fully conscious. All these cases involve changes in the intention context and therefore fit our previous characterization of the conditions under which components of a context become conscious. The "internal monologue" that we often use to command ourselves can be viewed as a way in which a processor able to broadcast a conscious command can trigger the creation of an intention by other processors. The intention then can serve to prepare and execute an action. It is to be noted that such conscious commands are never as complete as the intention: they seem to involve only what is new and different about an intention. Most of the content of the command is tacitly understood, just as the bulk of our communications with each other are tacitly understood (viz., Baars & Mattson, 1981).

Finally, we can deal with the closely related issue of attention. Attention involves a set of systems able to *select and maintain* some particular conscious content, either voluntarily or involuntarily. In voluntary control of attention, we may give a conscious command that triggers an intention that can control future conscious contents. In the involuntary case, specialized processors act to control the contents of consciousness. The experience of mental effort is thought to result from conflict between voluntary and involuntary means of controlling consciousness. Finally, the ideas of the dynamic or "affective" unconscious fit in naturally with the notion of attention, with the difference that some specialized processors may exercise control of access to the blackboard in order to avoid certain conscious contents, while others may seek to display certain other contents.

B. Conclusion

A great deal of work needs to be done to expand and clarify this approach, and to test it for theoretical adequacy and consistency. There are very many empirical implications that have not been discussed in this paper and that must be considered in detail elsewhere. Nevertheless, the theory sketched here fits a large number of facts about consciousness.

No theory at this stage can be more than a thinking tool, to be falsified and changed as our understanding grows. If the present paper serves to define some of the issues with more precision, and if it helps to develop a vigorous and pointed debate about them, a large part of its purpose will have been achieved.

ACKNOWLEDGMENTS

The author gratefully acknowledges Michael A. Wapner (CSULA) for a number of the ideas presented in this paper, and Donald A. Norman (UCSD) for his welcome insistence on brevity and clarity, which helped to improve the paper immensely. Others whose comments were most helpful include Robert Buhr (UCSD, Cognitive Science Program), Lynn Nadel (UC Irvine), Michael Posner (University of Oregon), David Cross (SUNY Stony Brook), and Michael T. Motley (UC Davis). The comments of Robert Monk (Chicago), Richard J. Davidson (SUNY Purchase), Daniel Dennett (Tufts University), and Walter Ritter (Einstein College of Medicine) were most helpful as well.

REFERENCES

ANDERSON, J. A., SILVERSTEIN, J. W., RITZ, S. A., & JONES, R. S. Distinctive features, categorical perception, and probability learning: Some applications of a neural model. *Psychological Review*, 1973, *84*(5), 413–451.

ARBIB, M. A. Perceptual structures and distributed motor control. In V. B. BROOKS (Ed.), *Handbook of physiology* (Vol. 3). American Physiological Society, 1982.

ASRATYAN, E. A. *Compensatory adaptations, reflex activity, and the brain.* Oxford: Pergamon Press, 1965.

BAARS, B. J. *What is the role of consciousness?* Unpublished manuscript, 1980.

BAARS, B. J., & MATTSON, M. E. Consciousness and intention: A framework and some evidence. *Cognition and Brain Theory*, 1981, *4*(3), 247–263.

BAARS, B. J., & KRAMER, D. N. Conscious and unconscious components of intentional control. *Proceedings of the Fourth Annual Cognitive Science Conference.* Ann Arbor: University of Michigan Program in Cognitive Science, 1982.

BAARS, B. J., MOTLEY, M. T., & MACKAY, D. G. Output editing for lexical status in artificially elicited slips of the tongue. *Journal of Verbal Learning & Verbal Behavior, 14,* 1975, 382–391.

BRANSFORD, J. D., & MCCARRELL, N. S. A sketch of a cognitive approach to comprehension: Some thoughts about what it means to comprehend. In W. B. WEIMER & D. S. PALERMO (Eds.), *Cognition and the symbolic processes.* New York: Wiley, 1974.

BRANSFORD, J. D., & JOHNSON, M. K. Consideration of some problems of comprehension. In W. G. CHASE (Ed.), *Visual information processing.* New York: Academic Press, 1973.

BREWER, W. F. There is no convincing evidence for operant or classical conditioning in adult humans. In W. B. WEIMER & D. S. PALERMO (Eds.), *Cognition and the symbolic processes.* Hillsdale, N.J.: Lawrence Erlbaum, 1974.

BRUNER, J. S., & POTTER, M. C. Interference in visual recognition. *Science,* 1964, *144,* 424–425.

DAWSON, M. E., & FUREDY, J. J. the role of awareness in human differential autonomic classical conditioning: The necessary-gate hypothesis. *Psychophysiology*, *13*(1), 1976, 50–53.

DENNETT, D. C. Toward a cognitive theory of consciousness. In D. C. DENNETT (Ed.), *Brainstorms*. San Francisco, Calif.: Bradford Press, 1978.

DIXON, N. F. *Subliminal perception: The nature of a controversy*. London: McGraw-Hill, 1971.

DUNCKER, K. On problem solving. *Psychological Monographs*, 1945, *58* (5, Whole No. 270).

ECCLES, J. C. Brain, speech, and consciousness. *Naturwissenschaften*, 1973, *60*, 167–176.

EIMAS, P. D., & CORBIT, J. Selective adaptation of linguistic feature detectors. *Cognitive Psychology*, 1973, *4*, 99–109.

ERMAN, L. D., & LESSER, V. R. A multi-level organization for problem solving using many, diverse, cooperating sources of knowledge. *Proceedings of the 4th International Joint Computer Conference*, Georgia, USSR, 1975, 483–490.

FROMKIN, V. A. (Ed.). *Speech errors as linguistic evidence*. The Hague: Mouton, 1973.

FROMKIN, V. A. (Ed.). *Errors of speech and hearing*. New York: Academic Press, 1981.

GAZZANIGA, M., & LEDOUX, J. P. *The integrated mind*. New York: Plenum Press, 1978.

GESCHWIND, N. Specializations of the human brain. *Scientific American*, 1979, *241*(3), 180–201.

GHISELIN, B. *The creative process*. New York: Mentor, 1952.

GLOBUS, G., & FRANKLIN, S. Prospects for a scientific observer of perceptual consciousness. In J. M. DAVIDSON & R. J. DAVIDSON (Eds.), *The Psychobiology of consciousness*. New York: Plenum Press, 1980.

GREENE, P. H. Problems of organization of motor systems. In R. ROSEN & F. M. SNELL (Eds.), *Progress in theoretical biology* (Vol. 2). New York: Academic Press, 1972.

GREGORY, R. L. *Eye and brain: The psychology of seeing*. New York: McGraw-Hill, 1966.

HAYES-ROTH, F., & LESSER, V. R. Focus of attention in the Hearsay II speech understanding system. *Proceedings 5th International Joint Computer Conference*, Cambridge, Mass., 1976, 27–35.

HILGARD, E. R. Neodissociation theory of multiple cognitive control systems. In G. E. SCHWARTZ & D. SHAPIRO (Eds.), *Consciousness and self-regulation: Advances in research* (Vol. 1). New York: Plenum, 1976.

HILGARD, E. R. *Divided consciousness: Multiple controls in human thought and action*. New York: Wiley, 1977.

HORNBY, P. A. Surface structure and presupposition. *Journal of Verbal Learning Verbal Behaviour*, 1974, *13*, 530–538.

JAMES, W. *The principles of psychology*. New York: Holt, 1890. (Reprinted by Dover, New York, 1950.)

JENKINS, J. J. Remember that old theory of memory? Well, forget it! *American Psychologist*, 1974, *29*(11), 785–95.

JOHN, E. R. A model of consciousness. In G. E. SCHWARTZ & D. SHAPIRO (Eds.), *Consciousness and self-regulation: Advances in research* (Vol. 1). New York: Plenum Press, 1976.

KAPLAN, R. M. A general syntactic processor. In R. RUSTIN (Ed.), *Natural language processing*. New York: Algorithmics Press, 1973.

KÖHLER, I. Experiments with goggles. *Scientific American*, 1962, *206*, 62–75.

KUHN, T. S. *The structure of scientific revolutions* (2nd ed.). Chicago: University of Chicago Press, 1970.

LABERGE, D. Acquisition of automatic processing in perceptual and associative learning. In P. M. A. RABBITT & S. DORNIC (Eds.), *Attention and Performance* (Vol. 4). London: Academic Press, 1974.

LEVINE, M. Hypothesis theory and nonlearning despite ideal S-R reinforcement contingencies. *Psychological Review*, 1971, *78*, 130–140.

Lewis, F. L. Semantic processing of unattended messages using dichotic listening. *Journal of Experimental Psychology*, 1970, *85*, 225–228.

Lindsay, P. H., & Norman, D. A. *Human information processing* (2nd ed.). New York: Academic Press, 1976.

Luchins, A. S. Mechanization in problem solving. *Psychological Monographs*, 1942, *54*(6, Whole No. 248).

MacKay, D. G. Mental diplopia: Towards a model of speech perception at the semantic level. In G. B. Fores d'Arcais & W. J. M. Levelt (Eds.), *Advances in psycholinguistics*. Amsterdam: North Holland, 1970.

MacKay, D. M. *Information, mechanism and meaning*. Cambridge, Mass.: MIT Press, 1969.

Mandler, G. Consciousness: Respectable, useful, and probably necessary. In R. Solso (Ed.), *Information processing and cognition: The Loyola Symposium*. Hillsdale, N.J.: Lawrence Elrbaum, 1975.(a)

Mandler, G. *Mind and emotion*.New York: Wiley, 1975.(b)

Miller, G. A. *Psychology: The science of mental life*. New York: Harper & Row, 1962.

Minsky, M. A framework for representing knowledge. In P. H. Winston (Ed.), *The psychology of computer vision*. New York: McGraw-Hill, 1975.

Nadel, L. Cognitive and neural maps. In P. Juscyzk & R. Klein (Eds.), *Essays on the nature of thought: In honor of D. O. Hebb*. Hillsdale, N.J.: Lawrence Erlbaum, 1981.

Naranjo, C., & Ornstein, R. E. *On the psychology of meditation*. New York: Viking, 1971.

Neisser, U. *Cognitive psychology*. New York: Appleton-Century-Crofts, 1967.

Newell, A., & Simon, H. A. *Human problem solving*. Englewood Cliffs, N.J.: Prentice-Hall, 1972.

Norman, D. A. *Memory and attention: An introduction to human information processing* (2nd ed.). New York: Wiley, 1976.

Norman, D. A. Categorization of action slips. *Psychological Review*, 1981, *88*(1), 1–15.

Norman, D. A., & Shallice, T. Attention & action: Willed and automatic control of behavior. Unpublished paper, UCSD, La Jolla, Calif., 1980.

Offir, C. E. Memory for presuppositions of relative clause sentences. *Journal of Verbal Learning and Verbal Behavior*, 1973, *12*(6), 636–643.

Paivio, A. Perceptual comparisons through the mind's eye. *Memory and Cognition*, 1975, *3*, 635–647.

Posner, M., & Warren, R. E. Traces, concepts and conscious constructions. In A. W. Melton & E. Martin (Eds.), *Coding processes in human memory*. Washington, D.C.: Winston, 1972.

Reddy, R., & Newell, A. Knowledge and its representation in a speech understanding system. In L. W. Gregg (Ed.), *Knowledge and cognition*. Potomac, Md: Lawrence Erlbaum, 1974.

Schwartz, G. E. Biofeedback and physical patterning in human emotion and consciousness. *American Scientist*, 1975, *63*, 314–324.

Shaffer, L. H. Intention and performance. *Psychological Review*, 1976, *83*(5), 375–393.

Shallice, T. Dual functions of consciousness. *Psychological Review*, 1972, *79*(5) 383–393.

Shallice, T. The Dominant action system: An information-processing approach to consciousness. In K. S. Pope & J. L. Singer (Eds.), *The stream of consciousness: Scientific investigations into the flow of experience*. New York: Plenum Press, 1978.

Shiffrin, R. M., & Schneider, W. Controlled and automatic human information processing: II. Perceptual learning, automatic attending, and a general theory. *Psychological Review*, 1977, *84*, 127–190.

Smith, K. *Behavior and conscious experience: A conceptual analysis*. Athens, Ohio: Ohio University Press, 1969.

Sokolov, E. N. *Perception and the orienting reflex*. New York: MacMillan, 1963.

Sperling, G. The information available in brief conscious presentations. *Psychological Monographs*, 1960, *74* (Whole No. 11).

Straight, S. H. Consciousness as a workspace. *SISTM Quarterly*, 1979, *1*, 11–14.

Tart, C. *States of consciousness*. New York: Dutton, 1975.

Thompson, R. F. The search for the engram. *American Psychologist*, 1976, *31*, 209–227.

Turvey, M. T. Preliminaries to the theory of action with reference to vision. In R. Shaw & J. D. Bransford (Eds.), *Perceiving, acting, and knowing: Toward an ecological psychology*. Hillsdale, Md.: Erlbaum, 1977.

Williams, M. D., & Hollan, J. D. The process of retrieval from very long-term memory. *Cognitive Science*, 1981, *5*(2), 87–119.

3 Event-Related Brain Potentials in the Study of Consciousness

Emanuel Donchin, Gregory McCarthy, Marta Kutas, and Walter Ritter

I. Introduction

A. A Phenomenological Approach to Consciousness

The electrical activity of the brain has always tantalized investigators interested in developing a psychobiology of consciousness. Hans Berger had been driven to his pioneering studies of the human electroencephalogram (EEG) by his interest in "psychic energy." Jung (1975) reported that Berger "believed that the chemical energy of brain metabolism was transported into heat, electrical and 'psychic' energy, and he hoped to extrapolate the latter by measuring the heat production and electrical activity of the brain" (p. 484). The EEG, which Berger discovered, promised to allow insights into the mechanisms underlying consciousness. The rationale for this promise is evident. Because the phenomena of consciousness make themselves most readily available in the human, consciousness is best studied in the awake, alert, speaking individual. As electrical brain activity is one of the few means available for the observation of neural activity in the intact human, it is a natural object of interest to the student of consciousness.

EMANUEL DONCHIN • Cognitive Psychophysiology Laboratory, Department of Psychology, University of Illinois, Champaign, Illinois 61820. GREGORY MCCARTHY • Neuropsychology Research Laboratory, Veterans Administration Hospital, West Haven, Connecticut 06516. MARTA KUTAS • Department of Neurosciences, University of California, San Diego, La Jolla, California 92093. WALTER RITTER • Albert Einstein College of Medicine and Lehman College, City University of New York, Bronx, New York 10468. The research reported here has been supported, in part, under the Office of Naval Research Contract #N00014-76-C-0002 with funds provided by the Defense Advanced Research Projects Agency, as well as by Wright Patterson Air Force Base.

In this chapter, we review studies of event-related brain potentials (ERPs) that address, either explicitly or implicitly, the phenomena of consciousness. An analysis of the methodology and findings of these studies leads to an examination of their conceptual foundations. It is our contention that these studies can benefit from recognizing the fundamental difference between the data on consciousness and the data on brain potentials. The data on consciousness take the form of introspective reports. That is, subjects report, either in words or by the manipulation of mechanical devices, about their consciousness. They may press a button labeled *red*, or state "the red light was on," or report the number of times the red light was illuminated over a period of time. The datum provided by the subject is the *product* of multiple brain processes, conscious and nonconscious. Electrical brain activities recorded on the scalp are, on the other hand, data on one or more of the *processes* that may be involved in conscious experience. We shall endeavor to show how this distinction between processes and their products, if used to guide research in cognitive psychophysiology, might lead to a firmer foundation for the development of a psychobiology of consciousness.

We adopt in this chapter a phenomenological approach to consciousness. That is, we accept that the data generated by our own and by others' reports about consciousness define a *phenomenon*. This phenomenon is as valid an object for analysis as any other phenomenon defined by any other data base. The individual's statement "I am aware . . ." is as valid a datum as the observation that a rat has locomoted on all fours down an alley in a maze. Observations define phenomena and it is the scientists' privilege to select those that appear to be—perhaps for personal reasons—the most exciting or promising. It is the scientists' responsibility, however, to treat the phenomenon chosen for study with ruthless objectivity, untrammeled by religious or philosophical predilections.

Our use of the term *introspection* requires a word of explanation. This perfectly appropriate word, which lexically means "self-report," carries to the psychologist a load of excess meaning. It invokes introspectionism, the once dominant force in American and German psychology (Boring, 1957). Yet the difference between contemporary cognitive psychology and Titchenerian introspectionism is not that one does, and the other does not, abjure introspection. Rather, the two differ in the way that they use introspective data. For both disciplines, the prime data are the reports an individual makes about his or her consciousness. The Titchenerians, however, viewed themselves as observers of the phenomenon. Their introspective reports described consciousness in the same way that Lewis and Clark described the North-west. Here, for example, is Titchener's (1905) psychologist:

> A man keenly interested in mind, with no purpose beyond mind; a man
> enamored of introspection; a man to whom the most fascinating thing in the
> universe is the human consciousness; a man to whom successful analysis of
> an unresolved mental complex is as the discovery of a new genus to the
> zoologist or a new river to the explorer; a man who lives with his mental
> processes as the naturalist lives with creatures which are ordinarily shunned
> or ignored. (p. 220)

According to this view, it is the psychologist's task to become a skillful observer of his or her own consciousness. A psychologist who has achieved the status of a good observer can say, "This light has the quality of redness," and his statement must be taken as a valid description. The datum is "In Titchener's consciousness, this light has redness." For the contemporary student of introspection, on the other hand, the datum would be "Titchener *said* that the light is red." The difference between the two statements is fundamental. The cognitive psychologist views the introspective data not as if they were official reports about the state of consciousness but rather as an intelligence officer treats the multiple (often conflicting) reports received from the field. All need to be judged, compared, and sifted until a coherent view emerges. Therefore, the cognitive psychologist must rely on the highly structured framework of experiments to make sense of the data.

The reader will note that by emphasizing introspective reports, we are finessing a set of problems that lie at the core of a wondrously erudite philosophical literature. We do not presume to deny or affirm the importance and relevance of the philosophy of the mind and the fine distinctions between monism, dualism, interactionism, and various other approaches to the philosophical analysis of the concept of consciousness. Rather, we take in this chapter the position that this debate is not crucial to a discussion of the psychobiology of consciousness. We view the latter as an attempt to understand, in the terms of biology, the phenomena of consciousness. We leave the philosophically qualified to discourse on the reality of the mental, or on the possibility of mind–matter interactions. There is, however, one philosophical bias that guides our thinking that must be made explicit.

In considering the psychobiology of consciousness, we assume that the phenomena of consciousness are intimately associated with neural activity. This is hardly a novel statement. Yet, it will become important in our delineation of research programs utilizing ERPs to make it quite clear that we consider consciousness an aspect of neural activity. We view consciousness as a manifestation of brain activity that reveals itself through the methods of introspection. Depending on the measuring instrument, brain activity manifests itself as chemical events, graded and pulsatile electrical events, temperature changes, and a host of other observables. Introspective reports can be viewed as yet another of these measures of brain activity. The following analogy might clarify our view. Consider the neuronal impulse as it appears to two investigators. The first, an electrophysiologist, places two electrodes on a neuron and records a potential difference between these electrodes in response to a stimulus. Such a study results in a description of neuronal activities in terms of pulse trains. A biochemist observes the neuron with a different set of tools and describes the events in terms of the movement of ions across membranes, the opening of pores in the membranes, and other, essentially chemical, descriptors. The two views of the neuron would, in many ways, be discrepant. In fact, the different techniques might dictate differences in the questions raised by the two investigators. Yet, neither of the two descriptions is inherently more valid, more fundamental, or more "phenomenal" than the other. Different methodologies yield different descriptions of the same phenomenon. It is, of course, of interest, once one accepts the assumption that the chemical and the electrical description of the neuron are both manifestations of the "same" phenomenon, to try to elucidate the relation between the two sets of observations. Such an endeavor is the study of electrochemistry. Concepts are developed that relate electrical and chemical concepts. Methods must be devised that allow the concurrent and closely related measurement of electrochemical events. Ultimately, this approach leads to a better understanding of neuronal function. Yet, it would be wasteful of intellectual energies to debate whether the electrical or the chemical are "epiphenomenal" to the real phenomena of neural function. To argue that the electrical manifestations of neural transmission are epiphenomenal because the process is ionic in nature is not particularly edifying. Even if it were conclusively established that the voltages associated with neural transmission are without causal relation to neural activity, these voltages remain an important manifestation of the process, and in an appropriately designed research program, these "epiphenomena" can provide crucial data about the organization of the nervous system.

It is in the spirit of this analogy that we approach the psychobiology of consciousness. Introspective reports are only one way of approaching brain activity. Reports of conscious experience become, in this view, a set of measurements of brain activity. Other measures of brain activity yield a different view of the brain. The two different ways of looking at the "same thing" must somehow be related. The relations will be elucidated through the forging of concepts that can deal with the joint variances of the two bodies of measurement. Techniques must be developed that will allow the study of such variance, and ultimately, given success, a more comprehensive understanding of the brain will emerge as the disparate phenomenal descriptions of its activity are unified.

This, then, is our object in pursuing the relation between ERPs and consciousness. It is because introspective reports can be obtained most readily from humans that the study of consciousness has the human at its focus. Neural activity in the human can be observed by other means only under fairly severe restrictions. It is not possible to subject human nervous systems to the mechanical, electrical, or chemical interventions that have been found so useful in the study of the nervous systems in nonhuman species. Neuropathology has provided richer data on human nervous activity. The administration of drugs is another important neuropsychological tool. Yet, these approaches are strongly limited by obvious ethical considerations. There remains only one rich source of data on neural activity in the awake, alert, behaving human: the recording from the scalp of the electrical activity of the brain.

B. The Event-Related Brain Potential: A Brief Survey

We limit ourselves in this chapter to a discussion of event-related brain potentials (ERPs). There is a large and interesting literature that focuses on the relation between the "ongoing" EEG and consciousness (see Lindsley, 1960; John, 1967). Work in that tradition dates to Berger's original studies. It tends to express the electrophysiological measurements in terms of their spectral composition and the observations on consciousness in terms of general states ("Is this person conscious? alert? comatose?"). Our research has focused on a different aspect of scalp-recorded electrical brain activity: event-related brain potentials. The ERP is a transient series of voltage fluctuations generated in brain tissue immediately preceding or following the occurrence of an event. This activity appears as a sequence of positive and negative peaks whose timing and relative magnitudes depend on the eliciting event, the state of the subject, and the placement of the recording electrode on the scalp (see Callaway, Tueting, & Koslow, 1978, for a comprehensive review of the ERP literature).

A central concept in the interpretation of the ERP waveform is the "component." Each peak-to-trough, or base-to-peak, deflection appearing in the ERP at a consistent interval following the eliciting event is often considered a component. More recently, components have been defined somewhat more rigorously as segments of the variability of the ERP waveform that are demonstrably controlled by experimental manipulations (Donchin, Ritter, & McCallum, 1978). The ERP waveform should definitely be treated not as a unitary object but as a sequence of overlapping components, each reflecting the activity of a neural processor.

A useful, heuristic distinction can be made between two classes of ERP components. Some components are *exogenous*. They represent an obligatory response of the brain to input in sensory channels. A series of seven wavelets can be recorded, for example, from the top of the head immediately following an auditory stimulus. The amplitude of these components is so minute that a signal average based on thousands of stimuli must be used for their extraction. These components seem to represent activity in the earliest stations of the auditory pathway (Starr, Sohmer, & Celesia, 1978). These brain-stem potentials have proved robust to manipulations of the subject's state. No matter how aroused, alert, asleep, relaxed, or attentive is the subject, the brain-stem evoked responses maintain their amplitudes and, generally, their latencies. However, damage to the auditory nuclei in the brain stem frequently causes specific distortions in the waveform of these evoked responses. It is for this reason that these early components have become important tools in neurological diagnosis.

The exogenous components are often followed by the *endogenous* components. These components represent information processing *invoked* by the psychological demands and the context in which a stimulus is presented, rather than that *evoked* by the presentation of stimuli. The amplitude, latency, and scalp distribution of these components reflect, in a systematic manner, variations in the underlying psychological substrate. It is characteristic of the endogenous components that they are *not* obligatory responses to stimuli. The same physical stimulus may, or may not, elicit an endogenous component, depending on several variables: the degree to which that stimulus is relevant to the task that the subject is performing, the attention the subject invests in the stimulus, and the extent to which the stimulus requires, or does not require, shifts in the subject's strategy. Such variables as the payoffs for task performance, the anticipated difficulty of the task, and the span of the short-term memory determine the amplitude, the latency, and the scalp distribution of the endogenous components. (For reviews of the endogenous components see Hillyard, Picton, & Regan, 1978; Donchin *et al.*, 1978; Tueting, 1978; Donchin, 1979).

The following endogenous components have been identified with some consistency. Components are labeled with letter–number combinations. The letter indicates the polarity of the component (negative or positive). The number represents the usual temporal interval, in milliseconds, from the eliciting stimulus to the peak of the component (the "latency").

1. N100

This negative component is present in ERPs elicited by almost all stimuli of moderate and high intensity. While N100 has many of the attributes of exogenous components, recent evidence suggests that its amplitude is modulated by the degree to which the subject is selectively attending to the eliciting stimuli. Particularly well known is the work of Hillyard and his associates (Hillyard et al., 1978). They presented stimuli at a high rate to each of the ears, or at different loci in space. Such physical cues were assumed to define input "channels." The subject was instructed to process stimuli that arrived in one channel and to ignore the input to other channels. The N100 elicited by stimuli in the attended channel was larger than the N100 elicited by the unattended stimuli. It now appears that the amplitude of N100 varies because Nd, a negative component that coincides in time with N100, is affected by attention (Naatanen & Michie, 1979).

2. N200

This ERP component is elicited whenever a rare or unexpected event occurs. It is of particular interest because it covaries on a trial-to-trial basis with reaction time (Ritter, Simson, Vaughan, & Friedman, 1979; Renault & Lesevre, 1979) and becomes longer in latency in conventional ERP averages when target stimuli are made more difficult to discriminate from nontarget stimuli (Goodin, Squires, Henderson, & Starr, 1978; Towey, Rist, Hakerem, & Sutton, 1980; Naatanen, Hukkanen, & Jarvilehto, 1980). In all of the studies cited, changes in the latency of N200 were accompanied by roughly equivalent changes in the latency of the P300 component to be discussed below. The significance of N200 has been overlooked until recently because this endogenous component is often obscured by exogenous components that occur in a similar time region. The most direct examination of N200 occurs when subjects perform a task with respect to infrequent, random omissions in a train of stimuli delivered at a constant rate of about one stimulus per second. The stimulus omissions elicit an N200, in the absence of any exogenous potentials, followed by a P300. However, subtraction procedures have been successfully used to remove overlapping exogenous components to uncover N200 elicited by physically present target stimuli. The N200 component has been shown to be modality-specific in its scalp distribution for auditory and visual stimuli (Simson, Vaughan, & Ritter, 1976, 1977) and is generally regarded as being related to the process of discrimination.

3. P300

This is a large-amplitude, endogenous component reliably recorded in association with task-relevant, unexpected stimuli. It will be discussed in detail in Section IV.

4. Response-Preceding Negative Waves

The contingent negative variation (CNV) and the readiness potential (RP) are both clearly endogenous. These two components, antecedent to an event, apparently represent anticipatory processes. The RP, discovered by Kornhuber and his associates in Germany (Kornhuber & Deecke, 1965), is a slow negative potential that appears up to 800 msec prior to the execution of a response (see Kutas & Donchin, 1977, for a review). It gradually increases in amplitude and peaks just prior to the response, then shifts to a rapid change in the positive direction. The RP tends to be larger over the hemisphere contralateral to the responding hand. Its onset depends on the point in time at which the choice between the responding hands is made. The CNV is a similar component that appears when one stimulus heralds the arrival of a second, imperative stimulus to which the subject must respond. Again, a slow negative potential emerges some 400 msec following the warning stimulus and gradually increases to a peak just prior to the imperative stimulus. While the CNV can be recorded reliably, it has been somewhat difficult to interpret, as its amplitude and waveform are sensitive to many different variables.

Attempts to assess the joint variance of consciousness and ERPs have taken a number of forms, which may, for convenience, be classified in three categories. These are attempts to distinguish between brain responses to supra- and subliminal stimuli, to relate aspects of the ERP to the contents of consciousness, and to relate ERPs to human information-processing. In the following sections, we review these approaches to the psychobiology of consciousness. Our intent is not an exhaustive review of the literature. Rather, we shall illustrate in each case the approach and the methodological and conceptual problems it encounters by focusing on a few typical studies.

II. ERPs, Threshold, and Subliminal Perception

Consideration of the relationship between ERPs and behavioral measures of stimulus detection or threshold provides a useful starting point for our discussion of ERPs and consciousness. Are there measurable differences in ERPs to stimuli that are above the threshold for conscious perception as compared with those elicited by stimuli presented below this threshold? Indeed, do stimuli presented below this threshold for consciousness evoke any brain activity?

Experiments designed to answer these questions have come from many quarters and from a variety of interests. In many clinical settings, the ERP is used as an objective measure of sensory threshold that is independent of the need for overt responses. Witness, for example, the use of ERPs in audiometry (Picton, Woods, Baribeau-Braun, & Healy, 1977). To determine if the auditory system is intact, the audiologist must first determine if a patient "can hear." When direct questions cannot be addressed to a patient, the audiologist may utilize ERP measures. It is important, in this context, to determine what can be inferred about a patient's awareness of a tone from the obtained ERPs. A similar interest in threshold measurements comes from the psychophysicist, who may be interested in the degree to which ERPs manifest the various relationships that have been established between the physical parameters of stimulation and the subjective judgments of sensation (see Hillyard *et al.*, 1978, for a discussion of these relationships). Investigators who have conducted studies relating ERPs to threshold measures have been motivated by an interest in the phenomena of subliminal perception. In these studies, ERPs have been used to validate, or test, the claim that stimuli too weak in energy, or too short in duration, for conscious perception can nevertheless influence behavior. These studies of ERPs for threshold and subthreshold are most germane to our present discussion; a brief review of this literature follows.

A few general remarks are in order. In all of the studies of threshold and ERPs, the investigators examine the relationship between subjective reports of stimulus detection and measures of the ERP. Although these experiments may seem to be straightforward, they are fraught with methodological difficulties. The problems encountered in such studies have been discussed by Donchin and Sutton (1970), Regan (1972), and Sutton (1969).

The concept of *sensory threshold*, in the sense of an absolute limit for conscious perception, has proved inadequate to account for the human's performance as a signal detector. The task assigned in "threshold" or signal-detection studies is more conveniently modeled as a decision task. Whether any given stimulus will be "detected" depends not only on a subject's sensitivity to the stimulus but also on the subject's criterion for stimulus detection. This criterion (labeled *response bias* in the signal-detection literature; Green & Swets, 1977) is affected by the relative probability of a signal as well as by the perceived payoffs and costs associated with correct and incorrect decisions. The "threshold," then, is a statistical abstraction rather than a physical entity in the sensory system. The decision mechanisms control the subject's behavior whether or not they are explicitly addressed in the experimental design. Thus, experiments that ignore the distinction between sensitivity and criterion are suspect.

The measurement of the ERP presents additional problems for the threshold paradigm. The ERPs must be extracted from the larger-amplitude "background" EEG activity. The purity of the extraction depends on the relative amplitude of the EEG and the ERP. The extraction process is also affected by the degree to which the ERPs are synchronized with the eliciting event. Low-intensity ("liminal") stimuli evoke minuscule and poorly synchronized ERPs, which are, therefore, difficult to extract. This problem is compounded in scalp recordings as the scalp attenuates ERP amplitudes and distorts the relative contributions from near and distant neural sources (Goff, Allison, & Vaughan, 1978).

Additional problems arise when investigators ignore the componential nature of the ERP. Much of current ERP research is concerned with elucidating the "vocabulary" of ERP components and identifying which physical and psychological manipulations control the variance of particular ERP components (see Callaway *et al.*, 1978; Otto, 1978). As we have noted, different components are affected in different ways by experimental manipulations. It is therefore quite inappropriate to discuss the effects of variables on "the" ERP. Studies that have treated the ERP waveform as a unitary entity, ignoring the detailed structure of the waveform, are of limited value. Lastly, given the trial-by-trial changes evident in detection behavior, it is necessary to record behavioral and ERP measures simultaneously and to sort the ERP trials on the basis of behavioral outcome. These considerations should be borne in mind as we proceed to discuss some of the attempts to relate ERPs to the detections of weak stimuli.

Shagass and Schwartz (1961) reported that an ERP appeared at the scalp whenever the eliciting stimulus exceeded the threshold for conscious awareness. Schwartz and Shagass (1961) extended their work by recording directly from the cortex of cats while simultaneously recording from thalamus and peripheral nerve. They found that shocks of an intensity sufficient to evoke a response in the peripheral nerve also evoked responses at the thalamus and cortex. The authors concluded from these two studies that there was no physiological substrate for subliminal perception: all stimuli that excited the peripheral receptor evoked a cortical response (in the cat), and all stimuli that evoked a cortical response could be consciously perceived (in the human).

The conclusions of Schwartz and Shagass were supported by Domino, Matsuoka, Waltz, and Cooper (1964), who recorded somatosensory ERPs simultaneously from the scalp and the epidural surface of the cortex. These investigators reported that the ERP became identifiable at threshold levels. Unfortunately, no information was provided regarding how the thresholds were determined or whether an attempt was made to record ERPs elicited by subthreshold stimuli.

Another attempt to relate ERPs to subliminal perception was made by Shevrin and Fritzler (1968; see also Shevrin, Smith, & Fritzler, 1969), who reported that a positive component at 175–275 msec latency, recorded from a frontal-occipital bipolar derivation, discriminated between two stimuli presented at subliminal durations. The stimuli consisted of a rebus figure composed of a pen and a knee and an abstract figure matched with the rebus figure for size, color, general configuration, and brightness but devoid of complex internal contours and specific content. These stimuli were presented in blocks for durations of 1 msec, 30 msec, and then 1 msec again. There were 60 stimulus presentations in each exposure block; after each 10 stimuli (5 rebus and 5 abstract), the subjects were asked to describe what they saw and then free-associate for 2 min. These free associations were the behavioral data; they were scored in three categories for their relationship to the rebus figure.

Libet, Alberts, Wright, and Feinstein (1967, 1972; see also Libet, 1965, 1966; Libet, Alberts, Wright, Lewis, & Feinstein, 1972; Libet, Alberts, Wright, Delattre, Levin, & Feinstein, 1964) examined ERPs to stimuli whose intensity was either above or below the threshold for conscious perception. Libet et al. (1967) reported that the difference between perceived and unperceived stimuli was manifested by both qualitative and quantitative differences in the ERP. Recording directly from the pia–arachnoid surface of the postcentral gyrus, Libet et al. found that stimuli that were below the threshold for conscious perception did elicit an ERP. These ERPs were smaller than those elicited by suprathreshold stimuli. Furthermore, only the early ("primary") ERP components were elicited by the "unconscious" stimuli. Libet et al. attributed the difference between their results and those mentioned above to the greater resolution afforded by recording directly from the cortex. In fact, their scalp and epidural recordings did not reveal these subthreshold ERPs. In contrast to Schwartz and Shagass (1961), Libet et al. claimed that their data indicate a possible physiological basis for subliminal perception: the nervous system responds to stimuli that are not consciously perceived. Presumably, stimuli invoke activity that is available for unconscious processing; Libet (1965, 1966, 1973) has elaborated a theory of unconscious and conscious processing of stimuli based on these results and other data relating to direct cortical stimulation.

While certainly intriguing, Libet et al.'s (1967) data, as well as the data reported by Shagass and Schwartz (1961), are somewhat difficult to interpret (Donchin & Sutton, 1970; Sutton, 1969). Particularly troubling is the manner in which the subject's "threshold" was assessed. Libet et al.'s subjects were instructed to attend for possible presentations of stimuli and to report if they had *consciously* perceived, or had not perceived, the stimuli. They were also allowed to report that they were "uncertain" whether a stimulus had been presented. Libet (1965, 1966, 1973) was explicitly critical of the forced-choice measures of threshold prevalent in contemporary psychophysics as methods for assessing subjective experience. He apparently feels that the subject may be able to respond manually to the presentation of a stimulus without, in fact, consciously perceiving that stimulus. However, the fact that Libet's subjects made a very small number of "false alarms" suggests that the subjects adopted a strict response criterion. It is conceivable, therefore, that with a more relaxed response criterion, subjects would have "detected" some portion of the subliminal stimuli. Libet, to be fair, insisted that he was measuring something quite different from what one tries to measure by employing signal-detection procedures. Libet was interested in "subjective experience," not in "detection." Subjective experience was defined by him to be whatever causes a subject to report that she or he "feels" the stimulus. Thus, the subject's reports are the "primary"—and according to Libet, the only—data on subjective experience. Yet, the evidence is overwhelming that an individual's report on subjective experience, whether spoken or otherwise communicated, is determined by both "sensitivity" and "criterion" (Green & Swets, 1977). It is therefore difficult to interpret data that ignore this distinction.

The studies reviewed in the preceding paragraphs attempted to determine if a physiological substrate exists for subliminal perception. To this effect, the investigators tried to ascertain if ERPs can be elicited by stimuli presumed to be below the "threshold" of consciousness. Other investigators have considered ERPs and the sensory threshold for quite a different purpose. Their intent has been to evaluate the validity of the claim that the ERP is a "correlate" of psychological processes. Their testing has been based on the assumption that any supraliminal stimulus must elicit an evoked potential. Further, they have assumed that the absence of ERPs after a supraliminal stimulus indicates that ERPs are not useful as correlates of information processing, or as measures of perception or sensation.

Clark, Butler, and Rosner (1969) made this latter argument as they observed a dissociation between sensation and ERPs. They recorded ERPs from seven male subjects who were anesthetized to different depths, through the inhalation of different concentrations of cyclopropane. The subjects' thresholds for the perception of mild electric shocks at the right ulnar nerve were determined by the descending method of limits prior to inhalation of the drug. Each subject indicated whether he had perceived the shock by pressing a button with his left hand. After threshold was determined in this manner, the subjects were administered the anesthetic.

The subjects' sensory thresholds were assessed for each concentration of cyclopropane. The ERPs elicited by stimuli presumed to be supra- and subliminal were also recorded at each level of anesthesia. However, the psychophysical and the electrophysiological data were recorded on separate occasions, under somewhat different circumstances. In general, the amplitude of the ERPs diminished with deepening levels of anethesia and, in three subjects, disappeared altogether at the time that the high concentrations of the anesthetic were administered. The sensory thresholds increased slightly during the anesthetic sessions. Of particular importance, according to Clark *et al.* (1969), was the finding that some stimuli that were definitely supraliminal (that is, those of which the subjects were presumably "conscious") failed to elicit any ERP. On the basis of these data, the authors asserted that, at best, the ERPs are unnecessary for at least some sensory experiences. Clark *et al.* suggested that the evoked potential may be "full of sound and fury signifying nothing" and may play "no essential or important role" in determining perceptual reactions to those parameters that might be encoded.

Donchin and Sutton (1970) found Clark *et al.*'s study wanting on many grounds. A particularly important weakness in Clark *et al.*'s study was that it measured the subject's sensory threshold using a technique that ignored the subject's decision criterion. Thus, it was quite possible for the subjects to use different decision criteria when in different levels of anesthesia. If the subjects relaxed their criterion with increasing levels of the drug, then the number of correct detections might not change, although the number of false positives (values not obtained with the procedure of Clark *et al.*, 1969) would also increase.

Another serious weakness in the study by Clark *et al.* is that they obtained the ERPs on different occasions than were used to measure the sensory threshold. The procedures used during threshold measurements were designed to focus the subjects' attention on the stimuli. The procedures used when the ERPs were recorded did not prod the subject to be attentive. Thus, the behavioral and the electrophysiological data were recorded while the subjects were in quite different attentional states. It is well known that attentional state plays a major role in determining the amplitude and the latency of ERPs (Haider, Spong, & Lindsley, 1964). It should also be noted that the disappearance of ERPs from scalp recordings does not eliminate the possibility that ERPs are present but are too small in amplitude to be measured without recording from inside the cranium.

A number of experiments have since been performed to clarify the relationship between ERP components and threshold-level stimuli in the context of the theory of signal detection (Hillyard, Squires, Bauer, & Lindsay, 1971; Paul & Sutton, 1972, 1973; Squires, Hillyard, & Lindsay, 1973; Squires, Squires, & Hillyard, 1975; Squires, Squires, & Hillyard, 1975). Hillyard et al. (1971) established that the amplitude of the P300 component of the ERP bore a systematic positive relationship to the subject's auditory "sensitivity" (the d' of signal-detection theory). Furthermore, Hillyard et al. (1971) established that while P300s were reliably elicited by detected threshold-level stimuli in the signal-detection task, no visible ERPs were elicited by stimuli of the same intensity when the subjects were not actively attending to the stimuli.

Paul and Sutton (1972, 1973) examined the relationship between response criterion and ERP components in an auditory signal-detection paradigm. In their studies, criterion was manipulated by varying the monetary value of correct responses and the penalties for false positives. Paul and Sutton also varied the probability that the signal would be present on any trial. Their results indicated that the amplitude of the P300 component increased with the increasing strictness of the subjects' criterion, no matter what caused the criterion to vary. Both Hillyard et al. (1971) and Paul and Sutton (1972, 1973) have interpreted their data in terms of the subject's confidence. The more confident the subject is in the detection of the signal, the larger the amplitude of P300.

The relationship of confidence to P300 amplitude in the signal-detection paradigm was studied in a series of papers by Squires and his colleagues (K. Squires et al., 1973, 1975; N. Squires et al., 1975). Using a cue light to synchronize the ERP to the presence or absence of an auditory signal, Squires was able to demonstrate that the amplitude of P300 was equal in both correct and incorrect signal-present decisions. Large P300s could also be elicited to high-confidence correct rejections, but only when these signal-absent decisions were relatively infrequent.

Thus, it seems that the P300 varies systematically with the nature of the subjects' decisions in a task of detecting threshold-level stimuli. This systematic variation is best seen when appropriate behavioral measures are taken and the ERP data and overt responses are obtained simultaneously and sorted on the basis of the subjects' decisions. It makes little sense in this context to inquire if supraliminal stimuli do or do not evoke an ERP. Whether they do depends on the processing activities invoked by the stimuli as the system goes about the business of deciding whether to report a detection. The subject's report is a product of the processes affecting the sensitivity and the response bias on any trial. The ERPs reflect some of these processes. In fact, different ERP components reflect different processes. Thus, it is not particularly meaningful to ask, as Clark *et al.* (1969) did, if ERPs in general are related, under poorly specified conditions, to the sensory "threshold." The studies conducted within the framework of signal-detection theory by Hillyard, Sutton, and their associates have been more fruitful.

In general, the ERP data and threshold data generated by Clark *et al.* (1969) are in agreement: ERP amplitudes diminish and thresholds increase as the level of anesthesia deepens. Clark *et al.* erred in expecting behaviorally determined thresholds to covary in a one-to-one manner with their physiological measures. Clark *et al.*'s conclusions were based on the implicit assumption that the brain processes manifested by the ERP components must be identical to a behavioral product: a button press. This assumption is not valid. Although some ERP measures appear to be related to parameters of sensations, these relationships are often nonlinear (Hillyard *et al.*, 1978). Of particular note is the tendency of the ERP components to saturate—that is, to reach maximum amplitude—before behavioral measures of sensation asymptote.

The studies reviewed in this section have established that stimuli that subjects deny perceiving sometimes elicit an ERP. Even when the ERPs are elicited by subthreshold stimuli, they tend to be restricted to early components. Whether one accepts these data as relevant to the issue of subliminal perception depends on one's point of view. Libet is essentially Titchnerian. He accepts the subjects' introspections as veridical descriptions of experience. If one accepts this view, then Libet's data are indeed fascinating. A particularly striking aspect of these data is that the difference between the ERPs elicited by conscious and unconscious stimuli is that the conscious stimuli elicit both early and late components, whereas only early components are elicited by the unconscious stimuli. These data are consistent with the view of the early components as "specific" and the late components as "nonspecific," but crucial for conscious perception (Hernandez-Peon, Scherrer, & Jouvet, 1956; Lindsley & Wicke, 1974).

It must be recalled, however, that this distinction does not hold up well under close scrutiny. Williamson, Goff, and Allison (1970) were able, for example, to show that the so-called primary vertex potential is quite diffuse. Vaughan (1974) and his associates have, on the other hand, presented data supporting the "specificity" of this wave. Furthermore, the structure and the functional significance of the reticular function have proved quite a bit more complex than presumed by the early models. Libet's data provided a very useful framework for elucidating this problem. Regrettably, his Titchnerian orientation makes it difficult to use his data. Much as Libet disagrees, the evidence is strong that individuals' reports in a detection task are subject to response bias. As the bias was not measured by Libet, it is not possible to know if the changes he observed were changes in sensitivity or in response bias. Until such data are available, this unique source of information on consciousness and ERPs has not fulfilled its promise. While we are not convinced by Libet's interpretation of his data, we do not deny the value of the paradigm he adopted. There is a point in recording, and analyzing, ERPs within the context of the signal-detection experiment. Libet's opportunity to do so, during surgery, from the exposed cortex is enviable.

What should be noted, we think, in designing such experiments, is the distinction we have made between process and product. The overt report that a subject makes on a given trial is the final product of a complex of interacting processes. These may include the activity in the sensory systems, leading from receptor to cortex, as well as the confluence of heuristic, motivational processes, the demands of concurrent tasks, and the changing strategies that the subjects adopt to deal with their environment. The ERPs measured in response to the stimulus may reflect any of these processes; therefore, the relation of the ERPs to the final product may depend on the extent to which this process affects the variance in this product. It is for this reason that one cannot declare the ERP to be, or not to be, "related" to the subject's overt report without considering the total complex of the factors that determine this report.

III. THE CONTENTS OF CONSCIOUSNESS AND ERPs

In the previous section, we discussed the extent to which the presence of an ERP component reflected a person's conscious awareness of the evoking stimulus, and we found the results equivocal. The investigators whose work is reviewed in this section have focused on supraliminal stimuli. Their basic assumption has been that specific aspects of conscious experience are reflected in the ERP. Studies designed to obtain such correlations generally take one of two forms. One version tests the hypothesis that the same physical stimulus presented on different occasions may lead to different percepts and that the ERPs recorded in association with the different percepts will be different. The difference in the ERPs is then attributed to the differential meaning ascribed to the stimulus. Such studies generally analyze the ERPs elicited by the same physical stimulus when endowed, naturally or by the experimenter, with different meanings.

Several experimenters presented the same physical stimulus in different contexts in order to test the hypothesis that the form of the ERP would vary with percept (Thatcher, 1977; Johnston & Chesney, 1974; Sandler & Schwartz, 1971; Brown, Marsh, & Smith, 1976; Teyler, Harrison, Roemer, & Thompson, 1973). Sandler and Schwartz (1971) employed ambiguous figures, thereby changing content but not the physical characteristics of the stimuli. They noted small waveform differences in the occipital ERPs, depending on which of the percepts was dominant. There were, however, major difficulties with the experiment (recognized by the authors) that restrict interpretation of the results. The stimulus they used was the "gypsy girl" ambiguous figure. It is generally the case that there is a bias about which figure is seen on initial presentation of the figure. As the male figure turned out to be dominant, the subjects reported difficulty in maintaining a perceptual set (of the alternate percept) during the ERP recording. In addition, there were no controls over attentional factors, which have been shown to have profound effects on ERP waveforms (Hillyard *et al.*, 1978).

Johnston and Chesney (1974) used a very similar approach. They presented an ambiguous figure that could be identified either as the letter *B* or the number *13*, depending on context. They reported, on the basis of a principal-component analysis of the waveforms, that the ERPs to the ambiguous stimulus differed, depending on whether it was perceived as a number or a letter. Because of the localization of the effect to the frontal electrode sites, they concluded that the visual cortex was more involved in the representation of the physical characteristics of stimuli, whereas the frontal areas were more concerned with the representation of meaning. The study has been criticized (Galbraith & Gliddon, 1975) on the grounds that the subjects' task was to say what they saw as quickly as possible after seeing it. This requirement could easily have led to a confounding of the stimulus ERP with vocalization potentials, both neural and muscular. The differences between the frontal and occipital recordings cannot be assessed from the data presented, as concurrent recording from both sides was accomplished in one subject only. Furthermore, as in Sandler and Schwartz's (1971) study, there is a tendency to perceive the ambiguous figure, when presented out of context, as the letter *B* rather than as the number *13*. As Johnston and Chesney used fairly short presentation intervals, it is possible that they avoided this bias.

Yet another problem with this study is that it lacked a very important control. Consider Johnston and Chesney's claim that the ambiguous stimuli elicit different ERPs when perceived as *B* or *13*. If there is, as they claimed, a difference between the ERP associated with the perception of a number and the ERP associated with a letter after the presentation of ambiguous stimuli, they should have established their point by showing that the ERPs to a class of unambiguous numbers is distinct from the ERPs elicited by a class of unambiguous letters. Furthermore, the ERP elicited by the figure when perceived as *B* should be more "lettery" than "numbery." Without these data, it is not possible to tell if the effect is due to unspecified interactions within the contexts or is indeed due to the manner in which the brain responds to numbers or letters.

A similar study in which meaning was determined by the linguistic context in which stimuli were presented was carried out by Brown *et al.* (1973, 1976) and Teyler *et al.* (1973). These studies were designed to assess hemispheric utilization induced by stimuli requiring linguistic analysis, yet they do bear on the issues at hand. Teyler *et al.* (1973) reported that different ERPs were elicited by clicks associated with ambiguous words, depending on whether the subject was thinking about the noun or the verb meaning of the word. Brown *et al.* reported a similar study, in which they recorded ERPs elicited by words rather than by clicks. They found that the ERPs elicited by the word *fire* in the phrases "sit by the fire" and "ready, aim, fire," were different, whereas the ERPs elicited by the same word in the phrases "fire the gun" and "fire is hot" were quite similar, because at the time the word *fire* was presented, the subjects could not tell if it served as a noun or a verb. These differences in the brain's response to the word *fire* in different contexts appeared only in recordings from electrodes placed over the "speech" areas in the left hemisphere. On the basis of such results, Brown *et al.* (1973) concluded that "context-produced differences in the meaning of a word" produced systematic differences in the waveform of the ERP. Not enough of the data are presented, so the differences in waveform cannot be evaluated with certainty. There are also some problems in the analysis used (see Friedman, Simson, Ritter, & Rapin, 1975; Donchin, Kutas, & McCarthy, 1977, for criticism). Subsequent work by this group (Brown *et al.*, 1976) extended the analysis and the range of data considered. It appears now that there are differences between ERPs elicited by words presented at the beginnings and at the ends of the sentences. However, these differences are somewhat hard to interpret in terms of specific components of the ERP, as the entire ERP waveform seems to disappear. In a subsequent report, Marsh and Brown (1977) described a principal-component analysis of their data. They reported effects of "meaning" on three different components. Such analyses, if pursued, will be of considerable value.

Not all such studies have reported positive results. There have been reports that decisions about the meaning of stimuli can occur without concomitant changes in the ERP. Rem and Schwartz (1976) recorded ERPs elicited by anaglyph versions of Julesz patterns. They recorded ERPs from occipital-parietal and vertex-mastoid sites that were elicited by a square imposed on a textured ground, a T-shape on a background, and a figureless textured area. They varied exposure durations and used different-colored filters. They reported that the ERP waveforms were sensitive to the microstructure of the Julesz patterns and were affected by the color and depth cues in the figures. They found, however, no differences between the ERP waveforms that could be attributed to the figural content of the stimuli.

When successful, the above studies share the claim that if the same physical stimulus is presented in different contexts that cause it to be perceived differently, it will elicit different ERPs. A much stronger statement of this position has been derived from the assumption that unique ERP waveforms reflect the specific perception elicited by specific stimuli. In its extreme version, this view can lead to the assertion that there is a unique ERP for Grandma's red Volkswagen. As stated by Sandler and Schwartz (1971), "Taken to their logical conclusion, our findings suggest that every percept amenable to study by ER methodology should have its individual electrophysiological code." The original attempt to search for such a close correspondence between stimulus content and the ERP was made by John, Herrington, and Sutton (1967), who compared ERPs to square, diamond, words, etc. They reported that (1) the ERPs elicited by a blank flash differed from those elicited when a geometric form or word was present in the visual field; (2) different shapes of equal area evoked different ERPs; (3) similar shapes of different area evoked similar responses; and (4) different words, equated for area, elicited different ERPs. The study, however, is not convincing. The differences reported were slight and difficult to see. Only 60% of the subjects showed any systematic effects. There was a great deal of inter- and intrasubject variability. The subjects were not assigned a task that required that they differentiate stimuli according to their meaning. Further, there are ample data confirming the role of the size, and the shape, of stimuli in determining ERP waveforms. The effects of "meaning" can probably be attributed to the fact that different retinal elements were stimulated by the different visual stimuli.

There have been several attempts at partial replication of the John et al. (1967) study (e.g., Purves, Low, & Baker, 1979; Purves & Low, 1978). In particular, a replication by Gringberg-Zylberbaum and John (unpublished, referenced in John & Schwartz, 1978), included controls intended to deflect some of the criticisms of John et al. (1967). John and

Schwartz felt that the new data supported the early conclusions that stimulus content is encoded in the waveform of the ERP. Further, Gringberg-Zylberbaum and John found that the differences observed in ERPs were particularly evident in certain brain regions in a manner consistent with the presumed functional anatomy of the brain: differences in letter size were represented in ERPs recorded over the occipital area, whereas the differences in meaning were observed in ERPs recorded over the parietal and temporal lobes.

From studies of differential generalization in cats, John (1967) has concluded that stimulus meaning is encoded by the wave morphology of the ERP. John reported that the ERP after response to a novel stimulus closely resembles the ERP usually caused by the stimulus to which the animal has learned to respond in the same manner. From work reviewed in detail elsewhere, John (1972) concluded that when the same physical stimulus has different meanings, the difference is reflected in the shape of the EP: "Waveshape of the EPs elicited by a neutral test stimulus in a differential generalization paradigm actually reflects readout of memory about specific stimulus-response contingencies."

Studies analogous to John's work with cats have been reported by Begleiter and his associates using human subjects (Begleiter, Porjesz, Yerre, & Kissin, 1973; Porjesz & Begleiter, 1975; Begleiter & Porjesz, 1975). They designed their experiments to show that "certain aspects of the EP reflect previous experiences of the organism . . . activation of memory traces . . . released from memory rather than evoked." Begleiter *et al.* (1973) used a warning stimulus to inform the subject of the intensity (low, medium, or high) of the following flash; in some instances, however, the flash presented was either brighter or dimmer than indicated to the subject. Thus, the authors could compare the ERPs elicited by the same physical stimulus following different cues. They found that the ERP waveform was determined by the expected intensity of the flash, rather than by the intensity of the flash actually presented. When a stimulus of medium intensity was preceded by a signal indicating that a bright flash would be presented, the resulting ERP was more similar to the ERP evoked by bright flashes (the cued stimulus) than by medium flashes (the actual stimulus presented). Similar results were obtained even when the subject predicted which intensity would be used on the next trial, or when the subject detected the intensity by pressing one of two appropriate buttons. In both cases, the expected intensity was reported to have a profound effect on the perception of the flash. The amplitudes of the N100–P200 components of the ERP elicited by the same physical stimulus were significantly different, depending on whether the subject predicted a bright or a dim flash.

Begleiter and his colleagues have reported success in replicating these results with several groups of subjects, under slightly different experimental setups (Begleiter & Platz, 1969, 1971). Their interpretation of the data presents some problems. The waveforms associated with the medium-intensity flashes are indeed somewhat different, depending on the expected intensity. However, this difference is slight in comparison with the difference between ERPs associated with bright or dim flashes. Furthermore, inspection of the waveforms presented in the papers (see, for example, p. 154 in Porjesz & Begleiter, 1975) indicates that the ERPs evoked by the medium flashes are more similar to each other than to either of the ERPs elicited by the bright or the dim flash. Begleiter *et al.*'s techniques are insufficiently sensitive to allow confident acceptance of their interpretation. It would have been of interest to know if a pattern recognition procedure applied to the ERPs elicited by the medium-intensity flashes had indeed classified them as predicted by Begleiter's theory.

John and Begleiter have maintained that their results demonstrate that ERP waveforms represent a neural readout from memory. Such claims are based on their findings, in the paradigm described above, that different ERP waveforms can be elicited by the same physical stimulus, depending on the "meaning" or "significance" attributed to the event. However, even if one accepts their empirical assertion about the ERP waveforms, one need not conclude that the ERP waveform encodes the *content* of consciousness. Alternative explanations can be invoked for the similarity between the ERPs elicited by a novel stimulus and the ERPs elicited by the test stimuli.

For example, the similarity of the ERP waveforms to the test and novel stimuli may be due to the similarity in the manner in which they are processed, rather than to the fact that the two stimuli evoke the same percept. That is, stimuli may share some attributes (defined by the subject or the experimenter) that lead to similar processing activities. It may be this equivalence in the processing strategy employed in dealing with the various stimuli that is reflected in the ERP waveform. As shown in the next section, there is an abundance of data showing that many physically dissimilar stimuli elicit ERPs with similar waveforms as long as the stimuli are considered identical or equivalent *in terms of the subject's task*. John's and Begleiter's results, viewed within this framework, are in accord with those reviewed below, demonstrating the importance of expectancy, stimulus significance, and other task variables in determining the waveform of the late components of the ERP.

IV. THE ERP AND INFORMATION PROCESSING

The studies reviewed in the previous two sections attempted to establish a correlation between attributes of the ERP and specific behavioral products. In virtually all cases, the investigators were trying to demonstrate a correlation between aspects of the subject's performance and electrophysiological measures. Behavior, however, is almost always the terminal product of a variety of converging processes. An investigator may determine if a subject reports "awareness" of a stimulus or reports a stimulus to be bright or to be triangular or square. In each of these examples the "behavioral" measure that supplies the variable that enters into the correlation computation is a consequence of attentional, perceptual, and cognitive processes invoked by the joint demands of external inputs, the instructions to the subject, and the subject's past history. These are correlated with measures of some attribute of the ERP. The resulting correlation is considered a correlation between "behavior" and ERPs. A positive, or negative, correlation is presumed to indicate that the ERP is a "correlate" of the behavior. When the correlations are weak, difficult to replicate, and therefore hard to interpret, one questions the degree to which the ERP is indeed a proper "correlate" of behavior (Uttal, 1973).

The inevitable weakness of the correlations may become clear if due attention is paid to the important distinction between *products* and *processes*. The studies we have reviewed attempt to correlate the properties of a product with attributes of a subset of the processes that have produced it. As usual, when comparing apples with pears, the results are confusing. The subject's report that "a stimulus is bright" is the terminal point of the following processing activities, at least. The pattern of stimulus energy impinging on the receptors must be transduced and conveyed via the sensory nerves through the geniculate relay to the more central nodes of the cortical processing system. The stimulus must be identified and its level of energy determined and compared with stored information about brightness levels. This comparison is required if the system is to determine the absolute, or the relative, brightness of the stimulus. The outcome of that determination is somehow translated into an appropriate overt response. This process involves control of the musculature, selection of the appropriate verbal or motor components, and their emission. In turn, this process leads, perhaps, to the deposition in memory of the consequences of this particular interaction between the environment and the subject and the determination of its implications in the contents of memory relevant to the task that the subject is performing. Thus, the specific response "The stimulus is bright," emitted on a specific occasion, is a product that depends on the course of these different processes and on their interactions.

If we monitor one, or a few, of the component processes, we cannot expect a strong deterministic relationship between the monitored process and the final product. The final product is affected, to a larger or smaller extent, by processes we do not monitor that succeed or accompany the process we do monitor, and by the interaction between the monitored process and the other processes. The degree to which any given process affects the final product varies with the circumstances. Sometimes, a process is strongly related to the product; on other occasions it is minimally related to the product. In general, the correlation between the process and the product depends on the share of the product's variance that is explained by the process's variance. It is often not possible to predict this share in advance.

The attempt to hang theoretical conclusions on the correlation between the ERPs and behavioral measures is doomed to fail if one ignores the need to consider other processes that contribute to the product's variance. In the present section, we illustrate this point by considering the P300 component of the ERP. This component is a manifestation, at the scalp, of neural activity that is intimately related to important stages in human information-processing activities (Donchin *et al.*, 1978). We shall try to show that the distinction between product and process is crucial to an understanding of the observed correlation between P300 and "behavioral" measures.

Specifically, we shall show that uninterpretable results are obtained when one attempts to relate the amplitude, latency, or scalp distribution of the P300 to specific behavioral products, disregarding the circumstances under which the observations are made. On the other hand, when the psychological terrain over which the information-processing system is traveling is taken into consideration, the data on the P300 fall into a coherent pattern (McCarthy & Donchin, 1978, 1979). We also examine here the degree to which information about the P300 enhances our understanding of the relationship between performance and consciousness. It will turn out that the important cognitive processes manifested by P300 are not necessarily conscious processes, even though the elicitation of P300 does depend on the subject's conscious awareness of a distinction between stimuli. Thus, at one and the same time, the P300, looked at from different points of view, appears to be "related" and "unrelated" to consciousness. The implications of these considerations in relation to the psychophysiology of consciousness are considered in the following section.

The P300 component was discovered by Sutton and his co-workers (Sutton, Braren, Zubin, & John, 1965; Sutton, Tueting, Zubin, & John, 1967). They noted that stimuli that, as they put it, "reduce the subject's uncertainty" elicit an ERP characterized by a large positive-going peak, with a latency of approximately 300 msec measured from the eliciting stimulus. The results, published formally by Sutton *et al.* (1965), were remarkable. It was dramatically evident that the same physical stimulus,

presented to the same subject, under virtually identical physical circumstances, elicits quite different ERP waveforms when the stimulus is
presented in different psychological circumstances. As Sutton *et al.*
noted, the neural activity manifested by the P300 is clearly endogenous.
That is to say, it is not an obligatory response to a stimulus but is
induced, or invoked, in the nervous system by the demands imposed
on the subject by the task. In the decade and a half since the discovery
of the P300, considerable effort has been invested in an attempt to
elucidate the behavior and the functional significance of this component.
Detailed reviews of the literature have been published by Tueting (1978),
Donchin *et al.* (1978), and Donchin (1979).

In the main, the evidence is strong that the P300 is elicited by task-
relevant stimuli that are, in some sense, unexpected. The relationship
between these two variables is illustrated in the study reported by Duncan-Johnson and Donchin (1977). These investigators utilized an experimental paradigm that has been used frequently in studies of P300.
The subject is presented with a Bernoulli series of events and is required
to make a differential response to each of the two events that can occur
in the series. A Bernoulli series, it will be recalled, is a sequence of trials
on each of which one of two events may occur. The probability of one
of the events occurring is P and the probability of the other event is
$(1 - P)$. In a Bernoulli series, the two probabilities are constant for all trials
in the sequence and are independent of the serial position of the trial.
The Bernoulli series used by Duncan-Johnson and Donchin were constructed from a high-pitched and a low-pitched tone. In each of the
series, each of the tones occurred with the indicated probability. The
subject was instructed to count the number of times that high-pitched
tones occurred. The amplitude of the P300 elicited by the stimuli varied
with the probability of the tones. The rarer the stimulus, the larger the
P300 it elicited. This basic finding has, of course, been repeatedly reported (Tueting, Sutton, & Zubin, 1971; K. Squires *et al.*, 1975; Roth,
Ford, Lewis, & Kopell, 1976).

Another important attribute of P300 can be seen by comparing ERPs
elicited when the subject was instructed to count the tones with those
elicited by the same tones when the subject was required to solve a
word puzzle rather than to listen to the tones. Such "ignored" tones do
not elicit a P300. Thus, the rarity of the tones is not a sufficient condition
for the elicitation of P300. The tones must also be relevant in some sense
to the subject's task (see Johnson & Donchin, 1978).

While these data suggest that it is the relative frequency of events
in the series that affects the P300, much evidence has been developed
that it is not the objective relative frequency of the stimulus that deter-

mines the P300 amplitude but the probability assigned to the stimulus by the subject (see Donchin, 1979). A detail of crucial importance is that the probabilities to be considered are not probabilities associated with specific *physical* events but the probabilities associated with the *categories* into which these events are classified by the subject's task. The Bernoulli series used to elicit the P300 must, by definition, constitute sequences of two events. However, these two events need not be unique physical stimuli. In fact, each event can be realized by one of many distinct physical stimuli as long as the subject's task, and the instructions to the subject, impose a dichotomy on this diversity of stimuli. Johnson and Donchin (1980), for example, have shown that when a series is constructed from *three* stimuli, one of which is to be counted and the others of which are to be ignored, the two uncounted stimuli are treated as if they belong to one category, that of the irrelevant events. Friedman *et al.* (1975) found a similar result for five stimuli, whether they consisted of five words or five nonverbal human sounds. Kutas, McCarthy, and Donchin (1977) have shown that the Bernoulli series could be constructed from many different words divided according to some semantic rule (e.g., synonyms of some word, or names of males vs. names of females). Courchesne, Courchesne, and Hillyard (1978) have shown that one can assemble Bernoulli series from two classes of letters distinguished only by the instructions given to the subject prior to the presentation. In work in progress by Towle and Donchin (in preparation), covers of *Time* and *Newsweek* were used and divided on different runs according to different categorization rules (for example, politicians vs. entertainers, male figures vs. female figures). The same physical stimulus did or did not elicit a P300, depending on the category to which it was assigned. The categories, of course, varied from one condition to another with the instructions to the subject.

It appears reasonable to suggest that the P300 is a manifestation, at the scalp, of neural action that is invoked whenever the need arises to update the "neuronal model" (Sokolov, 1969) that seems to underlie the ability of the nervous system to control behavior. We assume the existence of a mental model (or a world map, or an image, or a schema). This model is continually reviewed to determine action because inputs must be continually compared against this model to determine outcomes and the possibilities of various action consequences. The appearance of a discrepancy between inputs and the model has been defined by Sokolov as the event eliciting the orienting reflex. As a consequence of the recognition that a discrepancy occurred, the model may or may not be modified. The P300 may represent the updating of the model. Whether the model will be updated and the extent to which it will be updated depends on the surprise value, and on the relevance, of the events (see Pribram & McGuinness, 1975; Donchin, 1975; McCarthy & Donchin, 1979; Stuss & Picton, 1978).

The corollary of this concept important to the present review is that P300 represents the activation of a component process in the scheme of information-processing activities. This process is activated in parallel with the specific actions that subjects may take on any given trial. This process has more to do with the establishment of neuronal models than with the active utilization of information on any given trial. The process is likely to begin at any point during a trial, to proceed for any length of time, and to terminate after unspecified intervals.

The dissociation between the overt behavioral products and the attributes of the processes that are manifested by P300 can be illustrated by an analysis of the latency of P300. It is immediately obvious, on perusing the literature, that the value *300*, which appears in the component's label is a misnomer. The *minimal* latency with which P300 appears is in fact 300 msec. Very frequently, especially in experiments using "simple" stimuli, the latency is indeed 300 msec. Yet, there are numerous reports of P300 with latencies considerably longer than 300 msec. The label *P300* has been applied to positive-going peaks with a latency of 400, 500, and even 900 msec. Some investigators view peaks that appear with different latencies as representing different ERP components. But despite the diverse latencies of these peaks, they share most of the important attributes of P300. It is parsimonious to regard as instances of P300 all positive-going peaks whose scalp distribution is similar to that of the "classical" P300 (that is, those that are largest in the parietal electrode, smaller in central electrodes, and quite small in frontal electrodes), and which respond to experimental manipulations in the manner characteristic of P300.

The variable latency need not be puzzling if one recalls the endogenous nature of the P300. If the component is a manifestation at the scalp of cortical activity invoked by the need to update the neuronal model, then, unlike the exogenous components, whose latency is determined essentially by the time course of the primary activity elicited in relatively fixed sensory pathways and relays, the P300 depends on the activation of *internal* processes. As the elicitation of the P300 depends on the probability associated with the *category* into which the eliciting event is classified, the events must be fully categorized before the P300 can be elicited. Otherwise, the probability of the category could not be checked against the external model. This checking process involves, no doubt, contacts between sensory and memory processes and a fairly elaborate evaluation of strategies, purposes, and intentions. Therefore, one cannot expect the activity manifested by P300 to appear with a relatively fixed latency following a stimulus. The latency of P300 varies naturally as a function of the time course of the many processes that must precede the elicitation of the P300 (for a more detailed discussion of this issue, see Donchin *et al.*, 1978).

The distinction between products and processes has proved quite important in disentangling the confusing pattern of the results that are obtained when the latency of an overt motor response to a stimulus (the "reaction time") is compared with the latency of the P300 elicited by that same stimulus. The overt response is, of course, the terminal product of a multiplicity of processes (Posner, 1978). The relationship between the variance of P300 latency and the variance of the reaction time depends on the circumstances of the experiment. The two measures will be correlated (that is, the variance in one will be fully accounted for by the variance in the other) if, and only if, the component process that leads to P300 is predominant in determining the latency of the motor response. This will not be so if the subsequent processes that determine the duration of the reaction interval are affected by factors that do not affect the P300 process. The reaction time and P300 latency will then be uncorrelated (that is, the variance in the reaction time could not be accounted for by the variance in P300).

Kutas *et al.* (1977), for example, have studied the relationship between P300 latency and reaction time in an experiment utilizing the odd-ball paradigm. A Bernoulli series, constructed from male or female names, was presented to a subject, the female names with a probability of .20. These rare names, as expected, elicited a large P300. An algorithm adopted from Woody (1967) was used to measure the latency of P300 on each trial of the experiment (Ruchkin & Sutton, 1978). The subjects performed the task under two different instructional regimes: accuracy was emphasized in one; speed, in the other. The correlation between reaction time and P300 was found to be significantly different from zero when the subjects were trying to be accurate. Not so when they were trying to be fast; in that case, small, insignificant correlations were observed between reaction time and P300 latency. When subjects are trying to be accurate, their P300 and reaction time processes are more tightly coupled than when the subjects try to be fast. It is as if the response during the accuracy conditions is contingent on the results of the processing that ultimately lead to the P300. In the speed condition, the process associated with the P300 appears to be decoupled from the processes that ultimately lead to the reaction.

McCarthy and Donchin (1981) have provided a confirmation of our postulate that P300 latency is proportional to stimulus evaluation processes and is relatively independent of response selection processes. Subjects were presented on each trial the word *right* or the word *left*.

These were embedded either in a matrix of other characters, randomly selected, or in a matrix of # signs. A cue word preceding these matrices indicated to the subject whether to make a compatible or an incompatible response to the stimulus. When a compatible response was called for, the subjects responded to the word *right* by pressing a button with the right thumb, and to *left* with the left thumb. Incompatible response called for pressing the left button with the left thumb when the stimulus was *right*, and vice versa for the command *left*. The subjects' reaction times were increased both when the command stimulus was embedded in a distracting matrix ("noise"), and when an incompatible response was required. The effect of these two variables on reaction time was additive, indicating that each operates at a different "stage" of processing. There are good grounds for assuming that distracting characters affect the evaluation of the stimuli, while response compatibility affects the response selection and execution processes. It turned out that P300 latency was affected solely by the presence of the distracting characters. The need to perform an incompatible response, while increasing reaction time, had no effect on P300 latency. This pattern of results provides strong support for our interpretation of P300 latency.

The relation between reaction time and P300, when investigated, is quite complex. McCarthy, Kutas, and Donchin (1979; McCarthy & Donchin, 1979) were able to show in a similar experiment that when subjects err, the latency of P300 is increased by some 150 msec. The subjects' errors lead to the insertion of an additional processing stage whose nature at this time is not clear (see Rabbitt & Rodgers, 1977). We cannot tell, from the data on hand, if the subjects were aware that they erred and if the longer latency of P300 on error trials is related to the subject's consciousness that she or he has erred. It has, however, been the case that on all the error trials, the subjects responded faster than they did on other trials. It is as if on these trials, the final terminal product (the response) is emitted without the subject's full control. The subject is displaying a "response bias." Yet, the subjects read the names correctly even when they err. Whether the delay in P300 is induced by the conscious recognition or the conflict between the response emitted and the correct reading of the names is a matter for further research. This unsolved problem does illustrate, however, the specific questions that can be raised within the context of the psychophysiological study concerning the nature of conscious processing. This matter is discussed in Section V.

The importance of distinguishing between products and processes must also be recalled in attempts to interpret changes in the amplitude of the P300 component. Consider, for example, a subject who is confronted with a Bernoulli series of events and who is instructed to predict which of two events will occur on that trial. Let us label the two events A and B and consider a subject who has just now predicted that a B will occur on the next trial. No doubt, the subject is aware of the prediction. One might even be tempted to consider the overt prediction an introspective report by the subject on the contents of consciousness. The subject, in this view, apparently believes that a B will, or at least is more likely to, occur on the next trial. It is easy to rephrase the statement and say that the subject "expects" the B to occur on the next trial. Let us assume that the event that actually occurred on that trial is an A. The subject has been proved wrong. The prediction was *not* confirmed. We might be tempted to say that the subject's expectancy was violated and to predict that such disconfirmations would elicit a larger P300 than confirmations of the subject's predictions. We have claimed above, citing much evidence, that P300 is large if the eliciting stimulus violates the subject's expectations. Sutton, Tueting, Hammer, and Hakerem (1978) investigated the relationship between the degree to which stimuli confirm or disconfirm subjects' predictions and the amplitude of the related P300. The results they obtained were somewhat equivocal. In general, the relationship between "confirmation" or "disconfirmation" and the amplitude of the P300 has proved inconsistent. In a recent study by Chesney and Donchin (1979), no difference could be observed between the P300 elicited by confirming and by disconfirming stimuli. Even so, when the trials were sorted by the sequence of preceding stimuli, large variations in the amplitude of P300 were observed. That is to say, the pattern of results that has led Donchin and his colleagues to assert that the amplitude of P300 is proportional to the degree to which a stimulus violates the subject's expectancies was again observed in these data. Yet the subjects' expectations, as reflected by the subjects' predictions, failed to affect P300.

This finding can, of course, be interpreted as indicating that the generality of the assertion concerning the relationship between expectancy and P300 is limited. It is also possible to assert that these data suggest that the subject's predictions are *not* reflections of his or her expectations. Even though the subject is "predicting," the predictions cannot be taken, under the instructions given to the subject, as a necessarily veridical introspective report of the subject's beliefs concerning future events. The subject's explicit predictions may be determined by a host of factors, only a subset of which is the subjective probability assigned to the occurrence of an A or a B on the next trial. The overt predictions are generated in an interaction between the subjective probability assigned to the events and such factors as heuristics (Tversky & Kahneman, 1974), motivation, attention to the experiment, and the utility of risk taking (Cohen, 1972). The amplitude of P300 thus reflects only one of the many processes that determine the prediction. Therefore, P300 amplitude need not stand in a direct relation to the subject's predictions. These predictions may or may not be veridical reports about the subject's consciousness. Detailed analyses of the relationship between the amplitude of P300 and the subject's prediction conducted by Chesney and Donchin (1979) suggest that the subject's perception of the probability of events is, in fact, reflected by the amplitude of P300 and that any relationship between the amplitude of P300 and the overt predictions is fortuitous.

What does such a pattern of results imply for the analysis of consciousness and for our interpretation of electrophysiological data? First, of course, it underlines the futility of simpleminded attempts to relate the behavioral terminal points, the "products," to electrophysiological data. It is more profitable to consider the vast complexity of human information-processing and the detailed nature of the component processes that lead to various behavioral outcomes. Electrophysiology can be useful in supporting a detailed componential analysis of human information-processing because it provides data about some of the component processes whose existence and behavior are opaque to the traditional technologies. But electrophysiology will be of service only if it is not forced to bear unsuitable explanatory burdens. We do not wish to imply that it will never be of use to try to relate aspects of consciousness to the patterns of electrophysiological data. We agree with Posner's assertion (1978) that it is in the province of psychology to try to ascertain the attributes of those information-processing activities that become conscious, and to find how unconscious activities affect the conscious. It is within this context that careful analyses of the component processes based, where possible, on the analysis of ERP data become crucial.

As a final example of the manner in which ERP data patterns are used to address specific issues relating to the degree with which awareness affects information processing, consider the results reported by Johnson (1979). Johnson presented subjects with a Bernoulli series whose parameter, the probability of event A, was varied every 40–80 trials. A series began with $P(A) = .33$ and $P(B) = .67$. After a randomly selected number of trials, no less than 40 and no more than 80, $P(A)$ was set equal to .67, and $P(B)$ was set equal to .33. This state of affairs continued for another 40–80 trials, and again the probabilities were reversed. In the first experimental condition, the subject was not informed that the probabilities were reversed. In fact, as far as the subject was concerned, he or she was presented with a long Bernoulli series where $P(A) = P(B) = .50$. The P300 elicited by both A and B were analyzed. At issue was the degree to which the "local" probability of events in the series would affect the P300 without the subject's awareness of the probability reversals. Johnson found that even though the subjects were not aware of the changes in probability, the pattern of P300 amplitudes reflected the probability of the events within the short segments of the series. That is, the local computations of expectancy, if such are indeed reflected by P300, continued even though the subject was not aware that the basic probability parameters were changing.

One would conclude from this finding that the subject's awareness of the circumstances is not necessary for the information-processing activity reflected by the P300. This conclusion is reasonable, and true, as far as it goes. However, in a second experimental condition, results were obtained that also need to be considered. In that second condition, the subjects were told that the parameters of the Bernoulli series were reversed every so often. The subjects were instructed to detect the points at which the probabilities reversed. The fact that the subjects were now aware of the probability reversals did change the pattern of ERPs. These changes appeared, however, only in the segments of the series that began immediately after the probability parameter was changed, and they continued until the subject reported the detection. When the subject *became aware* of the reversals and *was trying* to detect them, the amplitude of P300 began to increase gradually from trial to trial. This increase was detectable some five trials before the subject reported the detection. The amplitude of P300 was largest just as the subject was about to report the detection. The amplitude returned to its expected value immediately after the detection. During the remaining trials, till the next transition point, the amplitude of P300 was determined by the local probability of the stimuli.

It appears, then, that the amplitude of P300 recorded during the transition phase does reflect the fact that the subject is aware of the changes. The interpretation of these data was discussed by Johnson (1979). The details are not germane to the present discussion. What is germane is that *while the pattern of ERP data is variable, the specific behavioral outcomes remain similar*. The differences in the ERP data can be explained by considering the detailed structure of the information-processing activities that underlie the contents of the limited-capacity system that is consciousness. The work reviewed in the previous two sections suffered because it attempted to ignore this important distinction between overt performance—the *final product* of information processing—and the rich content of the human mind.

V. THE ERPs AND CONSCIOUSNESS

As noted in the introduction, we assume that a conscious experience indicated by an introspective report implies activity in a neuronal population. This population is, of course, unspecified. There is, at present, no information about which brain events constitute conscious experience. The studies we reviewed did not succeed in locating, or in otherwise identifying, these processes. The evidence, however, is strong that the endogenous components of the ERP are manifestations of brain processes that are involved in what are clearly "cognitive" activities. There is, of course, no necessary relationship between cognition and consciousness. Yet, information processing does affect consciousness, at least in the sense that these cognitive processes play a significant role in determining the contents of consciousness or in modifying states of consciousness. Furthermore, brain processes that manifest themselves in introspective reports (i.e., are conscious in our terms) probably influence information processing by determining which information will be processed or by assigning relative weights to particular aspects or channels of information. Consequently, even though it is not known which brain events constitute consciousness, it is possible to discuss tentatively the manner in which the processes manifested by certain ERP components may be related to consciousness. This analysis has at least two purposes. It may help in bracketing the conscious process. As more is learned about the origin and the functional significance of the ERP, we might be led to an examination of the conscious processes. But even if this remote goal is not achieved, the ERP components might be used to judge the degree to which consciousness has entered into specific behavioral acts. In this way, the ERP becomes a tool for assessing, rather than understanding, consciousness.

A consideration of the circumstances in which the P300 component is observed suggests that whenever P300 occurs, the subject is conscious of the task-relevant information carried by the eliciting stimulus. In this sense, P300 can be used to index the occurrence of conscious processing. Under certain circumstances, ongoing EEG activity can also be used as an index of conscious processes, and a comparison of the inferences that can be derived from the EEG and from ERP components is instructive. The EEG, of course, can be used to infer the general state of consciousness of the subject.(Is the subject awake or asleep?) In the awake subject, the EEG can serve to index the subject's state of arousal. If the subject is asleep, the EEG may index the existence of dreams, though this point is controversial. The EEG, however, provides no data about the content of consciousness. This, as we have shown above, is also true of the ERP. When the experimenter knows about, or has control over, environmental stimuli, both the EEG and the ERPs can be used to indicate that certain kinds of conscious processing have occurred. For example, if the occurrence of a stimulus has caused a change from alpha to beta frequencies in the EEG, it may be inferred that the subject was conscious of the stimulus (Sokolov, 1969). If, however, the subject is already generating EEG in the beta range, the experimenter cannot decide to which of several stimuli in the environment the subject is attending. In fact, there is no way of determining whether the subject is consciously aware of *any* aspects of stimuli in the environment, since the subject could be immersed in a fantasy that is associated with an activated EEG. In this regard, the EEG is more limited than ERPs. By contrast, in a situation where there are several sources of stimulation (e.g., in the famous cocktail party that so many cognitive psychologists seem to have attended), it is possible to infer from ERPs to which source of stimulation the subject is paying attention, based on the proportion of the stimuli coming from a given source that is associated with P300.

Consider the following experiment by Ritter and Vaughan (1969). Tones were delivered once every 2 sec. On the average, 1 in 10 of the tones was slightly reduced in intensity. The subject's task was to detect the weaker tones (targets) and to signal to the experimenter whenever a target was noticed by pressing a button. (In the terminology of this chapter, this response represented a subjective report that a target had been detected.) As expected, the rare targets were associated with P300, whereas the frequent stimuli did not elicit P300. While it is clear that the subject must have consciously perceived the detected targets, the absence of P300 on presentation of the nontargets does not indicate that the subject was unaware of them. Thus, the presence or absence of P300 does not uniquely indicate whether the subject is aware of the stimuli. Rather, the elicitation of P300 by some stimuli in the series indicates that task-relevant information has been extracted from the series. These points may perhaps be best summarized by a consideration of the circumstance in the Ritter and Vaughan study that nondetected targets were *not* associated with P300. The latter, in other words, elicited only the obligatory components and thus were similar in waveshape to the ERPs elicited by the nontargets. The absence of P300 on presentation of the nondetected targets does not necessarily indicate that the subject did not hear them. What can be inferred is that the subject did not consciously perceive the *change* in intensity. Thus, presence of P300 indicates that the subject must have been conscious of the stimulus (in order to perceive the change and report it by the motor response), but the absence of P300 is uninformative, by itself, on this question.

Up to this point, the emphasis has been on ERP components that index the conscious awareness of task-relevant information (P300). However, whereas the ERP component can index brain events that affect the brain processes that constitute conscious experience, brain processes also can affect brain events, related to information processing, that do not constitute conscious experience. The "selective attention" effect, for example, that was reported by Hillyard and his associates (Hillyard, Hink, Schwent, & Picton, 1973) could not occur unless the subject consciously understood the instructions given by the experimenter to count the targets in particular channels and also had a conscious intention of cooperating and performing the experimental requirements. The stimulus selection process indexed by the ERP, which presumably occurs outside awareness, can thus be modulated by brain processes associated with consciousness. A somewhat similar situation pertains to P300. As reported in Section IV, when a list of names, 80% male and 20% female, was presented, and subjects were asked to count the male names, P300 was larger in amplitude for the male names than for the female names (Kutas *et al.*, 1977). This result could occur only if the subjects consciously understood the categories involved and the meaning of the words presented (cf. presenting the names in an alphabet unfamiliar to the subject). In another study, the subjects were presented with 15 numbers in random fashion and were instructed to press a button whenever any of the numbers was repeated on two trials in a row (Friedman, Ritter, & Simson, 1978). All of the numbers were potential targets and occurred with equal probability, but the repeated numbers elicited larger P300s than the other numbers. The subjective expectation in these two experiments, therefore, was determined by the nature of the class of stimuli that the subjects were attempting to identify, and not by the probability of the specific stimuli. Thus, the subject's conscious understanding of the stimulus categories in both of these experiments established the nature of the subjective expectations; this understanding modified the brain activities that processed the task-relevant information in such a way as to produce the differential P300 results for the two classes of stimuli.

Another ERP component that appears to be related to consciousness is the contingent negative variation (CNV). As we noted in Section I, the CNV is a slow negative shift that occurs between two stimuli, for example, in warned reaction-time (RT) studies where there is a constant interval of 1 sec between a warning stimulus and a target stimulus. The CNV is an endogenous ERP because mere presentation of stimuli is not sufficient to elicit the CNV; the subject must be performing a task in which the stimuli play a role (Walter, Cooper, Aldridge, McCallum, & Winter, 1964). Thus, the appearance of the CNV indicates that the subjects have comprehended the task requirements and intend to cooperate in the performance of their task. Cooper, Pocock, McCallum, and Papakostopoulos (1978) have suggested that "subjective awareness might well be considered a key factor in experimental conditions in which the CNV is observed." In developing their theory, Cooper *et al.* reported that overlearning in a warned, simple RT task is associated with diminution of the CNV, whereas RT performance in this task remains relatively constant. These data are interpreted by Cooper and colleagues in the following way. In the beginning of the experiment, the subjects must pay attention to the stimuli and their responses in order to learn and perform the task efficiently. As overlearning progresses, the subjects shift to an automatic mode of handling the task that occurs mainly or entirely outside awareness. An analogy outside the laboratory is the degree to which a novice must consciously pay attention to driving a car, compared with that paid by people after extensive experience in driving. In commenting on the Cooper *et al.* (1978) position, Naatanen (1978) suggested that the CNV appears to "mainly reflect conscious effort," which may overlap, and at times even interfere with, performance, depending on the circumstances (cf. paying too much attention to one's feet while dancing). The CNV, therefore, can be thought of as reflecting brain activity modulated by conscious involvement in certain experimental tasks.

In summary, whereas the current evidence indicates that ERPs do not reflect brain activity that constitutes consciousness, certain ERP components do appear to be related to such brain activity, either by affecting it, by being affected by it, or by indexing its occurrence in relation to task-relevant information. This is, of course, only a small contribution of ERPs to the development of a psychobiology of consciousness, but it is a beginning. For further discussion of the relationship between ERPs and consciousness, see Ritter (1978, 1979).

ACKNOWLEDGMENTS

We appreciate the comments of Ben Libet, Henri Begleiter, and E. Roy John, even when they disagreed with our treatment of issues and data dear to their hearts. Leo Towle, John Polich, and Ted Bashore have also provided useful insights. Julian Davidson, of Stanford University, has triggered this review. We regret that the consummation was so delayed.

REFERENCES

BEGLEITER, H., & PLATZ, A. Evoked potentials: Modifications by classical conditioning. *Science*, 1969, *166*, 769.

BEGLEITER, H., & PLATZ, A. Electrophysiological changes during stimulus generalization. *Psychonomic Science*, 1971, *23*, 373–374.

BEGLEITER, H., & PORJESZ, B. Evoked brain potentials as indicators of decision-making. *Science*, 1975, *187*, 754–755.

BEGLEITER, H., PORJESZ, B., YERRE, C., & KISSIN, B. Evoked potential correlates of expected stimulus intensity. *Science*, 1973, *179*, 814–816.

BORING, E. G. *A history of experimental psychology.* New York: Appleton-Century-Crofts, 1957.

BROWN, W. S., MARSH, J. T., & SMITH, J. C. Contextual meaning effects on speech evoked potentials. *Behavioral Biology*, 1973, *9*, 755–761.

BROWN, W. S., MARSH, J. T., & SMITH, J. C. Evoked potential waveform differences produced by the perception of different meanings of an ambiguous phrase. *Electroencephalography and Clinical Neurophysiology*, 1976, *41*, 113–123.

CALLAWAY, E., TUETING, P., & KOSLOW, S. (Eds.). *Brain event-related potentials in man.* New York: Academic Press, 1978.

CHESNEY, G. L., & DONCHIN, E. Predictions, their confirmation and the P300 component. Proceedings of the 18th Annual Meeting, Society for Psychophysiological Research. *Psychophysiology*, 1979, *16*, 174.

CLARK, D. L., BUTLER, R. A., & ROSNER, B. S. Dissociation of sensation and evoked responses by a general anesthetic in man. *Journal of Comparative Physiological Psychology*, 1969, *68*, 315–319.

COHEN, J. *Psychological probability or the art of doubt.* London: Allen and Unwin, 1972.

COOPER, R., POCOCK, P. V., MCCALLUM, W. C., & PAPAKOSTOPOULOS, D. Potentials associated with the detection of infrequent events in a visual display. In D. OTTO (Ed.), *Multidisciplinary perspectives in event-related brain potential research* (EPA-600/9-77-043). Washington: Government Printing Office, 1978.

COURCHESNE, E., COURCHESNE, R., & HILLYARD, S. A. The effect of stimulus deviation on P3 waves to easily recognized stimuli. *Neuropsychologia*, 1978, *16*, 189–200.

DOMINO, E. F., MATSUOKA, S., WALTZ, J., & COOPER, I. S. Simultaneous recordings of scalp and epidural somatosensory-evoked responses in man. *Science*, 1964, *145*, 1199–1200.

DONCHIN, E. Brain electrical correlates of pattern recognition. In G. F. INBAR (Ed.), *Signal analysis and pattern recognition in biomedical engineering.* New York: Wiley, 1975.

DONCHIN, E. Event-related brain potentials: A tool in the study of human information processing. In H. BEGLEITER (Ed.), *Evoked brain potentials and behavior.* New York: Plenum Press, 1979.

DONCHIN, E., & SUTTON, S. The "psychological significance" of evoked responses: A comment on Clark, Butler, & Rosner. *Communications in Behavioral Biology*, 1970, *5*, 111–114.

DONCHIN, E., KUTAS, M., & MCCARTHY, G. Electrocortical indices of hemispheric utilization. In S. HARNAD (Eds.), *Lateralization in the nervous system.* New York: Academic Press, 1977.

DONCHIN, E., RITTER, W., & MCCALLUM, C. Cognitive psychophysiology: The endogenous components of the ERP. In E. CALLAWAY, P. TUETING, & S. KOSLOW (Eds.), *Brain event-related potentials in man.* New York: Academic Press, 1978.

DUNCAN-JOHNSON, C. C., & DONCHIN, E. On quantifying surprise: The variation in event-related potentials with subjective probability. *Psychophysiology*, 1977, *14*, 456–467.

FRIEDMAN, D., SIMSON, R., RITTER, W., & RAPIN, I. Cortical evoked potentials elicited by real speech words and human sounds. *Electroencephalography and Clinical Neurophysiology*, 1975, *38*, 13–19.

FRIEDMAN, D., RITTER, W., & SIMSON, R. Analysis of nonsignal evoked cortical potentials in two kinds of vigilance tasks. In D. OTTO (Ed.), *Multidisciplinary perspectives in event-related potential research* (EPA-600/9-77-043). Washington: Government Printing Office, 1978.

GALBRAITH, G. C., & GLIDDON, J. B. Electrophysiological correlates of meaning: Vocalization artifact. *Science*, 1975, *190*, 292–294.

GOFF, W. R., ALLISON, T., & VAUGHAN, H. G., JR. The functional neuroanatomy of event related potentials. In E. CALLAWAY, P. TUETING, & S. H. KOSLOW (Eds.), *Event-related brain potentials in man*. New York: Academic Press, 1978.

GOODIN, D. S., SQUIRES, K. C., HENDERSON, B. H., & STARR, A. An early decision-related cortical potential. *Psychophysiology*, 1978, *15*, 360–365.

GREEN, D. M., & SWETS, J. A. Signal detection on theory and psychophysics. *Quarterly Journal of Experimental Psychology*, 1977, *29*, 727–743.

HAIDER, M., SPONG, P., & LINDSLEY, D. B. Attention, vigilance, and cortical evoked-potentials in humans. *Science*, 1964, *145*, 180–182.

HERNANDEZ-PEON, R., SCHERRER, H., & JOUVET, M. Modification of electrical activity in cochlear nucleus during "attention" in unanesthetized cats. *Science*, 1956, *123*, 331–332.

HILLYARD, S. A., SQUIRES, K. C., BAUER, J. W., & LINDSAY, P. H. Evoked potential correlates of auditory signal detection. *Science*, 1971, *172*, 1357–1360.

HILLYARD, S. A., HINK, R. F., SCHWENT, V. L., & PICTON, T. W. Electrical signs of selective attention in the human brain. *Science*, 1973, *182*, 177–180.

HILLYARD, S. A., PICTON, T. W., & REGAN, D. Sensation, perception, and attention: Analysis using ERPs. In E. CALLAWAY, P. TUETING, & S. H. KOSLOW (Eds.), *Event-related brain potentials in man*. New York: Academic Press, 1978.

JOHN, E. R. *Mechanisms of memory*. New York: Academic Press, 1967.

JOHN, E. R. Switchboard versus statistical theories of learning and memory. *Science*, 1972, *177*, 850–864.

JOHN, E. R., & SCHWARTZ, E. L. The neurophysiology of information processing and cognition. *Annual Review of Psychology*, 1978, *29*, 1–29.

JOHN, E. R., HERRINGTON, R. N., & SUTTON, S. Effects of visual form on the evoked response. *Science*, 1967, *155*, 1439–1442.

JOHNSON, R. E., JR. *Electrophysiological manifestations of decision making in a changing environment*. Unpublished doctoral dissertation, University of Illinois, 1979.

JOHNSON, R. E., JR., & DONCHIN, E. On how P300 amplitude varies with the utility of the eliciting stimuli. *Electroencephalography and Clinical Neurophysiology*, 1978, *44*, 424–437.

JOHNSON, R. E., JR., & DONCHIN, E. P300 and stimulus categorization: Two plus one is not so different from one plus one. *Psychophysiology*, 1980, *17*, 167–178.

JOHNSTON, V. S., & CHESNEY, G. L. Electrophysiological correlates of meaning. *Science*, 1974, *186*, 944–946.

JUNG, R. Some European Neuroscientists: A personal tribute. In F. G. WORDEN, J. P. SWAZEY, & G. ADELMAN (Eds.), *The neurosciences, paths of discovery*. Cambridge, Mass.: MIT Press, 1975.

KORNHUBER, H. H., & DEECKE, L. Hirnpotentialanderungen bei Willkurbewegungen und passiven Bewegungen des Menschen: Bereitsschaftpotential und reafferente Potentiale. *Pflugers Archiv für die gesamte Physiologie des Menschen und der Tiere*, 1965, *284*, 1–17.

KUTAS, M., & DONCHIN, E. The effect of handedness, the responding hand, and response force on the contralateral dominance of the readiness potential. In J. DESMEDT (Ed.), *Attention, voluntary contraction and event-related cerebral potentials* (Vol. 1). Basel: Karger, 1977.

KUTAS, M., MCCARTHY, G., & DONCHIN, E. Augmenting mental chronometry: The P300 as a measure of stimulus evaluation time. *Science*, 1977, *197*, 792–795.

LIBET, B. Cortical activation in conscious and unconscious experience. *Perspectives in Biology and Medicine*, 1965, *9*, 77–86.

LIBET, B. Brain stimulation and the threshold of conscious experience. In J. C. ECCLES (Ed.), *Brain and conscious experience*. Berlin-Heidelberg-New York: Springer, 1966.

LIBET, B. Electrical stimulation of cortex in human subjects, and conscious sensory aspects. In A. IGGO (Ed.), *Handbook of sensory physiology* (Vol. 2). Berlin: Springer-Verlag, 1973.

LIBET, B., ALBERTS, W. W., WRIGHT, E. W., JR., DELATTRE, L. D., LEVIN, G., & FEINSTEIN, B. Production of threshold levels of conscious sensation by electrical stimulation of human somatosensory cortex. *Journal of Neurophysiology*, 1964, *27*, 546–578.

LIBET, B., ALBERTS, W. W., WRIGHT, E. W., JR., & FEINSTEIN, B. Responses of human somatosensory cortex to stimuli below threshold for conscious sensation. *Science*, 1967, *158*, 1597–1600.

LIBET, B., ALBERTS, W. W., WRIGHT, E. W., JR., & FEINSTEIN, B. Cortical and thalamic activation in conscious sensory experience. In G. G. SOMJEN (Ed.), *Neurophysiology studied in man*. Amsterdam: Excerpta Medica, 1972.

LIBET, B., ALBERTS, W. W., WRIGHT, E. W., JR., LEWIS, M., & FEINSTEIN, B. Some cortical mechanisms mediating conscious sensory responses and the somatosensory qualities in man. In H. H. KORNHUBER (Ed.), *Somatosensory system*. Stuttgart: Georg Thieme, 1972.

LINDSLEY, D. B. Attention, consciousness, sleep and wakefulness. In J. FIELD, H. W. MAGOUN, & V. E. HALL (Eds.), *Handbook of physiology* (Vol. 3). Washington: American Physiological Society, 1960.

LINDSLEY, D. B., & WICKE, J. D. The electroencephalogram: Autonomous electrical activity in man and animals. In R. F. THOMPSON & M. M. PATTERSON (Eds.), *Bioelectric recording techniques: Part B. Electroencephalography and human brain potentials*. New York: Academic Press, 1974.

MARSH, J. T., & BROWN, W. S. Evoked potential correlates of meaning in the perception of language. In J. E. DESMEDT (Ed.), *Language and hemispheric specialization in man; cerebral ERPs. (Progress in Clinical Neurophysiology*, Vol. 3). Karger: Basel, 1977.

MCCARTHY, G., & DONCHIN, E. Brain potentials associated with structural and functional visual matching. *Neuropsychologia*, 1978, *16*, 571–585.

MCCARTHY, G., & DONCHIN, E. Event-related potentials—Manifestations of cognitive activity. In F. HOFFMEISTER & C. MULLER (Eds.), *Bayer-Symposium VII, Brain Function in Old Age*. New York: Springer-Verlag, 1979.

MCCARTHY, G., KUTAS, M., & DONCHIN, E. Detecting errors with P300 latency. Proceedings of the 18th Annual Meeting, Society for Psychophysiological Research. *Psychophysiology*, 1979, *16*, 175.

MCCARTHY, G., & DONCHIN, E. A metric for thought: Comparison of P300 latency and reaction time. *Science*, 1981, *211*, 77–80.

NAATANEN, R. Significance of slow potential shifts in anticipation of and during task performance. In D. OTTO (Ed.), *Multidisciplinary perspectives in event-related brain potential research* (EPA-600/9-77-043). Washington: Government Printing Office, 1978.

NAATANEN, R., HUKKANEN, S., & JARVILEHTO, T. Magnitude of stimulus deviance and brain potentials. In H. H. KORNHUBER & L. DEECKE (Eds.), *Motivation, motor and sensory processes of the brain: Electrical potentials, behavior and clinical use*. Amsterdam: Elsevier, 1980.

OTTO, D. A. (Ed.). *Multidisciplinary perspectives in event-related brain potential research* (EPA-600/9-77-043). Washington: Government Printing Office, 1978.

PAUL, D. D., & SUTTON, S. Evoked potential correlates of response criterion in auditory signal detection. *Science*, 1972, *177*, 362–364.

PAUL, D. D., & SUTTON, S. Evoked potential correlates of psycho-physical judgments: The threshold problem. A new reply to Clark, Butler, and Rosner. *Behavioral Biology*, 1973, *9*, 421–433.

PICTON, T. W., WOODS, D. L., BARIBEAU-BRAUN, J., & HEALY, T. M. G. Evoked potential audiometry. *Journal of Otolaryngology*, 1977, *6*, 90–119.

PORJESZ, B., & BEGLEITER, H. The effects of stimulus expectancy on evoked brain potentials. *Psychophysiology*, 1975, *12*, 152–157.

POSNER, M. I. *Chronometric explorations of mind: The third Paul M. Fitts lectures.* Hillsdale, N.J.: Erlbaum, 1978.

PRIBRAM, K. H., & McGUINNESS, D. Arousal, activation, and effort in the control of attention. *Psychological Review*, 1975, *82*, 116–149.

PURVES S. J., & LOW, M. D. Effects of stimulus shape on visual evoked potentials. *The Canadian Journal of Neurological Sciences*, 1978, *5*, 313–319.

PURVES, S. J., LOW, M. D., & BAKER, M. Evoked potential correlates of stimulus information content. In J. E. DESMEDT (Ed.), *Cognitive components in cerebral event-related potentials and selective attention* (*Progress in Clinical Neurophysiology*, Vol. 6). Karger: Basel, 1979.

RABBITT, H. P., & RODGERS, B. What does a man do after he makes an error? An analysis of response programming. *Quarterly Journal of Experimental Psychology*, 1977, *29*, 727–743.

REGAN, D. *Evoked potentials in psychology, sensory physiology and clinical medicine.* London: Chapman & Hall, 1972.

REM, M. A., & SCHWARTZ, M. Retinal versus central processes in determining averaged evoked response waveforms. *Physiology and Behavior*, 1976, *16*, 705–709.

RENAULT, B., & LESEVRE, N. A trial by trial study of the visual omission response. In D. LEHMANN & E. CALLAWAY (Eds.), *Human evoked potentials.* New York: Plenum Press, 1979.

RENAULT, B., RAGOT, R., & LESEVRE, N. Correct and incorrect responses in a choice reaction time task and the endogenous components of the evoked potential. In H. H. KORNHUBER & L. DEECKE (Eds.), *Motivation, motor and sensory processes of the brain: Electrical potentials, behavior and clinical use.* Amsterdam: Elsevier, 1980.

RITTER, W. The place of consciousness in brain research. In D. OTTO (Ed.), *Multidisciplinary perspectives in event-related brain potential research* (EPA-600/9-77-043). Washington: Government Printing Office, 1978.

RITTER, W. Cognition and the brain. In H. BEGLEITER (Ed.), *Evoked brain potentials and behavior.* New York: Plenum Press, 1979.

RITTER, W., & VAUGHAN, H. G., JR. Averaged evoked responses in vigilance and discrimination: A reassessment. *Science*, 1969, *164*, 326–328.

RITTER, W., SIMSON, R., VAUGHAN, H. G., JR., & FRIEDMAN, D. A brain event related to the making of a sensory discrimination. *Science*, 1979, *203*, 1358–1361.

ROTH, W. T., FORD, J. M., LEWIS, S. J., & KOPELL, B. S. Effects of stimulus probability and task-relevance on event-related potentials. *Psychophysiology*, 1976, *13*, 311–317.

RUCHKIN, D. S., & SUTTON, S. Equivocation and P300 amplitude. In D. OTTO (Ed.), *Multidisciplinary perspectives in event-related brain potential research* (EPA-600/9-77-043). Washington: Government Printing Office, 1978.

SANDLER, L. S., & SCHWARTZ, M. Evoked responses and perception: Stimulus content versus stimulus structure. *Psychophysiology*, 1971, *8*, 727–739.

SCHWARTZ, M., & SHAGASS, C. Physiological limits for "subliminal" perception. *Science*, 1961, *133*, 1017–1018.

SHAGASS, C., & SCHWARTZ, M. Evoked cortical potentials and sensation in man. *Journal of Neuropsychiatry*, 1961, *2*, 262–270.

SHEVRIN, H., & FRITZLER, D. E. Visual evoked response correlates of unconscious mental processes. *Science*, 1968, *161*, 295–298.

SHEVRIN, H., SMITH, W. H., & FRITZLER, D. Repressiveness as a factor in the subliminal activation of brain and verbal responses. *Journal of Nervous and Mental Disease*, 1969, *149*, 261–269.

SIMSON, R., VAUGHAN, H. G., JR., & RITTER, W. The scalp topography of potentials associated with missing visual or auditory stimuli. *Electroencephalography and Clinical Neurophysiology*, 1976, *40*, 33–42.

SIMSON, R., VAUGHAN, H. G., JR., & RITTER, W. Scalp topography of potentials in auditory and visual discrimination tasks. *Electroencephalography and Clinical Neurophysiology*, 1977, *42*, 528–535.

SOKOLOV, E. N. The modeling properties of the nervous system. In I. MALTZMAN & K. COLE (Eds.), *Handbook of contemporary soviet psychology*. New York: Basic Books, 1969.

SQUIRES, K. C., HILLYARD, S. A., & LINDSAY, P. H. Cortical potentials evoked by confirming and disconfirming feedback following an auditory discrimination. *Perception and Psychophysics*, 1973, *13*, 25–31.

SQUIRES, K. C., SQUIRES, N. K., & HILLYARD, S. A. Vertex evoked potentials in a rating-scale detection task: Relation to signal probability. *Behavioral Biology*, 1975, *13*, 21–34.

SQUIRES, N. K., SQUIRES, K. C., & HILLYARD, S. A. Two varieties of long-latency positive waves evoked by unpredictable auditory stimuli in man. *Electroencephalography and Clinical Neurophysiology*, 1975, *38*, 387–401.

STARR, A., SOHMER, H., & CELESIA, G. G. Some applications of evoked potentials to patients with neurological and sensory inpairment. In E. CALLAWAY, P. TUETING, & S. H. KOSLOW (Eds.), *Event-related potentials in man*. New York: Academic Press, 1978.

STUSS, D. T., & PICTON, T. W. Neurophysiological correlates of human concept formation. *Behavioral Biology*, 1978, *23*, 135–162.

SUTTON, S. The specification of psychological variables in an average evoked potential experiment. In E. DONCHIN & D. B. LINDSLEY (Eds.), *Average evoked potentials: Methods, results and evaluations*. Washington: Government Printing Office, 1969.

SUTTON, S., BRAREN, M., ZUBIN, J., & JOHN, E. R. Evoked-potential correlates of stimulus uncertainty. *Science*, 1965, *150*, 1187–1188.

SUTTON, S., TUETING, P., ZUBIN, J., & JOHN, E. R. Information delivery and the sensory evoked potential. *Science*, 1967, *155*, 1436–1439.

SUTTON, S., TUETING, P., HAMMER, M., & HAKEREM, G. Evoked potentials and feedback. In D. OTTO (Ed.), *Multidisciplinary perspectives in event-related brain potential research* (EPA-600/9-77-043). Washington: Government Printing Office, 1978.

TEYLER, T., HARRISON, T., ROEMER, R., & THOMPSON, R. Human scalp recorded evoked potential correlates of linguistic stimuli. *Journal of the Psychonomic Society Bulletin*, 1973, *1*, 333–334.

THATCHER, R. Evoked potential correlates of hemispheric lateralization during semantic information processing. In S. HARNAD, R. W. DOTY, L. GOLDSTEIN, J. JAYNES, & G. KRAUTHAMER (Eds.), *Lateralization in the nervous system*. New York: Academic Press, 1977.

TITCHENER, E. B. The problems of experimental psychology. *American Journal of Psychology*, 1905, *16*, 220.

TOWEY, J., RIST, F., HAKEREM, G., & SUTTON, S. N250 latency and decision time. *Bulletin of the Psychonomic Society*, 1980, *15*, 365–368.

TUETING, P. Event-related potentials, cognitive events, and information processing. In D. OTTO (Ed.), *Multidisciplinary perspectives in event-related brain potential research* (EPA-600/9-77-043). Washington: Government Printing Office, 1978.

TUETING, P., SUTTON, S., & ZUBIN, J. Quantitative evoked potential correlates of the probability of events. *Psychophysiology*, 1971, *7*, 385–394.

TVERSKY, A., & KAHNEMAN, D. Judgement under uncertainty: Heuristics and biases. *Science*, 1974, *185*, 1124–1131.

UTTAL, W. R. *Psychobiology of sensory coding*. New York: Harper & Row, 1973.

VAUGHAN, H. G., JR. The analysis of scalp recorded brain potentials. In R. F. THOMPSON & M. M. PATTERSON (Eds.), *Bioelectric recording techniques, Part B. Electroencephalography and human brain potentials*. New York: Academic Press, 1974.

WALTER, W. G., COOPER, R., ALDRIDGE, V. J., MCCALLUM, W. C., & WINTER, A. L. Contingent negative variation: An electric sign of sensorimotor association and expectancy in the human brain. *Nature (London)*, 1964, *203*, 380–384.

WILLIAMSON, P. D., GOFF, W. R., & ALLISON, T. Somatosensory evoked responses in patients with unilateral cerebral lesions. *Electroencephalography and Clinical Neurophysiology*, 1970, *28*, 566–575.

WOODY, C. D. Characterization of an adaptive filter for the analysis of variable latency neuroelectric signals. *Medical and Biological Engineering*, 1967, *5*, 539–553.

4   *Anxiety and Fear*

Central Processing and Peripheral Physiology

PETER J. LANG, GREGORY A. MILLER,
AND DANIEL N. LEVIN

The theory of emotions predominant in Western European culture describes affects as subjective states. Even the curious concept of unconscious emotion presumes a mind, albeit resistant to phenomenological analysis, which apes conscious experience in all its functional attributes. This view advances the primacy of subjectivity as the determiner of human behavior. Experienced intentions and affects are held to act through the effectors on the world of external objects. However, objective behavior is not the reality of the person; it is only a reflection of the subjective person within.

This general conception is shared by nearly all of us. No novelist would expect to communicate with the public without describing emotion and behavior to readers within this framework. Patients expect their psychiatrists to be concerned with their phenomenal experience of life, and they describe their therapeutic goals in terms of changing feelings of anxiety, dread, or depression. Our legal system is similarly predicated on the assumption that behavior is determined by humunculoid motives that we cannot know directly. In many civil and criminal cases, these private demons hold the law hostage. For example, two acts of violence may be given dramatically different definition (murder, manslaughter, or justifiable homicide), depending on the inferences that juries are instructed to make about the accused's subjective state (cooly rational, angry, or afraid for his or her life).

Human feelings are the private property of the experiencing person. Reports of subjective experience can never be shared observations. How, then, can feelings and emotions become the focus of systematic study?

PETER J. LANG • Department of Clinical Psychology, University of Florida, Gainesville, Florida 32611.   GREGORY A. MILLER • Department of Psychology, University of Illinois, Urbana, Illinois 61801.   DANIEL N. LEVIN • Medical School, Duke University, Durham, North Carolina 27706.

Philosophers have struggled with this epistemological problem through-out the last century. Psychology's solution has been similar to that of law: to examine behavioral phenomena (and physiology, if polygraph evidence is allowed) that appear to covary with the verbal report of emotion. These events (e.g., pale face, avoidance) that can be observed by the community are taken to be indexes of the true affects locked within human subjectivity. The model of emotion that most often guides lawyers and therapists, as well as many researchers, is as follows: External stress or an affective memory trace alters subjective state. This condition of feeling then mediates changes in the behavior and physiology of the person. Thus, the direction of causal effect is from internal experience to external behavior.

Around the turn of the century, William James (1884) proposed a theory that reversed this conceptual flow. He suggested that physiological and behavioral events acted back on subjective state. Indeed, he argued that feelings were actually the perception of visceral, postural, and facial responses. From this perspective, the experience of emotion is seen as a consequence rather than a cause of affective behavior. Contemporary tinkering with this view has restored some of the control function to subjectivity. For example, Schachter (1964) and others hold that affects are determined by an evaluation of physiological arousal and a judgment about its causal attribution. Thus, the experience of affect and functional affective behavior (e.g., avoidance) depend on the person's interpretation of his or her own physiology.

Whether seen as causes or consequences, feelings are beyond the pale of direct scientific inquiry. Furthermore, it has become increasingly apparent that their indexing observations—verbal report, behavioral acts or deficits, and physiological arousal—may not provide concordant information. It is not unusual to find patients with cardiovascular or intestinal upset in response to clear environmental stressors (social or occupational) who nevertheless report that they feel no anxiety, aggression, or fear. Or we may see behaviorally competent people, without visceral symptoms, who describe themselves as tortured by anxiety. Freud's (1938) invention of the unconscious was clearly an effort to cope with some of these mysteries, without giving up the notion that behavior is determined by subjective feelings, desires, and the like. For example, he proposed that a failure to report anxiety when a stress reaction was physiologically evident indicated that the experience of affect had been repressed into the unconscious. Adding the unconscious to the mental apparatus permitted Freud to retain the concept of psychic (subjective) determinism. However, the data base of the unconscious is unclear, constantly shifting to meet every explanatory need. It might be described as the replacement of the unmeasurable by the unreportable. Both science and clinical practice must consider alternative solutions.

I. THREE DATA SYSTEMS IN EMOTION

If we restrict our analysis of human emotion to a consideration of measurable responses (Lang, 1968, 1971, 1978), they organize themselves readily into a tripartite taxonomy. These are *verbal* responses (e.g., affective expressions, and judgments); behavioral *acts* (e.g., goal-oriented movements and performance deficits); and *physiological* patterns of arousal (e.g., change in the tonic activity of the somatic muscles and of the viscera). All these responses may be prompted by external events through the mediation of the central nervous system or may be occasioned directly by spontaneously occurring nervous or neurohormonal activity. A variety of data tell us that any of the responses described above can act back on the central nervous system through distance receptors and interoreceptors. Furthermore, the central organization of the brain may dictate system patterns. Thus, it is reasonable to hypothesize that there are interaction and covariation between the different responses in emotion, which are sufficiently consistent to define substantive affective states.

The central task for researchers is to define the conditions under which responding systems (language, acts, and expressive physiology) function in concert and under what conditions the systems operate independently, and to relate these phenomena to measurable antecedent events, both within the nervous system and, as far as possible, in the reactional biographies of individuals. The central task for theorists is to provide us with guiding explanatory constructs, models, or analogies that organize these data as affective states and that ultimately provide a basis for practical prediction and control. From this perspective, human experience of emotion is not considered part of our data base. Subjective experience is a theory of the organization of verbal, behavioral, and physiological events, which has no special status beyond that conferred by ubiquitous use in Western culture. Indeed, rather than a single theory, it is actually a host of theories, as the mental apparatus has received various descriptions by philosophers and psychologists and has variously woven itself into the fabric of the thought of every person. Despite the conviction of phenomenologists, there is no "raw experience," as the subjective life is inevitably rendered into theory by the act of examination itself. Thus, we should not be overly concerned that our explanations of behavioral or physiological data parallel phenomenological psychology. In fact, it may be argued that our failure to progress very far is a consequence of this concern. We should be more ready to accept models that promise prediction and control and that mathematically interrelate the objective data, even if their conceptual structure is quite alien to a psychology of experience.

A. Affective Behavior: Concordance and Discordance

The assumption of affective reponse unity receives inconsistent support in both the experimental and the clinical literature, in part because of differences in the sensitivity, level of developmental maturity, and unique effector characteristics of responding systems. It appears that verbal reports of feeling, for example, express subtle gradations of affect that are not apparent when measuring changes in the viscera. Thus, studies of semantic generalization (Lang, Geer, & Hnatiow, 1963) simply do not show autonomic gradients with the breadth and continuity implied by verbal associations. Furthermore, emotional responses in one system of expression may be well developed before another system is ontogenetically complete; for example, infants show well-organized avoidance responding and evidence of physiological arousal long before language development permits us to record reports of feeling. Finally, except perhaps for the facial muscles, effectors are not specialized or uniquely dedicated to the task of emotional expression. The cardiovascular system, as an example, is more occupied with the practical housekeeping of the body, responding to a variety of energy demands, and the impact of affective stimuli or cognitions is often difficult to perceive in the context of other activity.

The above facts by themselves argue that the three responding systems in emotion are very loosely coupled. We must also consider recent evidence that visceral, as well as motor and verbal, response can be separately shaped by the environment (Miller, 1969). It is clear that an increases in the sympathetic tone of an organ system can be produced through reinforcement and feedback (Lang, 1975). Thus, a mechanism is provided for that explains many discontinuities between response systems. Furthermore, the specific subresponse within the system may have unique characteristics that determine its concordance or discordance. Skin conductance, for example, is very responsive to the energy characteristics of external stimuli (e.g., loudness and temporal sequence). This particular sensitivity may obscure conductance changes to the affective tone of the stimulus. Similarly, it is not clear what characteristic of verbal responding should, in any given situation, covary with visceral arousal or performance deficits (see Lang, 1978). While we are inclined to study the relationship between systems with subjects set to respond in a perceptual mode (e.g., "How angry, fearful, depressed, etc., do you feel?"), the expressive language of subjects (e.g., "I hate you" or "Gee, this is a tough job!") may be much more relevant to a concordant systems response. In addition, it must be recognized that responses in different systems follow different time courses. In our own research, we have noted that phobic patients sometimes show reduced fearful posttreatment *behavior*, which is unaccompanied by reports of reduced *feelings* of fear. Often, the verbal behavior seems to catch up with performance at follow-up (Lang, 1968). On other occasions, it is the verbal or physiological responses that seem to move first. Rachman and Hodgson (1974) have referred to this phenomena as "response system desynchrony."

II. LANGUAGE AND AFFECT: THE EMOTIONAL IMAGE

Given the enormous complexity of affective behavior, it is difficult to know where best to begin its analysis. It seems clear that our research efforts have been scattered and unfocused, generating data that are inadequate to support the development of a general synthesis. We are ill prepared for the generation of broad theories of the emotions, even though our practical need for organizing concepts is great. Cognizant of this problem, we propose to address here only a small part of the larger issue. Specifically, a minitheory is proposed, designed to explain some aspects of emotional imagery as this phenomenon occurs in the context of the imagery therapies. The theory considers the circumstances in which the language of affect covaries with patterns of visceral arousal. However, instead of focusing on expressive verbal communications or the perceptlike reports of feeling states, this view examines the control function of language, that is, the variables that determine whether instructions to imagine an emotionally evocative scene are accompanied by an appropriate peripheral physiology. In undertaking this task, we will make use of research findings from the field of psychophysiology. The conceptual framework is consistent with the information-processing approach to cognitive psychology. The following description of our view is an abridgment of an address given at the 18th meeting of the Society for Psychophysiological Research (Lang, 1979).

A. Physiology of the Image

There is a large literature that shows that the pattern of peripheral physiological activity associated with the perception of an external stimulus is often reactivated when subjects are instructed to recall the same stimulus content. In 1940, Shaw demonstrated that subjects' imaginal recall of a weight-lifting task was accompanied by muscle tension in the arm previously used that was exactly proportional to the size of the weights. Even earlier, Jacobson (1930) reported that subjects recalling objects with extension in the vertical plane (e.g., the Eiffel Tower) showed perceptlike verticle eye movement. Deckert (1964) later reported that the recall of pendulum movements included oscillation of the eyeball at the same frequency as the original swaying pendulum. Similar relationships between perceptual eye movements and recall patterns of ocular activity have been described by Brown (1968), and Brady and Levitt (1966).

Nearly all investigators of this phenomenon have reported that the extent or verisimilitude of such perceptual responses, recorded at imaginal recall, was related to verbal reports of the vividness of the image. Furthermore, subjects preselected as good imagers (or good hypnotic subjects) tended to show the physiological phenomena more clearly and consistently than "poor" imagers. Investigators have described these imaginal responses as instances of *efferent outflow* from cognitive activity. More explicitly, it appears that perceptual response information is coded by the brain along with information about stimulus content. Furthermore, instructions to imagine an event accesses both types of information (at least, it does in good imagers). Accessing the response information also appears to initiate motor programs that run automatically as part of the act of recall.

Psychophysiological studies of emotional imagery have yielded results that in some ways parallel the findings with sensory image recall. When phobic subjects are instructed to imagine a feared stimulus, they generate a pattern of physiological arousal that is similar to that occasioned by actual presentation of the phobic object (e.g., Lang, Melamed, & Hart, 1970). Furthermore, as with Shaw's demonstration of a relationship between the size of a recalled weight and the amount of muscle tension, it has been shown that the amplitude of visceral response is monotonically related to reported increases in the extent to which variations of the phobic stimulus lead to avoidance or feelings of distress. However, in the same sense that the perceptual response in imaginal recall is degraded in amplitude and precision, visceral and somatic activation in emotional imagery appears to be less complete or intense. Furthermore, the extent of physiological change in imagery roughly covaries with reports of image vividness. In brief, there are sufficient parallels between the phenomena of sensory imagery and emotional imagery to suggest that both may be explained within a single theoretical framework.

B. Processing the Image: Definition and Theory

The view taken here is that while images are sometimes described as graphic mental displays, they are not represented in the brain in the iconic or analogue form implied by phenomenological report. Following the lead of theorists such as Pylyshyn (1973) and Kieras (1978), we hold that all information, including imagery, is coded in a single, uniform, abstract manner. It is further proposed that the unit of information appropriated for the analysis of imagery is the proposition.

Propositions are here understood to be logical relationships between concepts. It is important to emphasize that propositions are logical and not linguistic units. While they have been used to analyze written text, they represent the meaningful structure of that text rather than the text itself. For example, a proposition affirming that the concept *Mary* stands in the relationship *read* to the concept *book* gives the meaning of the sentence, "Mary reads the book." However, this same proposition is equally the meaning of other, syntactically different sentences, for example, "Mary is reading a book."

Kintsch (1974) has developed a notation system that would render the above proposition as: (READ, MARY, BOOK). In this system, the predictor (or the statement of the relationship between concepts) is listed first, followed by its relevant arguments. The word *argument* is used here in its meaning in formal logic, as one of the variables on whose value a function depends. Kieras (1978) described an alternative way to render propositions, as node-link relationships. He would diagram the same proposition in this way: MARY $\xrightarrow{\text{READ}}$ BOOK. MARY and BOOK are both nodes connected through the relational link, READ. Kieras's notation highlights the fact that propositions are not stored in isolation but are organized into networks. Concepts are nodes linked to other concepts, which are, in turn, nodes related to further arguments. Thus, the stimulus of a single word concept may prompt the retrieval of a finely woven tapestry of information. Kieras (1978) offers the diagram presented in Figure 1 as an example of such a propositional network.

Kintsch (1974), Anderson and Bower (1973), and others have employed propositional theories to explain how meaningful text is processed, stored in, and retrieved from the brain. Their efforts have been primarily directed toward the explication of semantic networks. However, as Pylyshyn (1973) has shown, a similar approach is applicable to the analysis of imagery. He defined the image as an internally constructed perceptual description. Such a description is readily reduced to a set of propositions—if we keep in mind that propositions refer to a general abstract form of representation and are not limited to semantic knowledge. The fact that propositions can represent perceptual and

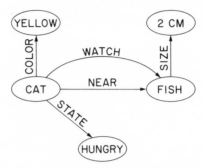

FIGURE 1. Example of a propositional representation using simplified notation. The network represents the information that a hungry yellow cat is watching a nearby fish that is 2 cm in size. (From Kieras, 1978.)

imaginal information has already been demonstrated, with the most dramatic evidence emerging from work in computer simulation. As Kieras (1978) noted:

> Visual scene analysis programs (e.g., Guzman, 1968; Winston, 1970, 1973; see recent papers, Winston, 1975) have advanced to the stage in which a computer accepts input from a television camera and uses intensity and shadow information to construct a propositional description of the objects in the scene and their spatial relations with one another. The description can then be used in learning perceptual concepts, solving, problems, or manipulating objects in response to verbal commands. (p. 535)

We may still wonder, however, what makes a stored description an image? Or rather, when should we describe the information retrieval process as involving the construction of an image? One answer to this question is that the propositional network of an image contains modality-specific information. We may further specify that image networks usually contain a large number of specific stimulus propositions. Thus, if asked to imagine a cat, the brain may process a long list of interconnected propositions, such as: (HAVE, CAT, FUR), (YELLOW, FUR), (LONG, FUR), (HAVE, CAT, PAWS), (HAVE, CAT, CLAWS), etc. We would then say that an image had occurred if subjects (after being given the instruction, "Imagine a cat," and after a suitable time period for retrieval) were able to report a great deal of specific, cat-relevant stimulus detail. Images of a cat would differ from other, exclusively semantic cat networks in the quantity of information of a specific type that had been processed. Vividness of imagery is here identified with how elaborate the verbal description is, within the processing capacity of the image generator.

While it seems likely that the above is relevant to many instances of image processing, the number of stimulus propositions is insufficient as a definition of an image. Indeed, the visual image of a single geometric figure might involve few propositions, despite reports of a great vividness. A more fundamental characteristic of the image is the fact that its information network includes propositions related not just to content, but to the modality-specific operations of perceptual processing. That is to say, the image network includes information about perceptual responses (e.g., sense organ adjustments, body orientation to the stimulus, postural set), as well as psychological processing factors such as ease in resolving the image or picking it out from a background.

Response propositions are a fundamental part of image structure. We firmly reject the dualism implied by phenomenological analysis: the image is not a stimulus in the head to which we respond; it is itself an active response process. Furthermore, as the psychophysiological studies amply demonstrate, imagery is accompanied by an efferent outflow appropriate to the content of the image. This statement may now be reformulated with more specificity: During active imagery, the pattern of effector activity is determined by the response propositions that are included in the image structure. Reciprocally, these proposition-determined motor patterns are a real-time index of the image processing going on in the brain. In addition, the extent to which perceptual response operations are represented in the image provides an estimate of image vividness (it is also independent of the interpretive bias that afflicts postimage verbal reports).

C. Emotional Imagery and Text Processing

The above comments are relevant to mental imagery in general. However, the focus of this analysis is emotional imagery. More specifically, we are interested in the imagination of meaningful situations, in which the imager appears as an active participant, and the context is one in which affective reactions occur. Imagery of this type is normally invoked in the course of psychotherapy and behavior therapy through the therapist's instructions. It is used in treatment methods that differ widely, ranging from systematic desensitization and behavioral approaches such as flooding or implosive therapy, to the psychodynamic methods of hypoanalysis and Gestalt therapy.

In psychological treatments, imagery is generally prompted by verbal input, that is, by a script. A script is the text base for an image, made up of sentences describing, in greater or lesser detail, the events to be imagined. The general path from text to image has been considered by Kieras (1978), who noted that both semantic and perceptual information may be retrieved from word concepts:

> For example, the word cat is connected to the node for the concept CAT, to which is connected propositions representing the facts that cats are animals, are usually pets, and are notorious for being independent. Notice that this semantic information consists of facts about cats that contain no direct information about the perceptual qualities of cats. On the other hand, also connected to cat are propositions about the characteristic colors, sizes, shapes, and other features of cats that allow one to distinguish a cat from a dog visually and to draw a recognizable picture of a cat. Thus, the memory lexicon allows access from words to both semantic and perceptual information about the denoted concept. (p. 538)

Our view takes ths line of reasoning one step further: we suggest that concept links such as WATCH are dually coded in the brain. This is similar to Paivio's hypothesis (1971) that concrete nouns are represented in memory both semantically and imagistically. However, our conception is more narrowly propositional. Thus, when given as part of an image script, the word *watch* has a clear semantic meaning and may be retrieved by subjects at a later time as part of a verbal report. However, the concept link WATCH—when it is evoked by a script, particularly if the script is administered under an instruction to imagine oneself as an active participant in the described events—this deeper structure of WATCH may also include coded motor patterns of sense organ and postural adjustment. These efferent events are evoked in parallel association with the semantic meaning of *watch*, and both aspects of the WATCH predicator may be tied to an even more elaborate semantic and motor propositional network. This is even more likely if WATCH links the imager himself to a stimulus object. Thus, as we illustrate in Figure 2, the proposition (WATCH, YOU, CAT) may include a motor program (Stelmach, 1978) that specifies scanning movements of the eyes. This motor program is even more likely to be included in

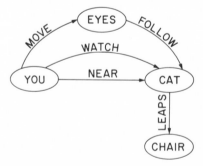

Figure 2. A propositional network which contains information that you are watching a cat and following the cat with the movement of your eyes as it leaps onto a chair. (From Lang, 1979.)

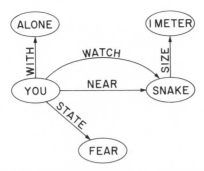

FIGURE 3. A propositional network which contains the information that you are alone watching a nearby snake, one meter in length, and you are afraid. (From Lang, 1979.)

the image if the text specifically describes visual scanning and the context renders it appropriate (e.g., a leaping cat).

The scripts used in therapy require a further explication in that they are designed to provoke emotion in the patient. Thus, they should not stimulate the processing just of stimulus-relevant semantic and perceptual response information, but they should also generate propositional networks that include the efferent output of affect. In Figure 3, we have replaced Kieras's "fishing cat" network with a script appropriate for a phobic subject that is reducible to the same basic proposition structure.

The proposition (STATE, YOU, FEAR) is, like (WATCH, YOU, CAT), susceptible of multiple coding. We have described elsewhere the efferent events that define an emotional response (Lang, 1978): they are verbal responses (expressive vocalization or reports of feelings), behavioral acts (avoidance, coping responses, and performance deficits), and patterns of somatovisceral arousal. Analogous to the way that perceptual response propositions are evoked in the perceptual memory image, we hold that response propositions from these three classes of behavior are generated as part of the emotional memory image, and that it is primarily these elements that define its affective character. In our view, the emotional image is an elaborate propositional network, including stimulus labels (e.g., a black snake) related to semantic information (e.g., snakes are dangerous!), perceptual response elements, and the motor program of affective expression.

In Figure 4, we have presented a script and a potential-fear image network in which response propositions contribute to its meaning. The image structure that it would actually prompt in a subject's brain might, of course, be quite different from that yielded by a formal analysis of the text. Certainly, there would be deletions and many more modifications and elaborations. The sequence and timing of events will vary,

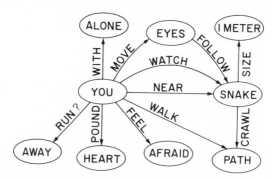

FIGURE 4. The propositional network derived from a fear imagery script. This network includes the conceptual information contained in the script and its conceptual structure would remain the same even with minor changes in script snytax. "You are walking alone. There is a snake one meter long. It is very near. Your eyes move following the snake as it crawls across your path. As you watch the snake, your heart begins to pound wildly. You feel afraid. You want to run away." (From Lang, 1979.)

and these variations are not noted in our analysis. Even under conditions of optimal instructional control, the subject's imagery response depends only partly on the script. As we have already seen, it is determined also by the subject's actual experience with the stimulus context, as well as the talent or ability to generate an emotional image that he or she brings to the task. Nevertheless, the script is one potentially powerful variable for controlling the image and its psychophysiological expression.

III. RESEARCH: SCRIPT, IMAGE, AND BEHAVIOR

Our initial explorations of the above model have focused on the script, as part of the instructional set delivered by a therapist intending to evoke an emotional image. We have tried to determine the conditions under which the script controls image content. More specifically, we have explored independent variables that influence the degree to which the pattern of physiological responding during image processing, as well as the postprocessing verbal report of affect, conforms to the conceptual structure of the initiating script.

We suggested earlier that a propositional analysis of affective imagery scripts permitted a division of conceptual content into stimulus and response propositions. The former propositions are descriptors of context, events, and agents that are to be "perceived" in the image. The latter propositions (concepts and their linkages) refer to things that the imager is doing in the scene. In the experiments to be described, the stimulus content of scripts was held constant, and all subjects were instructed to imagine the scenes "as if they were real." However, for some subjects, response propositions were added to the scripts. These additions to the text described visceral and somatomotor responses that are found when subjects actually confront the circumstances described in the script. Examples of stimulus-plus-response scripts and stimulus-only scripts are presented in Table 1. Some nonresponse filler has been added to the stimulus-only scripts to roughly equate both script types for length.

Under conditions of perfect instructional control, the propositional network of the script would be the same as the propositional network of the image schema in the brain. However, as we have seen in studies of both sensory and emotional imagery, such control is not the rule. Some subjects (so-called good imagers) do appear to respond in a way fully consistent with a script. They report vivid experience of the content and also generate, during imagery, patterns of physiological change consistent with the text's propositional structure. However, unselected subjects show this phenomenon much less clearly. Thus, the statement "you sweat with fear" will very likely be encoded semantically by the subject and retrievable on request as a verbal report; we are much less certain that the second, sudomotor program implied by this proposition will be part of the consequent emotional image.

In order to increase the probability that a script would occasion this

TABLE 1
A Sample Fear Script[a]

Stimulus propositions only

You are alone taking a steam bath and the temperature of the sauna starts to become unbearable. Thick clouds of white mist swirl around you, while droplets of the condensed steam accumulate on the walls, mingling in small riverlets of moisture which stream down the wooden walls and onto the floor. The heavy fog blankets the room with an almost impenetrable whiteness. The large wooden door is tightly closed, swollen from all the steam and jammed shut. The wooden walls of the small room surround you, closing you in with the oppressive steam.

Stimulus and response propositions

You are alone taking a steam bath and the temperature of the sauna becomes unbearable. You sweat great buckets[b] of perspiration, which roll down your skin and mingle with the condensed moisture from the swirling clouds of steam. The heavy fog hampers your breathing and you take deep rapid gulps of the seemingly liquid air. You tense all the muscles of your forehead, squinting to exclude the burning steam from your eyes, as they dart left and right to glimpse the exit. Your heart pounds wildly as you pull with all your strength on the door, which is jammed shut.

---

[a] Includes only stimulus propositions and the same fear content with both stimulus and response propositions in the text (from Lang, 1979).
[b] The response propositions are underlined.

processing of deep structure, we developed a training program designed to associate verbal descriptions of responses with the experience of these same responses occurring in imagery. Subjects were presented with sample scripts, containing response propositions, and asked to imagine the scenes suggested by the text. Following each imaging, the experimenter asked them to report what they had actually imagined. The trainer reacted to these descriptions by systematically reinforcing all statements that indicated that the subject experienced herself or himself behaving during imagery. Typical reinforced responses were "My muscles were tense," "I felt myself running," "My heart was racing," and "I was gasping for breath." Stimulus description was ignored by the trainer. Over trials subjects progressively increased reports of responding in their imagery and in the reported vividness of an imagined behavioral experience.

We also developed a second training program based on the counterhypothesis, that vivid imagery is characterized by the number, clarity, and specificity of stimulus elements in the image. In this "mind's eye" training, subjects were reinforced for reports of the color, form, and pictorial vividness of the things apprehended. The trainer pressed for more and more detailed content, while ignoring any reports of subject behavior in the scenes. These subjects also progressed under training and soon came to report rich tapestries of sense impression during imagery.

Thus, we have designed a methodology that molds the verbal report of imagery experience in predictable ways. It is our view that such changes in verbal report feed back to modify the propositional structure of the image. (A similar path back to the image might also be developed through the systematic shaping of physiological output.) We have performed several experiments in which the independent variables of script and training were manipulated (Lang, Kozak, Miller, Levin, & McLean, 1980; Lang, Levin, Miller, & Kozak, 1981).

A. Experiment I

In our initial study, three scripted contents were studied: neutral, action, and fear scenes. The neutral scripts were the same for all subjects: tranquil scenes with no response description. The action scripts described a context of activity but were not designed to arouse intense affect. The fear scripts specified situations involving danger, potential pain, and the confrontation of phobic objects. The scripts were written in the two forms: either stimulus propositions alone were included or the text contained both stimulus and response propositions.

In order to give ourselves the greatest chance of observing our phenomenon, the two independent variables (script and training) were applied additively in the first experiment. Thus, one group of subjects was given two sessions of stimulus training and tested at a third session on stimulus scripts. These subjects were compared with a group who had been response-trained for the same period and were tested on response scripts. An untrained group tested on stimulus scripts completed this initial design.

In Figure 5, the scores for changes in heart rate, respiration, and muscle tension are presented for the two trained groups. For neutral

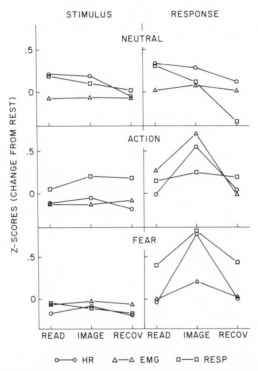

FIGURE 5. Mean heart rate, muscle tension, and respiration cycle length over *read, image,* and *recover* periods for Experiment I, represented as change scores from the immediately preceding *rest* period. Results are shown for the stimulus and response groups separately, during imagery of neutral, action, and fear scenes. The values shown in all figures are z scores, computed for each measure from the distribution of all raw change scores for the three periods for all subjects in Experiments I and II. The change values in respiration cycle length were multiplied by −1 for plotting. Average heart-rate change for the response group during the fear-content image period in Experiment I was +5.31 bpm. The change in muscle tension was +11.27 V/min, and the change in respiration cycle length was −1.25 sec.

scenes, which never included response propositions, there was a lack of physiological response and no differentiation between groups. This same absence of response was found for stimulus-trained subjects, reacting to fear and action scenes. A similar overall pattern was also found for untrained subjects, who also did not show an arousal response to either fear or action scenes.

In contrast, the response group generated significantly more activity to both arousing contents than to neutral scenes and significantly greater reactions to the arousing contents than did the stimulus-trained subjects. The response subjects showed a characteristic inverted-V pattern, with minimal change during the read period, then a clear, large imagery response, followed by recovery toward baseline. Response-trained subjects also showed a significant difference in pattern of physiological reaction during action and fear scene imagery. That is, cardiac rate increases were accompanied by an increased respiratory response during fear scenes, with a smaller increase in muscle tension. Action scenes generated a different physiological integration: heart-rate increases were associated with significantly more muscular activation, while respiration change was significantly less than to fear content.

The text of the response-action scripts contained more muscle response propositions than were included in the fear script; respiration responses were relatively more frequent in fear scripts. This covariation between physiology and script is consistent with the hypothesis that the manifest response structure of a script is a main determinant of the patterns of physiological activity in imagery. This hypothesis was supported, though less strongly, by the electro-oculogram (EOG) data: subjects tended to show more eye activity during those images occasioned by scripts containing eye movement propositions. A further implication of these results was that script stimulus content alone (even if emotional events are described) is a weak generator of response propositions in normal, unselected subjects.

Our subjects' verbal reports of imagery vividness were not significantly different for the two groups. However, as we observed previously (Lang et al., 1970; Weerts & Lang, 1978), neutral scenes were reported as more vivid than either fear or action scenes. The subjects may have reported this way because the neutral scenes were propositionally less complex and thus put less demand on the image processor, or, alternatively, they were simply more familiar. As expected, fear scenes occasioned higher ratings of fear than did action or neutral scenes. There was also a tendency for response subjects to report greater fear during imagery than stimulus subjects.

The above results provided strong support for the main hypothesis, that increased efferent activity is associated with an image structure that includes response information. These results also suggest that shaping language behavior (to increase semantic response propositions) significantly increases the probability that related motor programs will be activated by imagery instructions. The subjects provided with both response scripts and response training reacted to imagery instructions in a way usually seen only in subjects preselected for imagery ability or hypnotic susceptibility. The results suggest that instructional control over affective responding could be routinely obtained in the laboratory.

B. Experiment II

The second experiment was designed to accomplish three main goals: (1) to replicate the previous results; (2) to assess the *independent* effects of script and training on physiological response and verbal report; and (3) to determine if fear and action contents generate different patterns of physiological response intrinsically, independent of differences in the response propositional structure of the imagery script.

The procedure for the second experiment was essentially the same as that used in our first effort. However, the design of the research was expanded so as to unconfound script and training variables. Four groups were studied, each containing 16 subjects. Training orientation and script structure were crossed in the design, so that each group received a different combination of test script and training type, and all possible combinations of propositional training and script structure were examined. Furthermore, for action and fear scripts, the response propositions were equal in number, referring to the same physiological systems in each script.

In order to better compare the subjects' experience of the different scene contents and to obtain a more physiologically relevant, unvariate verbal report, we asked the subjects to rate their subjective arousal during imagery rather than to rate their fear. We found that the subjects who received response scripts reported greater subjective arousal during imagery than did the subjects administered stimulus scripts. However, the arousal ratings were unrelated to the training variable. Conversely, the reports of imagery vividness were greatest for the subjects who had been response-trained, while these vividness ratings were uninfluenced by the propositional structure of the script.

The results for the physiological responses are presented in Figure 6. It is immediately apparent that the response–reponse and stimulus–stimulus groups generally replicated our initial findings. The subjects who had been response-trained and were administered scripts that included response description as part of the text showed a dramatic

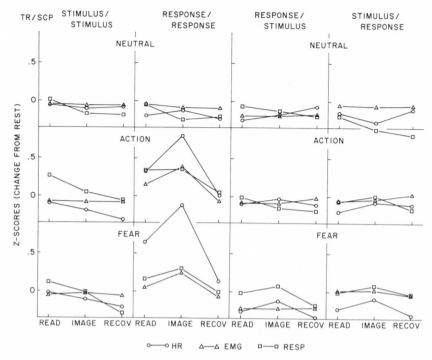

Figure 6. Mean change in median heart rate, muscle tension, and respiration cycle length over *read, image,* and *recover* periods for Experiment II. Results are shown for the four groups separately, during imagery of neutral, action, and fear scenes. The values shown are z scores, based on the combined data of Experiments I and II. Change values in respiration cycle length were multiplied by −1 for plotting. Average heart-rate change for the response-trained–response-script group during the fear content image period was +7.31 bpm. Muscle tension change was +15.58 V/min, and the change in respiration cycle length was −.64 sec. (From Lang, 1979.)

increase in physiological activity with imagery, whereas the response curves for the subjects with a stimulus orientation were relatively flat. Furthermore, it appears that response script and training generate a strong effect only when administered together, since neither occasioned much increase in heart rate when paired with a stimulus variable.

The difference in physiological pattern found previously for action and fear scripts appears again in these data, albeit in a somewhat less pronounced form. Thus, while respiration response did not differentiate action and fear scripts in this study, more muscle tension was observed during action script imagery than during fear imagery. A reversed pattern of difference was observed for heart rate. These results further clarify some of the conclusions reached on the basis of the first experiment. Response script and training exert a strong influence on the physiological configuration during imagery; however, the stimulus content of the image also plays a role. This effect of stimulus content was illustrated more vividly in subsequent experiments in which we studied subjects selected for specific fears.

C. Experiment III

Lang *et al.* (1981) reported results from two groups of subjects, one selected by questionnaire and interview to be high in snake phobia and the other distressed by social anxiety. In the first part of this study, we confirmed the expectation that the snake phobics would increase their heart rate more and report more arousal in the presence of a live snake than would the nonphobic, socially anxious subjects. However, when both groups were required to give a speech before an audience, the socially anxious subjects *did not show* larger increases in heart rate and reports of greater arousal than the snake phobics (see Figures 7 and 8). Instead, both groups reacted strongly on these variables before and

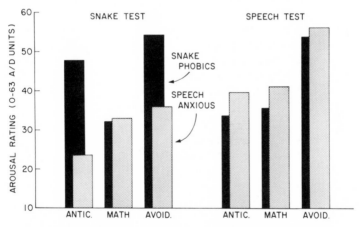

FIGURE 7. Two groups of subjects are shown. One group was selected by questionnaire and interview to be snake-phobic; the other was socially anxious and specifically fearful of giving a public-speaking performance. Both groups were required to confront a live snake, which was brought progressively closer to the subject until contact was made or the subject requested that the test be discontinued. Both groups also participated in a public-speaking test in the laboratory before a live audience. The subject rated his or her arousal, using a lever that controlled a scaled (0–63) computer display. Ratings were made after instructions were given that the avoidance test would take place (*anticipation period*); during a control task, which immediately preceded the avoidance test (subjects were asked to solve a series of *mathematical problems*); and after the last *avoidance test* step completed by the subject.

during the speech. Failure of a speech behavior test to clearly discriminate subjects reporting speech anxiety from subjects not reporting the problem has also been shown by Knight and Borden (1979). Apparently, either (1) the public-speaking situation is stressful for nearly all subjects (whether or not they so label it), or (2) the metabolic demands of the task itself (cognitive and motor activity associated with speech preparation and delivery) are so great as to obscure group differences in emotional response.

Both groups were also instructed to visualize snake and public-speaking scenes, prompted by scripts containing relevant stimulus and response propositions. Verbal report of arousal yielded results similar to actual confrontations; that is, both groups said that they were highly agitated while imaging the speech, but only the snake phobics reported high arousal to snake scenes. However, their physiological responses were inconsistent with these reports. As may be seen in Figure 9 (right panel), both fear groups failed to show a strong reaction to either context, and there was no group difference in response to snake scenes, as was found with actual confrontation.

The above results show that when confronting the fear context, there is concordance between verbal report of arousal and physiological arousal response for two types of fearful subjects. These results also point up a difference between fear types apparent in the behavioral test, but not revealed by the initial interviews and questionnaires used to

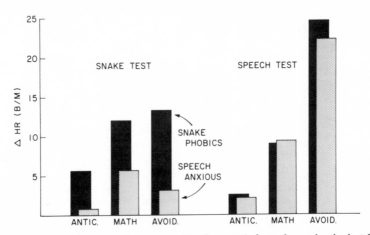

FIGURE 8. Heart-rate increases from a preceding base period are shown for the last 30 sec of the *anticipation period*, the last 30 sec of the *math task*, and the average of the final three 30-sec periods of the *avoidance test*. As with arousal reports, snake-phobic subjects showed a marked increase in heart rate during the snake avoidance test, while the speech-anxious subjects did not. Both fear groups showed large heart-rate increases during the speech test.

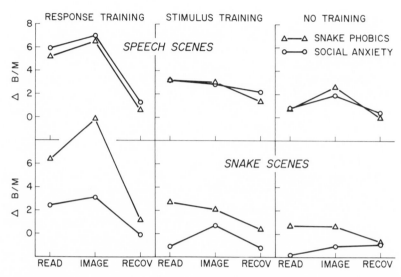

FIGURE 9. This graph combines data from Experiments III and IV, described in the text. The right panel shows heart-rate changes for untrained snake-phobic and speech-anxious subjects (Experiment III) while imagining public-speaking situations (upper figure) and during imagery of snake confrontations. The middle and left panels show the heart-rate change of the trained subjects (phobic and socially anxious) studied in Experiment IV, imagining similarly scripted materials. All subjects were administered stimulus-plus-response scripts. However, it is clear that only the response-trained subjects responded in imagery in a manner analogous to that observed in actual avoidance tests; that is, both fear groups showed a strong response to the speech scenes, but only the snake phobics reacted with a large heart-rate increases to the snake scenes.

select the two fear groups; that is, the speech tasks generated similar arousal patterns for all subjects, while the snake confrontation produced discriminably different activation responses.

Under imagery instructions, verbal report and physiological response were clearly discordant for this untrained sample (unlike the concordance seen with confrontation). In point of fact, there was little evidence that imagery instructions prompted any relevant efferent outflow to either scene. From our perspective, the imagery was not vivid. The propositional networks of script and image were not the same—an outcome frequently observed in small samples of subjects who are unselected for imagery ability.

D. Experiment IV

In the next experiment, two new samples of snake-phobic and socially anxious subjects were studied. Half of each fear group was stimulus-trained, and half were response-trained, following the method previously developed by Lang *et al.* (1980). All the subjects were then tested on scripts relevant to their own focal fear, as well as on scripts based on the dominant fear of the other group. The results for the heart-rate response are presented in Figure 9. Unlike untrained or stimulus-trained subjects, the response-trained snake phobics generated a significantly larger response to snake scripts than did the socially anxious group. These phobics also showed a larger response to their own more relevant snake scripts than they did to scripts that involved social confrontation.

As with snake scenes, imagery heart-rate responses to public-speaking scripts were little influenced by stimulus training. However, response-trained subjects, whether snake-phobic or socially anxious, showed a palpable heart-rate increase when imagining the speech context. It is interesting to note that these subjects did not produce the differential group response that would have been expected if they were behaving consistently with questionnaire assessment; but both groups generated a similar, strong heart-rate change, as the previous samples did when actually confronting the fear situation.

These results demonstrate that response training is *not* an artificial, instructional imposition on the psychophysiology of the subject. The effect of training is to produce a physiology in imagery that is more concordant with the physiology generated by actual exposure (if confrontation is depicted in the imagery script). The data also provide strong evidence that it is an interaction between script content and fear concepts already stored in the subjects' memory that determines arousal patterns in imagery. Training appears to act like an amplifier, increasing the magnitude of those responses that are part of an affective reaction to which the subject is already predisposed.

The above conclusion is further supported by correlational analysis. For example, we have found that untrained or stimulus-trained women tend to be more responsive than men to imagery instructions. Furthermore, across the four experiments reported above, women showed a substantial positive correlation between scores on a questionnaire measuring snake phobia (Klorman, Weerts, Hastings, Melamed, & Lang, 1974) and their heart-rate response in phobic imagery ($r = .51$ for untrained subjects, $N = 14$; $r = .46$ for stimulus-trained subjects, $N = 34$). In contrast, male subjects yielded a near-zero correlation ($r = -.22$ for the untrained subjects, $N = 14$; $r = -.08$ for the stimulus-trained subjects, $N = 34$) for the same two variables. However, with response training, the relationship increased for males to the level of the women ($r = .43$, $N = 34$). As a direct function of training, the males came to generate a physiology more concordant with their verbal report on the questionnaire.

To summarize, these results suggest that response training has the effect of causing average subjects to respond to imagery instructions in a way that is similar to that of subjects who have been selected, through questionnaire or perceptual recall tests, for their inherent imagery ability. Thus, like the "good" imagers of the perceptual and hypnosis studies, response-trained subjects report their images to be more vivid. They also react more strongly to the response content of the instructions, showing a substantial efferent outflow during imagination. Furthermore, the physiological response patterns that they generate in imagery are consonant with an emotional response to the thematic content of the script, as determined by an independent assessment of emotion through actual stimulus confrontation.

IV. Clinical Implications of Imagery Theory

These preliminary findings provide considerable support for the bioinformational theory of emotional imagery that we outlined in Section II. The assumption that the image is a propositional structure and the hypothesis that some of these propositions are elements in a motor program have led us to a specific analysis of imagery instructions, and to the development of an effective training procedure for the amplification of efferent outflow during imagery. We will now consider the function of the image in the production of behavior: We propose that the image is a prototype in the brain for overt responding, and that it has the status of a perceptual-motor set that controls contextual behavior. We further suggest that it is the processing of the affective image in therapy, the alteration of its cognitive and programmatic motor structure, that mediates significant behavior change. As we have previously argued (Lang, 1978), the relationship between image processing and behavior change is a fundamental issue in the evaluation of a therapy's process and outcome.

A. Imagery and Behavior Change

Behavior change is accomplished through the generation of new responses to stimuli, which replace habits evoked previously by these same stimuli. In ideal circumstances, this process is accomplished in the context of the objective events to which the new responses are to be attached. Thus, if our aim is to modify unwanted fear or anxiety, we presume that this modification is best achieved by confronting the patient directly with the provoking stimulus situation, in which the patient may rehearse new behaviors, and a therapist may instruct, or coach, or reinforce partial coping responses, which reciprocally inhibit, facilitate the extinction of, or implement whatever operation is presumed to alter fear.

While most behavior theorists would agree with the above, it is nevertheless true that most therapy is accomplished outside the context of the stimuli that are presumed to prompt the problem behavior because, first, it may not be known what are the relevant stimuli. They may not be obvious to therapist or patient. Thus, treatment often begins with a tedious exploration of the patient's verbally reported experience. Second, when the stimuli are known, they may not be readily brought under the administrative control of the therapist (e.g., a tyrannical boss or a dependent spouse).

Most psychotherapies depend on the medium of language and the patient's cognitive processing of the problem situations to accomplish the therapeutic task. The imagery therapies apply this procedure most explicitly, literally asking the subject to re-create in her or his mind an extratreatment environment, which then becomes the phenomenal field of action for both therapist and patient. The theoretical view taken by most psychotherapists is that the patient is bringing the stimuli to the therapy room in her or his "mind's eye."

In this chapter, we have presented an alternative view of mental imagery. We suggest that what is constructed in the patient's brain is not an internal stimulus, to which he or she learns new responses. Rather, what the subject does is generate a conceptual structure that contains stimulus and response information, both embedded in a more-or-less elaborate semantic network. Furthermore, to the extent that the emotional image involves efferent activity, it has the properties of a perceptual-motor response set. It represents a predisposition to respond, according to a specific pattern, in a defined stimulus setting, in a context of correct or incorrect knowledge of that behavioral field.

We tend to think of the stimulus object as the primary initiator of the brain's affective response program. However, emotional behavior may begin at other nodes in the conceptual network. Indeed, there is no inherent potency in a "fear" stimulus. While we often use the analogy of physical intensity to describe emotion, it is not, for example, a physical stimulus dimension that is represented by the desensitization patient's anxiety hierarchy; it is a dimension of response intensity. Thus, a snake-phobic subject who is alone in a dark room and is instructed that a snake is loose somewhere in the room generally shows a greater affective response than is evoked by an actual confrontation with the stimulus.

Similarly, obsessive patients who return repeatedly to check the gas or lock the door are terrorized not by valves or doorknobs but by the anticipation of harmful consequences, which is part of a fear prototype in the brain. In these cases, the tangible cues for fear may be unstable, seeming to change from day to day, but the pattern of the fear response persists. The patient is a victim of the brain's software, running in a self-defeating loop, treating a variety of inocuos stimuli as if they provided the same life-threatening information, and prompting as output the same incapacitating behavior.

The view presented here is that affective behavior change depends not on simple exposure to fear stimuli, but on the generation of the relevant, affective cognitive structure, the prototype for overt behavior, that is subsequently modified into a more functional form. The imagery therapies fail when the therapist has not achieved the first requirement, the primary processing of this affective program. This fact is illustrated most clearly in an experiment by Lang et al. (1970), in which physiological responses were recorded continuously during desensitization therapy. An important analysis was undertaken of heart-rate reports to those specific imagined scenes that the subjects said were maximally frightening, that is, too fear-inducing to be repeated without the opportunity to relax and recover. For these scenes, all subjects gave the same reports of maximum fear following imagery. The subjects were also assigned ranks according to the success of the therapy as defined by average change scores on all outcome measures. When fear-imagery heart-rate and outcome scores were correlated, it was shown that those subjects who were therapeutic successes displayed the most sympathetic arousal during the first presentation of a frightening scene, as well as a pattern of response reduction with repeated exposure. The less-successful cases showed almost no heart-rate change, despite a verbal report of intense fear.

From the perspective presented here, we can say that the patients who were unresponsive to the therapy processed only the verbal response propositions of the image structure. Those subjects who processed the motor and visceral response propositions showed a significant posttherapy reduction in phobic behavior. These latter subjects altered their response set to objective phobic stimuli through a modification of a conceptual structure in the brain (the fear prototype) without extensive exposure to actual feared objects.

B. Reality and Image: The Participatory Set

While our recent research tells us something about the relationship between scripts and such factors as physiological arousal and reported imagery vividness, we as yet know little about how an imagery-processing set is induced. Clinicians have argued that patients must take on the role of "active participants" in the scene if the image is to be vivid and therapeutically effective. In a recent paper (Lang, 1977), we similarly argued that the psychological set of being a participant in real events is important to the evocation of a relevant affective information structure:

> It is held that fundamental to the emotional response of fear is the prototype fear image contained in long term storage. This template can be evoked for processing in a variety of ways, e.g., through instructions, pictorial representations, or by objective stimuli. The stored descriptor propositions constitute a model against which external events are tested. If the stimulus does not closely match the prototype, fear is not evoked. However, instructions which provide more information (e.g., "image that it is real") can override a mismatch and prompt emotional processing. The processed image is a response set. Thus, an external stimulus which elicits descriptor elements and interpretive propositions will activate the total information unit, including the designated overt behaviors.
>
> It is possible to define the specific conditions which will encourage such processing. Clearly large parts of the unit can be generated by telling subjects to imagine they are interacting with real stimuli. It should come as no surprise that this is so, as the objective stimulus configuration of most phobic stimuli has no funamental nociceptive property. More intense fear stimuli will not burn the skin, or destroy the retina or basilar membrane. Whether a stimulus is present or absent becomes wholly academic, for example, under conditions of attenuated ambient light, when the crucial issue is whether the subject "believes" the stimulus is present. On the one hand, a useful avoidance response is not to "believe" in the fear object and thus not to invoke the image unit with its disruptive response components. However, the conditions prompt equivocation. Whether belief and the fear will be absent, or alternatively, fear will be augmented by the uncertainty, is here a function of idiosyncratic learning. The important consideration is that the objective stimulus is clearly not fundamental to the evocation of either the stimulus or response propositions of the image.
>
> We have already noted that despite the apparent importance of a reality set to the effectiveness of imagery therapy, there are limited objective data on the specific effect of such instructions. Furthermore, we do not routinely determine how well patients will respond to an "as if" set before we proceed to treatment. The large individual differences in the imagery ability of patients need to be investigated, and methods developed to increase patient responsivity to instructional control. (pp. 882–883)

Bauer and Craighead (1979) have recently reported an experiment relevant to some of these issues. They examined the significance of a "set of active participation" in generating physiological arousal during emotional imagery, and whether this instructional set is independent of the fact that response information is or is not processed in the image. In the Bauer and Craighead study, the subjects were told to image fearful events, and their physiological activity was monitored during image processing. The scripts appear to have contained mainly stimulus information and were the same for all subjects. Two main variables and their interaction were examined: (1) subjects were either told explicitly to focus on their "bodily reactions and feelings" in the image or to focus on stimulus content ("What objects can you visualize in the scene? Can you see colors?"); (2) subjects were told either to imagine that they themselves were actually participating in the events described in the image or to imagine that they were simply watching themselves "as in a movie." Bauer and Craighead found that the first variable produced the expected effects on verbal report of fear and on physiological response, that is, more physiological arousal (heart-rate increase) with a response orientation. However, the movie versus direct-experience variable (similar to our "engagement set") was not a potent manipulation. This finding suggests that engagement set as an imagery instruction may have no specific effects on affective imagery, and that it may have a general role only for some subjects in encouraging the processing of response information. That is to say, it may not be critical whether the subject imagines herself or himself to be (or is told to be) directly experiencing a real event. It is only important that she or he activate the motor programs associated with the affect that would be experienced in the referent reality context. This activation of the efferents of emotion would also be critical to the effectiveness of modeling and vicarious learning paradigms are sometimes effective in modifying emotional behavior. The implications of these new data are that like imagery therapy, these other procedures would change affective behavior, *not* to the extent that the subjects imagined these events were *really* happening to them, but to the extent that response information was processed along with the stimulus input. If Bauer and Craighead's finding is replicated, it suggests that the number of set variables can be reduced and an aspect of the theory simplified.

V. Summary and Conclusions

It is clear that much remains to be learned about the nature of emotional imagery and its role in affective response modification. However, the theory proposed here does provide an organizational framework for the objective study of imagery both within and outside the therapeutic setting. We have shown that predictions from the propositional view may be brought to experimental test and that specific changes in the text base of the image, as well as laboratory-induced change in the reported categories of image content, influence both the physiology of imagery and the apparent vividness and intensity of the affective experience.

We have only a beginning in understanding how imagery functions in the therapeutic modification of emotional states. However, we believe that a first step in this task is to be able to evoke reliably the conceptual program that controls aversive emotional behavior. It is not clear whether the next step is to modify the structure of related behavioral acts, the somatovisceral patterns of emotion, or the semantic information in the network, or whether the procedure will involve all three elements and vary from case to case, depending on the subject's response profile and reactional biography. Whatever the path, we appear to have a procedure for determining whether the relevant contents of the image are indeed being processed. In future research, we hope to discover how these affective information structures are modified in the brain, and to develop applications of this knowledge that will aid in assessing pathological emotional states and will provide for more efficient behavior therapy.

REFERENCES

ANDERSON, J. R., & BOWER, G. H. *Human associative memory*. Washington: Hemisphere Press, 1973.

BAUER, R. M., & CRAIGHEAD, W. E. Psychophysiological responses to the imagination of fearful and neutral situations: The effects of imagery instructions. *Behavior Therapy*, 1979, *10*, 389–403.

BRADY, J. P., & LEVITT, E. E. Hypnotically induced visual hallucinations. *Psychosomatic Medicine*, 1966, *28*, 351–353.

BROWN, B. B. Visual recall ability and eye movements. *Psychophysiology*, 1968, *4*, 300–306.

DECKERT, G. H. Pursuit eye movements in the absence of moving visual stimulus. *Science*, 1964, *143*, 1192–1193.

FREUD, S. *The basic writing of Sigmund Freud*, A. A. BRILL (Ed.). New York: Modern Library, 1938.

GUZMAN, A. *Computer recognition of three-dimensional objects in a visual scene* (Tech. Rep. MAC TR-59). Cambridge: Massachusetts Institute of Technology, Project MAC, December 1968.

JACOBSON, E. Electrical measurements of neuromuscular states during mental activities: III. Visual imagination and recollection. *American Journal of Physiology*, 1930, *95*, 694–702.

JAMES, W. What is emotion. *Mind*, 1884, *19*, 188–205.

KIERAS, D. Beyond pictures and words: Alternative information-processing models for imagery effects in verbal memory. *Psychological Bulletin*, 1978, *85*, 532–554.

KINTSCH, W. *The representation of meaning in memory*. Hillsdale, N.J.: Erlbaum, 1974.

KLORMAN, R., WEERTS, J. C., HASTINGS, J. E., MELAMED, B. G., & LANG, P. J. Psychometric description of some specific fear questionnaires. *Behavior Therapy*, 1974, *5*, 401–409.

KNIGHT, M. L., & BORDEN, R. J. Autonomic and affective reactions of high and low socially-anxious individuals awaiting public performance. *Journal of Psychophysiology*, 1979, *16*, 209–213.

LANG, P. J. Fear reduction and fear behavior: Problems in treating a construct. In J. M.

SHLIEN (Ed.), *Research in psychotherapy* (Vol. 3). Washington: American Psychological Association, 1968.

LANG, P. J. The application of psychophysiological methods to the study of psychotherapy and behavior modification. In A. E. BERGIN & S. L. GARFIELD (Eds.), *Handbook of psychotherapy and behavior change.* New York: Wiley, 1971.

LANG, P. J. Acquisition of heart-rate control: Method, theory and clinical applications, In D. C. FOWLES (Ed.), *Clinical applications of psychophysiology.* New York: Columbia University Press, 1975.

LANG, P. J. Imagery in therapy: An information processing analysis of fear. *Behavior Therapy,* 1977, *8,* 862–886.

LANG, P. J. Anxiety: Toward a psychophysiological definition. In H. D. AKISKAL & W. L. WEBB (Eds.), *Psychiatric diagnosis: Exploration of biological predictors.* New York: Spectrum, 1978.

LANG, P. J. A bio-informational theory of emotional imagery. *Journal of Psychophysiology,* 1979, *16,* 495–512.

LANG, P. J., GEER, J., & HNATIOW, M. H. Semantic generalization of conditioned autonomic responses. *Journal of Experimental Psychology,* 1963, *65,* 552–558.

LANG, P. J., MELAMED, B. G., & HART, J. D. A psychophysiological analysis of fear modification using an automated desensitization procedure. *Journal of Abnormal Psychology,* 1970, *76,* 229–234.

LANG, P. J., KOZAK, M. J., MILLER, G. A., LEVIN, D. N., & MCLEAN, A. Emotional imagery: Conceptual structure and pattern of somato-visceral response. *Psychophysiology,* 1980, *17,* 179–192.

LANG, P. J., LEVIN, D. N., MILLER, G. A., & KOZAK, M. J. *Fear behavior, fear imagery, and the psychophysiology of emotion: An information processing approach to affective response integration.* Manuscript submitted for publication, 1981.

MILLER, N. E. Learning of visceral and glandular responses. *Science,* 1969, *163,* 434–445.

PAIVIO, A. *Imagery and verbal processes.* New York: Holt, Rinehart & Winston, 1971.

PYLYSHYN, Z. W. What the mind's eye tells the mind's brain: A critique of mental imagery. *Psychological Bulletin,* 1973, *80,* 1–22.

RACHMAN, S. J., & HODGSON, R. I. Synchrony and desynchrony in fear avoidance. *Behavior Research and Therapy,* 1974, *12,* 311–318.

SCHACHTER, S. The interaction of cognitive and physiological determinants of emotional state. In L. BERKOWITZ (Ed.), *Advances in experimental and social psychology* (Vol. 1). New York: Academic Press, 1964.

SHAW, W. A. The relation of muscular action potentials to imaginal weight lifting. *Archives of Psychology,* 1940, *237,* 50.

STELMACH, G. E. (Ed.). *Information processing in motor control and learning.* New York: Academic Press, 1978.

WEERTS, T. C., & LANG, P. J. The psychophysiology of fear imagery: Differences between focal phobia and social-performance anxiety. *Journal of Consulting and Clinical Psychology,* 1978, *46,* 1157–1159.

WINSTON, P. Learning structural description from examples (Tech. Rep. MAC TR-76). Cambridge: Massachusetts Institute of Technology, Project MAC, September, 1970. (NTIS No. AD-713 988.)

WINSTON, P. Learning to identify toy block structures. In R. L. SOLSO (Ed.), *Contemporary issues in cognitive psychology.* Washington: Winston, 1973.

WINSTON, P. (Ed.). *The psychology of computer vision.* New York: McGraw-Hill, 1975.

5   *Meditation*

In Search of a Unique Effect

ROBERT R. PAGANO AND STEPHEN WARRENBURG

More than a decade has passed since initial reports of striking physiological changes during meditation stirred widespread interest in the scientific and public communities. Particularly influential were a series of articles by Wallace and his collaborators (Wallace, 1970a; Wallace, Benson, & Wilson, 1971; Wallace & Benson, 1972) on Transcendental Meditation (TM). Based on experimental results from measurement of oxygen consumption, electroencephalogram (EEG) and a variety of other variables, Wallace *et al.* (1971) made the following impressive claim: "The physiologic changes during meditation differ from those during sleep, hyponosis, auto-suggestion, and characterize a wakeful, hypometabolic physiologic state" (p. 795). Their report indicated that this state existed for most of the meditation period and was characteristic of meditators in general, even those having limited practice.

This and other claims of dramatic, beneficial effects have been used by the Students' International (Transcendental) Meditation Society (SIMS) to promote their recruiting efforts, resulting in remarkable numbers of persons learning the TM technique. Led by its founder, Maharishi Mahesh Yogi, the TM movement had reportedly grown from a few hundred in 1965 to over one million in 1977 (Orme-Johnson & Farrow, 1977). An important basis for making these promotional assertions was a body of experimental studies that have been recently collected together in the form of a book, titled *Scientific Research on The Transcendental Meditation Program* (Orme-Johnson & Farrow, 1977). However, the majority of these studies have never been published in peer-reviewed scientific journals. Furthermore, a number of these reports utilize design

Portions of this chapter have been taken from an article in the *Journal of Behavioral Medicine* (Warrenburg et al., 1980).

ROBERT R. PAGANO • Department of Psychology, University of Washington, Seattle, Washington 98195. STEPHEN WARRENBURG • Department of Psychology, Yale University, New Haven, Connecticut 06520. Portions of the research cited in this chapter were funded by a grant from the University of Washington (GSRS/PHS RR0709643).

and statistical methodologies that are inappropriate for distinguishing effects due to TM practice itself from those due to the voluntary self-selection of persons who learn TM, or from the nonspecific effects of the technique such as systematic timeouts, general relaxation, and positive expectancy, etc.

In this chapter, we describe our research on TM and how it has led our interests to broader concerns in behavioral medicine and the psychology of health. In the course of conducting these investigations , we have become increasingly convinced of the importance of using rigorous scientific methodology in evaluating claims made by organizations or individuals regarding TM, or indeed, any form of relaxation technique. For reasons described in the following pages, we believe that the initial claims about some of the most important beneficial aspects of TM were greatly exaggerated.

We concur with Davidson and Goleman (1977) that in order to properly comprehend meditation as a form of self-regulation, the investigator must study the predispositional factors affecting persons who learn to meditate, as well as the state and trait effects of the practice of meditation. An understanding of the former characteristics is particularly important if progress is to be made in predicting who is likely to adhere to the meditator's discipline over a long term, and consequently benefit from sustained practice. Discovery of these factors may also have broader implications for successful adherence to a variety of health-promoting regimens.

We chose to study TM because of our theoretical interest in altered states of consciousness and because we were interested in studying a meditative technique that could have widespread clinical application. TM was appropriate because (1) at the time of these experiments (1974–1979), there was a plentiful supply of TM meditators; (2) preliminary published reports on the effectiveness of TM were very promising; (3) the technique seemed effective with a minimum of practice; and (4) the meditation instruction was relatively brief and standardized. After a series of two orientation lecture-meetings, the novice is instructed on how to "passively" attend (Naranjo & Ornstein, 1971) to his/her covert repetition of a mantra (Sanskrit: *man* = "mind"; *tra* = "control"), a two- or three-syllable Sanskrit word with no literal meaning to the typical Westerner. A few follow-up meetings usually complete the training, and two daily meditation sittings of 15–20 minutes each constitute the prescribed regimen. Each meditation is to be practiced by taking time out from daily activity to sit in a quiet, nondistracting environment with eyes closed. As part of our interest in TM, we learned the technique ourselves, practiced it regularly for several years, and experienced subjective benefit.

In reviewing our meditation research over the past six years, we have selected a series of experiments whose common thread is best characterized as our search for a "unique" or dramatic effect directly attributable to the practice of TM. We have not, however, attempted to investigate TM as a means of pursuing spiritual development, nor have we investigated the more recent extraordinary claims of "siddhi powers." The reader is also referred to reviews by Schuman (1980) and J. M. Davidson (1976), that provide more explicit focus on the phenomenology of meditation. The research we report here fits into four topic areas: (1) psychophysiological state effects during meditation; (2) hemispheric dominance; (3) personality traits; and (4) clinical outcome effects.

I. Psychophysiological State Effects[1]

A. EEG Sleep Stages

Our first study involved a comparison between TM and napping (Pagano, Rose, Stivers, & Warrenburg, 1976). As mentioned above, at the time of this research, the dominant findings were those reported by Wallace and his co-workers, who found reduced oxygen consumption and carbon dioxide elimination, increased EEG alpha activity and skin resistance, and reduced heart rate during TM. Although many of these changes occur when a subject relaxes and/or falls asleep, Wallace and his colleagues characterized meditation as a wakeful hypometabolic state that differs from ordinary relaxed or sleep states, as well as from other "altered states of consciousness" such as hypnosis. Because of the qualitative similarity of these reported changes during TM to those observed during relaxed wakefulness and sleep, we decided to compare directly the EEG effects of TM and napping in one experiment. Rather than study a larger sample of meditators for one session each, we chose to study a small number of meditators over a greater number of sessions.

In this experiment there were five male subjects, each with over $2\frac{1}{2}$ years of practice; four of them were teachers of the TM technique. All were accustomed to 40-minute meditations and were not in the habit of napping. Each subject participated in 10 sessions, half of which were meditations and half of which were naps. The subject meditated for 40

[1] Although TM has become the "model" form of meditation in most Western research, other forms of Yogic meditation that involve more active concentration of attention have been shown to produce qualitatively different patterns of psychophysiological state effects, i.e., activation, that also merit further investigation (Das & Gastaut, 1955; Wenger & Bagchi, 1961; Corby, Roth, Zanone, & Kopell, 1977).

TABLE 1
Percentage of Time Spent in Each Stage, Averaged
over Sessions[a]

	Meditation				Nap			
Subject	W	1	2	3 & 4	W	1	2	3 & 4
1	19	12	42	27	32	17	40	10
2	44	46	6	0	7	14	62	14
3	53	15	16	15	15	12	31	41
4	37	6	28	27	31	8	51	9
5	43	17	23	15	1	7	54	36

[a] These percentages do not sum to 100 because some epochs were scored
as movement time.

minutes in his usual sitting position or napped for the same duration
while lying on a bed. Whether a subject napped or meditated was
randomly determined after his arrival. To eliminate the "first session
effect" (Agnew, Webb, & Williams, 1966), we did not include the first
napping or meditation session in our analyses. We monitored EEG recordings in order to make sleep-stage classifications throughout the
experimental periods. Our results (shown in Table 1) indicated that (1)
during TM, meditators spent 39.2% in Stage W (wakefulness), 19.2%
of the time in Stage 1 EEG sleep activity, 23.0% in Stage 2, and 16.8%
in Stages 3 and 4; (2) there were no significant differences between
meditation and nap sessions in the amount of time spent in Sleep Stages
2, 3, or 4; and (3) there was a great deal of variability in the time spent
in the various EEG stages both within subjects (from meditation to
meditation) and between subjects.

On the basis of these results, we challenged the view that TM
uniformly gives rise to a single, unique, wakeful hypometabolic state
which persists for most, or all, of the meditation period. We also raised
the issue of whether the beneficial effects reported for TM were due to
the ordinary rest a practitioner gets during the meditation period or due
to something unique about the process as was, at that time, claimed by
TM proponents.

These results were, of course, contrary to those reported by Wallace
and his co-workers and to the information disseminated to the public
for the purpose of enrollment in TM. In a letter to *Science*, Wallace (1976)
addressed the discrepancies. First, he agreed with our results that during
practice of TM subjects may experience Sleep Stages 1, 2, 3, and 4 and
that there may be considerable variability from meditation to meditation
and from meditator to meditator in the states of consciousness experienced. We were pleased that Wallace would publicly acknowledge these

results, because in our experience, they gave a more complete and accurate picture of what actually transpires during practice of TM.

The second point Wallace made was that during the meditation period there are times, albeit not necessarily throughout the entire period, that the meditator enters a "unique wakeful hypometabolic physiologic state." He did not directly address the important question of whether this allegedly unique wakeful hypometabolic state or the ordinary rest was responsible for the benefits of TM. Although this still remains an open question, as we shall see in a later section, subsequent research has further questioned his position by showing that the "hypometabolic" activity reported by Wallace and his co-workers may not actually have been hypometabolic.

The amount of Stage 1, 2, 3, and 4 EEG activity that occurs during TM obviously depends on many factors such as how tired the meditator is at the time of meditation, how conducive the environment is to sleep, and time of day when meditating. To date, the research shows the following. Younger, Adriance, and Berger (1975) have reported that advanced meditators spent 41% of their meditations in Sleep Stages 1 and 2. On the other hand, Hebert and Lehmann (1977) reported only 10% Stage 1, and no Stage 2, 3, or 4 activity. In a recent study (Warrenburg, Pagano, Woods, & Hlastala, 1980), we found long-term TM meditators showed 21% Stage 1, only 1.6% Stage 2, and no Stage 3 and 4 activity. Based on these results, the rather high incidence of Stage 3 and 4 activity reported in our initial experiment seems atypical. From a Sleep Stage analysis it seems most accurate to summarize the current state of research as indicating that there are many states of consciousness that occur during TM, the most common EEG stages being Stage W, 1 and 2, respectively. Several additional investigators of TM and other meditation techniques have also emphasized the unusual predominance of "nondescending theta" states, traditionally called Stage 1 sleep, or drowsiness, that occur during meditation (Elson, Hauri, & Cunis, 1977; Fenwick, Donaldson, Gillis, Bushman, Fenton, Perry, Tilsey, & Serafinowicz, 1977; Tebecis, 1975).

Since the EEG is a relatively crude measure, it is possible that when the subject manifests Stage 1 or 2 activity during meditation, he or she is not in the same central nervous system (CNS) states as when these stages are identified during ordinary sleep. It is a well-known phenomenon that a tone or stimulus presented during "ordinary" Stage 1 EEG often elicits a short burst of alpha activity (the alpha arousal response), and that during Stage 2 it elicits a K-complex. We reasoned that if the states of meditation and napping are, in fact, different even if the sleep-stage classifications were identical, the EEG response to tone probe stimuli might distinguish such a difference. In order to test this possi-

TABLE 2
Percentage of Tone Responses to Presentations

Subject	Stage 1		K-complex Stage 2	
	Meditation	Nap	Meditation	Nap
1	24	32	33	47
2	33	58	78	53
3	21	45	33	29
4	18	62	68	78
5	32	70	37	59
X̄	25.6	53.4	49.8	53.2

bility we collected tone-response data that were not reported in our original *Science* article. A 45-db, 600-Hz tone of 0.5-sec duration was presented during each of the meditation and nap sessions, using a randomized interstimulus interval of $1 \pm .25$ minutes. The results of the response rate to tone presentations (percentage of probes eliciting an alpha arousal or a K-complex) indicated no significant difference between napping and meditation when subjects exhibited Stage 2 EEG sleep (see Table 2). However, there was a significant difference ($p < .02$) between napping and meditation during Stage 1, with subjects responding more often during napping. These results suggest that when the TM meditator is in Stage 2 sleep during meditation, this probably reflects a normal sleep state. On the other hand, when Stage 1 activity is present during meditation, the CNS state appears to be other than that during ordinary drowsiness. Schuman (1980) reviews research suggesting that Stage 1 EEG during meditation may reflect a "freezing of the hypnagogic process (i.e., the physiological/phenomenological transition state between waking and sleeping).

B. Oxygen Consumption: Does TM Produce a Hypometabolic State?

One of the most dramatic findings of Wallace's early research was that a 16% drop in oxygen consumption ($\dot{V}O_2$) occurred during the first few minutes of the meditation period and was maintained until the subject stopped meditating. This remarkable decrease appeared to set TM apart from other ordinary relaxed or "altered" states and formed the basis for the author's postulation of a wakeful *hypometabolic* state during TM practice. In our second experiment, we attempted to replicate this finding with $\dot{V}O_2$, and in addition, to compare the physiological effects of TM to those of classical progressive muscle relaxation (PR) (Warrenburg, et al., 1980). We monitored a variety of other physiological measures in this experiment (minute ventilation [$\dot{V}_E$], respiration rate [RR], heart rate [HR], and frontalis electromyogram [EMG]) as well as recording EEG.

Three groups of 9 healthy subjects each participated in the study. There were 3 males and 6 females in each group. One group was comprised of regular, long-term TM (LTM) practitioners (mean practice = 3.4 years). A second group consisted of long-term PR practioners (LPR-mean = 6.4 years). Subjects in the third group were novice PR (NPR) trainees. The groups did not differ significantly with regard to age. All subjects participated in two identical sessions. Each session consisted of five periods of 13–15 minutes duration. As a baseline condition, during the first, third and fifth periods, all subjects sat in a straight-backed, soft chair and read from a travel book which was supported before them. During the second and fourth periods, subjects closed their eyes. In one of the eyes-closed (EC) periods, the treatment condition, subjects were instructed to practice their respective relaxation techniques. TM subjects practiced meditation and PR subjects practiced "zeroing down" (i.e., immediate muscle relaxation without the active tensing phase). The other EC period served as a control condition in which subjects were instructed to "sit quietly" without practicing their technique. The order of the two EC periods, treatment and EC control, was counterbalanced across subjects within groups.

The oxygen consumption results are shown in Table 3. Separate three-way ANOVAs (groups × days × conditions) were computed comparing (1) the TM and the long-term PR groups and (2) the two PR groups. For the comparison between TM and long-term PR groups there

TABLE 3
Oxygen Consumption ($cm^3/min \cdot m^2$)[a]

Group	Day	Condition		
		Reading	EC control	Treatment
Novice progressive relaxation	1	124.6	119.8 (3.9%)	118.7 (4.7%)
Basal $\dot{V}O_2$ = 122	2	123.6	120.4 (2.6%)	119.1 (3.6%)
Long-term progressive relaxation	1	118.8	116.7 (1.8%)	114.8 (3.4%)
Basal $\dot{V}O_2$ = 122	2	120.6	117.0 (3.0%)	116.2 (3.6%)
Long-term transcendental meditation	1	127.5	123.9 (2.8%)	122.4 (4.0%)
Basal $\dot{V}O_2$ = 123	2	122.3	117.9 (3.6%)	117.3 (4.1%)

[a] Percentage values in parentheses are decrements from the reading condition.

was a significant main effect ($p < .001$) for conditions, no significant group main effects ($p > .10$) and a marginally significant ($p < .06$), group × days interaction. The treatment mean and the EC control mean were both significantly lower than the reading mean. The treatment mean was also lower than the EC control mean at borderline significance ($p < .06$). Further examination of the group × days interaction effect revealed that the TM group, whose mean values were relatively high on Day 1, showed a significant decrease in $\dot{V}O_2$ on Day 2 ($p < .01$) whereas the long-term PR group did not ($p > .10$).

As one reviews the data of Table 3, the outstanding features are the similarity of and relatively small changes in $\dot{V}O_2$ which occurred during practice of TM and PR. The 4% decrease in $\dot{V}O_2$ found during treatment for the TM group is considerably less than Wallace's reported 16% decrease and calls into question his claim that the state produced by TM is "hypometabolic." There are two factors that we believe explain these conflicting results. The first factor involves differences in baseline $\dot{V}O_2$ levels between Wallace's and our study. In the present experiment we have attempted to create a "low-stress" environment, as well as reducing the metabolic increase in $\dot{V}O_2$ due to recent food ingestion. Apparently we were successful, since mean baseline values for the reading condition were within 4% of the predicted basal values for each group (see Table 3). This percentage is similar to that obtained during the reading baseline condition in the experiment by Benson, Steinert, Greenwood, Klemchuk, and Peterson (1975), who also found a mean decrement in $\dot{V}O_2$ during TM (4.5%) quite similar to ours. On the other hand, Wallace's baseline value of $\dot{V}O_2$ was 9% above its predicted basal values, possibly because of more stressful procedures followed in his study (e.g., arterial cannulation). Therefore, the large 16% decrement found by Wallace may be due mainly to the elevated baseline values in his study, rather than being a reflection of a profound hypometabolic state. It is likely that relaxed and fasting subjects encounter a "floor effect," or lower limit, as they engage in the relaxation technique, resulting in the modest 4.5% decrement from the baseline condition in both our study and that of Benson et al. (1975). This interpretation supports the conclusion of Fenwick et al. (1977) who showed that (1) mean $\dot{V}O_2$ decrements during TM were only 2% in subjects who were self-rated as "relaxed," whereas "tense" subjects had a mean decrement of 12%; and (2) meditation subjects who had been fasting since the previous evening manifested a nonsignificant 2% decrease in carbon dioxide elimination. We must point out, however, that although in our study TM subjects' baseline $\dot{V}O_2$ was elevated 5% on Day 1 relative to Day 2, the mean decrement during TM from baseline was only .8% higher on Day 1. The result is contrary to a baseline-differences explanation of Wallace's data.

Individual differences are a second factor which may account for the discrepancies in obtained $\dot{V}O_2$ decrements during TM. Hebert and Lehmann (1977), Pagano et al., (1976), Tebecis (1975), and Younger et al. (1975) have shown that striking individual differences exist in EEG activity during TM practice. Case studies of selected Yogi meditators (Anand, Chhina, & Singh, 1961a) and Zen meditators (Hirai, 1974) have found decreases in $\dot{V}O_2$ of 15–20% below predicted basal values during meditation. Since individuals no doubt differ in their ability to relax somatically during relaxation/meditation, it is possible that Wallace's TM subjects were more capable in this ability than ours. We have examined the distribution of mean decrement scores during comparable intervals during meditation in Wallace's study and ours. In his study $\dot{V}O_2$ of seven subjects fell to values more than 15% below predicted basal metabolic levels, whereas that of no subject in our study did so on either day. If we dichotomize the subjects in both studies at the -15% level, the distributions are significantly different ($p < .05$, by Fisher's exact test), thus supporting the individual differences hypothesis.

One obvious individual difference variable which might affect $\dot{V}O_2$ decrements is the length of practice with the technique. We have calculated the correlation between length of practice of Wallace's (1970b) subjects and their mean $\dot{V}O_2$ decrement from a predicted basal values, and this correlation is significant ($r = .46$). However, the average length of practice in our TM group (3.5 years) was longer than in Wallace's (2.5 years). Thus, if individual differences are an important factor, some variable other than length of practice must be responsible. We think it fair to summarize this line of research by saying that if TM does really produce a hypometabolic state, it has not yet been adequately demonstrated. At this stage of the research the dramatic decrement of 16% O_2 consumption reported by Wallace and his co-workers appears to have been largely due to an inflated baseline.

C. Relaxation Response or Multiprocess Model

The results of the present study (Warrenburg et al., 1980) are interesting in yet another light. Benson, Beary, and Carol (1974) have hypothesized that a variety of relaxation techniques, including TM, produces a common pattern of physiological changes, which they called "the relaxation response." In opposition to this view, Davidson and Schwartz (1976) have proposed a "multiprocess" model, in which relaxation techniques having a somatic attentional focus, such as progressive relaxation should yield greater somatic relaxation than techniques having a cognitive attentional focus, such as TM. In later writing, Schwartz, Davidson, and Goleman (1978) have attempted to integrate these two models by positing that "relaxation consists of (1) a generalized reduction in multiple physiological systems (termed the relaxation response by Benson) and (2) a more specific pattern of changes superimposed upon this general reduction, which is elicited by the particular technique employed" (p. 327).

In the present study, we have compared the somatic effects of TM and PR. In analyzing the data from the TM and the long-term PR practitioners, we found a highly significant main effect for conditions for each measure. For $\dot{V}_E$ and RR, the treatment mean was significantly lower than the reading mean (p's $< .001$) and the EC condition mean (p's $< .01$). For HR and EMG the treatment and the EC control means were both significantly lower than the reading mean (p's $< .01$ for HR; p's $< .001$ for EMG), but the EC control and treatment means did not differ significantly. Although significant, it is worth noting that the decreases were relatively small, with the exception of EMG. There were no significant *group* main effects except for HR ($p < .05$) and a near-significant main effect in $\dot{V}_E$ ($p < .06$). Inspection revealed that these effects were due to the long-term PR group having lower levels of those measures across conditions compared to the TM group. There were no significant group × condition interactions for any measure, indicating that these two groups did not differ in the changes in somatic activity from one condition to another.

Although of the five measures only HR differed significantly between groups, a closer examination of the data revealed that in 25 of 30 possible mean comparisons between the TM and long-term PR practitioners, the PR group had lower values than the TM group. This pattern of means was significant via the sign test, ($p < .01$) and suggested to us that a composite measure (combining all five measures) might yield a more sensitive parametric index of group differences in somatic relaxation. Average within-subject correlations between all five measures were positive (.32–.81) and significant (p's $< .025$), thus justifying the usage of a composite score as an overall measure of somatic relaxation. The composite measure (z score) yielded a marginally significant main effect for groups ($p < .09$) with the long-term PR group showing greater relaxation in each condition. Furthermore, this composite index was correlated substantially ($r = .78$, $p < .005$) with the number of weeks of practice in the novice PR group. Since it is well established in sleep laboratories that a subject's first session in the laboratory yields greater physiological arousal than subsequent sessions, and since Goleman and Schwartz (1976) have shown that long-term TM meditators are more responsive than controls to stressful stimuli (see "Relaxation Under Stress"), we also analyzed the data involving the composite measure separately for Day 1 and Day 2. Analysis revealed that the meditator brevity of their treatments, Schoickett *et al.* (1979) did not observe PR subjects to be more relaxed than controls, as we did with our long-term PR group. They did, however, observe enhanced reactivity in the meditation group, as compared both to controls and PR subjects.

A similar pattern of responding to stressful stimuli was observed in a study of long-term TM meditators by Goleman and Schwartz (1976). Groups of meditators and controls viewed a highly stressful shop accident film containing several discrete episodes of suspense leading to a vivid accident. TM meditators displayed increased responding in heart rate and SCFs during the anticipation and "impact" segments, and also faster recovery after impact. Meditators also reported less state anxiety both before and after viewing the film. The findings presented here are quite paradoxical from the conventional view of meditation as a relaxation technique, whether by the formulation of Benson, or Davidson and Schwartz.

We wish to note two other studies of stress reactivity in non-meditators that provide an interesting context for these meditation findings. In a study of parachute jumping, Fenz and Epstein (1967) found that experienced jumpers manifested an earlier, and considerably lower peak in physiological arousal prior to a parachute jump, as compared to novices. A similar curve was obtained for self-reported fear. Both groups recovered to the same physiological levels, but the former group showed a rebound of subjective fear after the jump. Our aim in bringing this study to the reader's attention is to point out the paradox of the contrasting parallel between the heightened physiological responsivity to stress in meditators and novice parachutists, yet the reduced psychological stress response in both meditators and experienced parachutists. Fenz and Epstein interpret the lowered responses of the experienced group to be the result of an adaptive psychological inhibitory process that operates first on the subjective fear response and later on the physiological component. Such an explanation, however, could not account for the heightened reactivity in meditators. Goleman and Schwartz (1976) speculate that paradoxical enhancement of meditators' physiological response to the accident film may represent "a defensive reaction that combines both a set to respond and a sensitization to incipient stimuli" (p. 464). Indeed, they propose that this dual component reaction may actually represent a more adaptive total response than one that omits either the former of latter component. The process by which meditation affects this type of dual component stress response clearly appears to be more than merely one of relaxation, and suggests that altered attentional processes may be responsible.

In later sections of this chapter we will discuss our findings, and those of other researchers, that point to a capacity for "absorbed attention" in meditators that appears to mediate important beneficial effects of meditation. Concerning stress reactivity, Tellegen (1981) cites J. R. Hilgard's suggestion that persons high in absorbtion are particularly sensitive to "intense traumatic experiences."

Results of another study of non-meditators suggests an altogether different interpretation of this paradoxical meditator pattern. Weinberger, Schwartz, and Davidson (1979) observed heightened physiological reactivity in subjects who scored high in defensiveness in reporting negative emotional states (on the Marlowe-Crowne Social Desirability Scale) as compared to low defensive subjects. Recovery was not measured in this study, however. We report in a later section (*Personality Traits*) that long-term TM meditators score higher than non-meditators in Tellengen's (1977) Social Desirability Scale. This suggests the possibility that meditators may be more reactive physiologically than non-meditators, yet report less stress, because they are defensive about reporting subjective anxiety. More research is clearly needed before we can draw definitive conclusions about the paradoxical nature of meditators' reactions to stress.

F. EEG Alpha and Theta Activity

We have recently conducted a third investigation of the state effects of TM, this time focusing on EEG integrated alpha activity and theta burst activity (Warrenburg & Pagano, 1982). Three groups of 16 subjects were studied: long-term TM meditators (LT-TM, range of 2–10 years of practice), novice TM meditators (Nov-TM, 1–5 weeks of practice), and non-meditators (Non-med, not interested in learning TM). These subjects participated in two sessions of meditation (LT-TM and Nov-TM) or self-instructed relaxations (Non-med) which were conducted after $1\frac{1}{2}$ hour sessions of performance testing (described in the next section on *Hemispheric Dominance*). Equal numbers of males and females were included in each group, and all subjects were fully right-handed with no known left-handedness in their immediate family.

Each of the two sessions involved the following A-B-A sequence: 5 minutes of sitting with eyes-closed (pre-control period), 20 minutes of meditation or relaxation (treatment period), and 5 minutes of sitting with eyes closed (post-control period). We monitored subjects' EEGs from left (L) and right (R) homologous parietal (P3 and P4) and frontal (F3 and F4) sites, using the tip of the nose as the reference.

From the EEG we derived measures of mean integrated alpha activity (8–12.5-Hz) from parietal and frontal regions ([L + R]/2), as well as indices parietal and frontal alpha asymmetry (R/L). Records were also during the baseline period, moderate increases in relaxation during meditation would probably produce increased alpha activity.

In our alpha results, individual differences were once again a notable aspect. Although group means of frontal and parietal alpha decreased during both sessions for all groups, a number of subjects in each group manifested increases during at least one session in the parietal and/or frontal regions. The number of such subjects was 8 out of 10 for the Nov-TM group, 9 out of 15 for the LT-TM group, and 7 out of 15 for the Non-Med group. On the other hand, only 1 (LT-TM) out of 35 subjects having complete data demonstrated an increase on both days in both channels.

The analysis of alpha asymmetry (R/L) during this experiment was conducted as it was for the integrated alpha amplitude data. Pre-postcontrol ANOVAs revealed no significant effects for either frontal or parietal asymmetry. ANOVAs for both the 20 minute and 5 minute parietal treatment data also yielded no significant effects (The mean index was 1.03). A similar lack of significant results was generally obtained for the frontal asymmetry index, as well, with one exception— the periods × days interaction (using 20 minute treatment means) was significant ($p < .04$). Frontal asymmetry decreased from control (1.03) to treatment (1.02) on Day 1, but increased from control (1.02) to treatment (1.03) on Day 2. The general absence of effects in alpha asymmetry was disappointing, both in terms of treatment changes and group differences. The data fail to support the theory (discussed in detail in the next section) that meditation causes a shift toward right hemisphere dominance that may underlie subjective reports of altered states of consciousness. The average asymmetry index in both parietal and frontal channels suggests a slightly greater relative activation of the left hemisphere that did not change appreciably when the subject engaged in meditation or relaxation.

Results of two prior studies of alpha asymmetry during meditation, unfortunately, are in conflict on this issue. Bennett and Trinder (1977) obtained results in meditating TM subjects that were essentially in agreement with ours. On the other hand, Ehrlichman and Weiner (1980) observed substantial relative right hemisphere activation during a meditation condition in unselected meditators and non-meditators. Procedural and subject selection differences among these investigations may explain their lack of agreement.

In the present study, as well as in a prior one (Warrenburg et al., 1980), we observed high amplitude sinusoidal theta activity (5–7.5 Hz) in TM subjects. This type of activity has been previously reported during TM by Wallace et al. (1971), Banquet (1973), Fenwick et al. (1977), and Hebert and Lehmann (1977). Likewise theta has been observed in Zen

Table 4
Theta Bursts above 75 μV Criterion (per Minute)

		Group		
		Nov-TM	LT-TM	Non-med
Day	Condition	$\overline{X}$ SD	$\overline{X}$ SD	$\overline{X}$ SD
1	EC-control	0.14 (0.36)	0.93 (1.88)	1.73 ((3.56)
1	Treatment	0.79 (1.19)	2.31 (4.00)	1.17 (2.50)
2	EC-control	0.14 (0.36)	1.06 (2.05)	0.73 (1.49)
2	Treatment	0.64 (1.23)	2.47 (5.09)	1.20 (1.58)

meditators (Kasamatsu & Hirai, 1969), Amanda Marga meditators (Elson, Hauri, & Cunis, 1977), and practitioners of autogenic relaxation (Luthe, 1969). We know of no past literature noting theta activity during PR. In our prior study we saw such waveforms in both TM and PR subjects. These groups did not differ significantly in theta activity, and individual differences within groups were a prominent feature.

In the present study 7 Nov-TM, 9 LT-TM and 8 Non-Med subjects displayed at least one theta burst above 75 μV during the treatment condition, and these numbers for the 100 μV criterion (used by Hebert & Lehmann, 1977) were 6, 7, and 8, respectively. As noted in our previous study, the incidence of this activity varied between individuals in terms of its appearance during Stage W or 1, and its scalp distribution (parietal and/or frontal sites). Analysis of these data (75 μV criterion) for all subjects revealed no groups main effects or groups × periods interaction, but did yield a main effect for periods ($p < .005$) and a groups × days × periods interaction at borderline significance ($p < .051$) (see Table 4). Overall, the number of bursts increased during the treatment condition as compared to the control condition. However, the Non-Med group exhibited the opposite pattern on Day 1, but not Day 2.

The general pattern of a higher incidence of theta bursts during treatment than control periods is interesting, and is supported by prior research (Fenwick et al., 1977; Hebert & Lehmann, 1977). This treatment effect suggests that subjects who show theta bursts at all are able to increase the occurrence of this type of activity by engaging in a deliberate attempt to meditate or relax. At first glance, the Non-Med control mean on Day 1 seems to contradict this generalization by the mean's unusual elevation. A closer look at this cell, however, revealed that this effect was due to two subjects only. Since the number of subjects showing this elevation is small, we feel it is premature to try to interpret this interaction. The significance of theta burst activity in regards to CNS processes can be said to be obscure at best, and yet is descriptive of the state produced by a number of techniques, including Zen, Ananda Marga, and autogenic training. In an effort to relate this type of activity to more clearly understood processes, we correlated the frequency of theta bursts during treatment to levels of alpha amplitude, asymmetry, skin conductance fluctuations, and changes in these measures during treatment. No correlations were significant. Likewise, no significant correlations for theta were obtained with a number of personality trait variables obtained for these subjects (described in a later section).

As in our previous experiment, we again noted that LT-TM subjects tended to display (although not significantly) more theta burst activity during treatment than both of the other groups (see Table 4). Moreover, if we compute means based only on subjects who manifest at least one criterion (100 μV) burst, our Session 1 mean for the LT-TM group (.44 bursts/min) is very nearly identical to the mean (.48) reported in a study of advanced TM meditators conducted at the Maharishi European Research Laboratory (Hebert & Lehmann, 1977). Inconsistent with their data is our observance of this activity in non-meditators. No non-meditators in the latter study by Herbert and Lehmann manifested criterion theta burst activity. Clinical EEG researchers consider this type of EEG waveform (at this criterion) to be quite rare in nonneurologically damaged subjects. We can only speculate that instructions to subjects, or population of subjects sampled, may play an important role in whether or not this type of activity is seen. Our non-meditators were healthy young (X = 28 years) students and professionals, for the most part, who had never learned or practiced a relaxation technique. They were recruited through notices inviting them to participate in a "brain wave experiment of hemispheric specialization," and each subject received only minimal payment for participation. Their instructions for the treatment condition were: "Deeply relax all your muscles and continue to relax as much as you can for 20 minutes." Hopefully, future investigations will uncover both the necessary conditions and significance of this unusual type of brain activity.

As a non-EEG measure of physiological relaxation, skin conductance fluctuations (SCF) were counted during each period. Criterion amplitude was .2 μmho for 1.27 cm^2 of active palmer contact area. The pre- and postcontrol means were first analyzed via a groups × periods × days ANOVA. Only the periods main effect was significant ($p < .001$). The postcontrol mean (2.36 min^{-1}) was higher than the precontrol mean (.96), partly due to increased movements of the subjects as they came out of the relatively long and quiescent treatment period. In subsequent analyses, therefore, we compared means of the precontrol period to those for the treatment period. An ANOVA of the 20 minute treatment means revealed a significant periods main effect ($p < .02$), but no other effects. The treatment mean (.69) was lower than the precontrol mean. A similar ANOVA involving the first 5 minutes of treatment ($\overline{X} = .80$) was not significant for periods. As true for the integrated alpha results, the SCF data indicating a lack of a "unique" effect for TM (compared to non-meditators) are supported by prior studies of several researchers (Goleman & Schwartz, 1976; Schoicket et al., 1979; Walrath & Hamilton, 1975) but not all researchers (Orme-Johnson, 1973).

II. Hemispheric Dominance

In the current section, we depart from the conventional analysis of meditation as a relaxation technique, and instead, we focus our interest on the study of TM as a technique for the self-regulation of attention. Although several theoretical papers have treated meditation as a process involving the redeployment of attention (Boals, 1978; Davidson & Goleman, 1977; Deikman, 1969; Goleman, 1976), this approach has led to surprisingly little empirical research. In one early American paper, Deikman (1969) applied the concept of "deautomatization" to meditation. He proposed that the alteration in consciousness experienced during meditation stemmed from a reorganization of habituated perceptual and cognitive functions, presumably by reinvestment of actions and percepts with attention" (p. 31). Ornstein (1972, p. 138) has expanded this idea and hypothesized that the "deautomatized" state of consciousness experienced during meditation becomes a generalized trait. According to this theory, with continued practice, the meditator shifts his or her dominant mode of attention from one which is verbal and analytical to one predominantly intuitive and holistic. Indeed, the goal of meditation has been traditionally described in terms of such a change in normal attentional processes, in order to create a more healthy, "unitive" awareness of experience (Goleman, 1976). Ornstein further speculated that the attentional alternation resulting from meditation reflects a relative shift in the brain's underlying dominant mode of information processing.

A growing, substantial body of scientific work on cognitive functioning has shown that the two cerebral hemispheres each process information in specialized modes. Currently, most researchers formulate the distinction as follows (Galin, 1974; Gevins, Zehlin, Doyle, Yingling, Schaffer, Callaway, & Yeager, 1979; Hecaen & Albert, 1978, p. 408 ff.; Nebes, 1974): The left hemisphere (in right-handed persons) processes information analytically, involving stimuli coded either linguistically or sequentially. In a complementary fashion, the right hemisphere (in right-handers) processes information synthetically, utilizing stimuli that are not readily coded linguistically, but that are easily perceived in terms of whole patterns, or "gestalts." The extensive evidence supporting this theory of hemispheric specialization has been amassed through clinical neuropsychological research on brain-damaged patients (Hecaen & Albert, 1978), experimental and clinical studies of patients having had brain surgery (Milner, 1962) or commissurotomy (Nebes, 1974), and experimental studies of normal subjects (Dimond & Beaumont, 1974).

Our interest in alterations in the attentional processes related to meditation centered on testing Ornstein's hypothesis that meditation induces a relative shift in hemispheric "dominance." This hypothesis predicts that meditators manifest a relative shift in their major information processing strategy from that mediated primarily by the left hemisphere (LH) to one involving more of the right hemisphere (RH). Such a "shift" implies an increased ability to process material patterned in gestalts. Does this shift actually occur in long-term meditators? Do RH dominant abilities such as tonal memory and spatial patterning improve as a result of more dominant RH processing? How specific or general is the improvement? Do LH-dominant abilities, such as verbal memory or logical reasoning, suffer a decrement? Questions such as these immediately offer themselves for empirical investigation. The practical importance of answering these questions is obvious.

A. Performance Measures

In the first series of experiments (Pagano & Frumkin, 1977), we attempted to test the meditation–laterality hypothesis using tonal memory, a task which had been previously found to primarily involve the RH. The specific task we employed was the Tonal Memory Subtest of the Seashore Music Battery. This subtest has consistently revealed a selective impairment due to ablation of the right temporal lobe (Chase, 1967; Milner, 1962). There were two experiments in this series. In the first experiment, we compared 8 practitioners of TM (range 1.4–3 years) and 9 non-meditators in performance on the tonal memory test. The meditation–laterality hypothesis would predict better performance on this task for meditators. All subjects had minimal or no musical training. The subjects were run on the tonal memory test for three days to eliminate any practice effects. The procedure was the same for each day. Each subject was given a pretest, followed by a treatment period, followed by a posttest. One form of the tonal memory test was given on the pretest and a second form on the posttest. During the treatment period, the meditators practiced their usual meditation for 20 minutes and the non-meditators sat comfortably with eyes closed. Table 5, part

TABLE 5
Performance on Tonal Memory

	Long-term meditators		Non-meditators	
	$\overline{X}$	SD	$\overline{X}$	SD
Experiment 1 (A)				
Pretest	92.13	8.20	70.66	19.89
Posttest	91.50	5.01	69.10	19.17

	Long-term meditators		Inexperienced meditators		Non-meditators	
	$\overline{X}$	SD	$\overline{X}$	SD	$\overline{X}$	SD
Experiment 2 (B)						
Pretest	89.00	4.50	70.50	15.24	74.00	17.49
Posttest	89.50	4.20	68.30	16.79	75.44	12.02

A, shows the pretest and posttest percentage of correct responses for both groups on Day 3. A two-way ANOVA revealed no significant pre-posttest main effect ($F < 1$). However, there was a highly significant difference ($p < .005$) between the TM and non-meditation groups, with the meditators being superior to non-meditators in both the pre and posttests (p's $< .01$).

The second experiment in this series was conducted to evaluate whether the above results were due to predispositional selection factors (i.e., to the attraction of TM for individuals having superior tonal memory prior to learning TM). In this experiment 28 new subjects were tested, 10 experienced practitioners of TM, 9 inexperienced TM practitioners (less than one month of TM experience and presumably prior to having developed traits characteristic of their more experienced counterparts) and 9 non-meditators. Materials and procedures were the same as in the first experiment differing only in that subjects were run in groups of three at a time (1 experienced meditator, 1 inexperienced meditator, and 1 non-meditator in each group). Table 5, Part B, shows the pre and posttest percentages of correct responses on the tonal memory test for all groups on Day 3. As can be seen, the results closely replicate those of the first experiment. There were no significant pre-posttest main effects ($F < 1$). There was, however, a highly significant groups effect ($p < .005$). As before, individual contrasts showed that the experienced meditators were superior to the non-meditators both in pre and posttest performance (p's $< .005$). There was no significant difference between non-meditators and inexperienced meditators. It is also worth noting that the variance of the long-term meditators was significantly lower than that of the nonmeditators. This could be due to either selection factors or the effect of meditation itself. To assess the stability of the experienced meditator trait effect, we have plotted in Figure 2 the data from all three days of testing for both experiments. As can be seen from the graphs, the superior performance of the experienced meditators was manifested on each day of testing. The results of these two experiments are consistent with the hypothesis that the relatively long-term practice of TM *produces* a shift in information-processing strategy toward greater involvement of the right hemisphere.

In the next series of three experiments, we investigated the effects of TM on iconic memory (Frumkin & Pagano, 1979). The task we employed was Sperling's (1960) tachistoscopic procedure using number matrices shown at brief exposure (50 msec). Although direct evidence regarding this task is not available, similar tasks have shown themselves to LH dominant.[2] We have included all three experiments in our discussion here to emphasize the importance of doing carefully controlled experiments when investigating the effects of meditation.

In the first study, there was 10 experienced practitioners of TM (range 6 months–13 years) and 10 non-meditators obtained from a University of Washington introductory psychology course. The same paradigm as in the tonal memory experiments was used; a pretest followed by a 20 minute treatment period, followed by a posttest. During the treatment period, the meditators practiced TM and the non-medi-

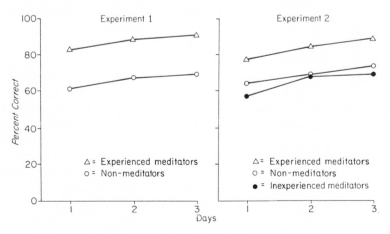

FIGURE 2. Tonal memory performance over days.

[2] We recognize that it is possible to argue that the configurational aspects of numbers implies RH processing.

Table 6
Performance on Iconic Memory Task

	Meditators		Non-meditators	
	$\overline{X}$	SD	$\overline{X}$	SD
Experiment 1 (A)				
Pretest	43.10	—	53.10	—
Posttest	67.40	—	52.10	—
Experiment 2 (B)				
Pretest[a]	58.88	11.28	65.66	13.64
Posttest[a]	63.22	10.83	70.78	13.82
Pretest[b]	66.00	10.61	66.56	16.76
Posttest[b]	70.00	9.55	72.00	16.75
Experiment 3 (C)				
Pretest	53.98	15.14	58.81	13.19
Posttest	58.18	13.96	65.03	10.21

[a] Auditory cue.
[b] Visual cue.

tators were run together as a group. The non-meditators were also run together as a group and the two groups were run separately. The pre and posttests consisted of two practice trials followed by 16 trials which determined the performance score. The experimenter was a meditator and the digit matrix was cued verbally by the meditator. Intertrial interval was fixed at 10 seconds. There was no warning signal. The results are shown in Table 6, Part A. There were no significant differences between TM practitioners and non-meditators on pretest ($p > .10$). However, on the posttest, the TM practitioners performed significantly better than the non-meditator group ($p < .05$).

Given the promising results of this pilot experiment, we decided to do a second experiment using appropriate controls. The following controls were added: (1) extrinsic motivation (a $10 reward for highest performance); (2) matching of groups; (3) individual rather than group running; (4) subject-paced presentation; (5) automatic rather than experimenter initiated cueing; (6) experimenter neutral regarding meditation (the experimenter was a non-meditator and unaware of whether the subject was a meditator or a non-meditator); (7) scoring "blind" with regard to subjects' condition; and (8) running subjects over many trials to eliminate practice effects and to stabilize the dependent variable.

The experiment followed standard procedures for this task using individual pacing (see Frumkin & Pagano, 1979). In the first part of the experiment cueing was auditory and in the second part, visual. The experiment lasted five days. On Days 1 and 2, subjects practiced the task using auditory cueing. Two hundred massed trials per day were run, requiring 30–60 minutes in the laboratory. Day 3 was the testing day and used auditory cueing. The subjects were pretested, followed by a treatment condition (meditation or relaxation), and then posttested. Days 4 and 5 were test days identical to Day 3, except visual cueing was used.

Table 6, Part B, displays the mean performance data for both the auditory and visual cues. The data shown are from Day 3 (auditory cue) and Day 5 (visual cue). Separate two-way ANOVAs were performed for the auditory and visual cues. There were no significant group main effects for either cue ($F < 1$). There was, however, a small but significant pre-post main effect for the auditory cue ($p < .01$) and for the visual cue ($p < .01$). Individual t-tests showed a significant pre-post effect for both the meditation and non-meditation groups for auditory and visual cueing. This effect could be due to something happening in the experimental period or to a practice effect. Figure 3 plots the group scores as a function of practice. Analysis of these data reveals some interesting features. First, it appears as though asymptote was not reached on Day 3. By Day 5, the curves were leveling off. The small Day 3 and Day 5 pre-post effects are most likely practice effects. The second rather strik-

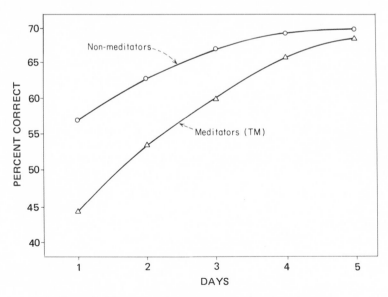

FIGURE 3. Mean percentage correct as a function of practice.

ing feature is that the meditators' performance seems to be inferior to the non-meditators. Indeed, a t-test on Day 1 showed that the meditators' performance was significantly lower than non-meditators ($p <$ .05).

In the second experiment, subjects were allowed to pace presentation of the stimuli, while in the first experiment the stimuli were experimenter-paced. There is the possibility that the increased performance of the meditators, after their meditation period in the first experiment of the series, might be due to a general increase in alertness relative to the non-meditation group. The self-paced procedure in the second experiment might have permitted all subjects to confine performance only to periods when vigilance had been brought to a maximum, thus canceling out possible differences in the level of alertness between groups. In addition, it is also possible that, by administering many practice trials in the second experiment, a possible meditation effect early in learning may have been obscured.

To investigate these possibilities, another experiment was run. Essentially, it was a replication of the first experiment except that the following controls were added: (1) extrinsic motivation ($10 prize); (2) running of heterogenous groups; (3) group matching; and (4) blind scoring. These controls were added to eliminate variables other than attention and practice (e.g., experimenter bias and differences in motivation) which may have caused the superior meditator performance in the first experiment. Fifty-nine subjects were run: 32 meditators and 27 non-meditators. Subject characteristics were similar to the previous experiment.

Table 6, Part C, shows the mean percentage of digits correctly recalled. Again, there was a significant pre-post main effect ($p <$ .005). As in the second experiment, individual t tests showed a significant pre-post effect for both meditation and non-meditation groups. In addition, the main effect for groups was at borderline significance ($p =$ .068). From Table 6, it is apparent that this effect was due to the superior performance of the non-meditator group. There were no significant interactions.

These three studies taken together graphically illustrate the need for careful research when evaluating the effects of meditation on performance. On the basis of the first experiment, it appeared that meditation facilitated performance on the appointed task. However, this experiment lacked important controls. The meditation and non-meditation subjects were run in separate groups, cueing was controlled by the experimenter who was a meditator, testing was not done blindly, and there was no attempt to equate motivation between the groups.

The study actually was of a pilot nature. When the appropriate controls were added, not only did the enhancement effect specific to meditation fail to occur, but meditators performed worse in the iconic memory task. This inferior performance even persisted in the final experiment. The possibility that meditation might lead to decreased performance, particularly on LH tasks, was mentioned earlier. It has also been raised by Schwartz (1974), based on unpublished data with TM practitioners using problem solving tasks which are usually associated with LH processes.

These initial results from our laboratory involving tonal and iconic memory, and the results of Schwartz led us to the next study which pursued the meditation—laterality hypothesis using a wider variety of tasks (Warrenburg & Pagano, 1982). We realized that even if this study confirmed the previous results, an adequate evaluation of this hypothesis would ultimately require a well-controlled longitudinal study to settle the issue of subject selection and consequent possible predispositional biasing variables. However, we felt that before undertaking such a lengthy study, we wanted to see if the results obtained with tonal and iconic memory would generalize to other RH- and LH-dominant tasks.

The study employed a battery of 7 tests; three that involved primarily linguistic (LH-dominant) skills and four involving spatial or musical (RH-dominant) abilities. The three LH-dominant tests were: (1) Watson and Glaser's Critical Thinking Appraisal (CTA), a logical reasoning test highly correlated with measures of verbal intelligence (Watson & Glaser, 1964); (2) a verbal memory test, composed of categorized abstract words, divided into cued and uncued portions; and (3) Wallach and Kogan's "Uses" Test (Wallach & Kogan, 1965), that was scored separately for fluency and originality. The four RH-dominant tests were: (1) Seashore's Tonal Memory test, employed in our previous research; (2) the Mental Rotations Test, a visuospatial perception test, adapted from Shepard and Metzler (Shepard & Metzler, 1971); (3) the Hidden Patterns Test (French, Ekstrom, & Price, 1963), involving detection of simple patterns embedded in complex designs; and (4) the Blocks Subtest of the Weschler Adult Intelligence Scale (WAIS) (Matarazzo, 1972).

The choice of tests to be administered was based on the following theoretical and methodological considerations: (1) Tests were of theoretical interest from the standpoint of addressing a fairly wide range of functions within each hemisphere's functional realm, including several tests (or similar tests) which had previously been given to TM meditators; (2) Test performance on the specific test to be given, or on similar tests, had previously been documented to require differential engagement of the cerebral hemispheres, as indicated in neuropsychological tests of unilaterally brain-damaged or commissurotomized patients; (3)

Test involvement reflected appropriate EEG asymmetries in pilot testing in our laboratory;[3] (4) Where possible, tests had been standardized using large samples of normal subjects, thereby allowing comparisons with estimates of population parameters; (5) All tests were compatible with EEG analysis, namely, (a) of sufficient duration to yield reliable samples of artifact-free data, and (b) containing periods of either no manual involvement or minimal, controlled manual activity; (6) Finally, all tests were designed to yield mean performance levels which would not be constrained by "floor" or "ceiling" effects (i.e., tests were chosen to be moderately difficult, 20–80% correct). One major reason that we have constructed our own testing battery is that most neuropsychological tests which are differentially sensitive to LH and RH damage (e.g., the Halstead–Reitan battery) are designed to reflect primarily impaired performance, and normal controls score near the top of the scale (Reitan, 1969).

In addition to assessing performance on the 7 tasks, cerebral dominance was measured during each task using EEG alpha asymmetry. Parietal sites, P3 and P4 were monitored separately using the vertex (Cz) and the nose as a reference. Manual activity was kept minimal and was carefully controlled and counterbalanced for each task (These data will be presented in the next section). Subjects were 3 groups of 16 healthy young adults, with equal numbers of males and females per group: (a) long-term TM meditators (LT-TM), (b) novice TM meditators (Nov-TM), and (c) non-meditators (Non-Med). (Additional characteristics of these subjects were described in the previous section, *EEG Alpha and Theta Activity*.) All subjects had minimal or no musical training. Due to incomplete data (performance measures) or recording difficulties (EEG measures), several subjects in one or more groups were deleted from analysis. Each subject participated in two laboratory sessions on separate days. To maximize test-taking motivation, subjects were paid a base fee ($4) plus a bonus amount proportional to their level of performance. The seven tasks plus an eyes-open baseline period (EOB) were counterbalanced for order over the two days of testing.

The 7 administered tests yielded 9 performance scores, as shown in Table 7. Preliminary analysis indicated that although the 3 groups were closely matched for age and education, the Non-Med group was

---

[3] Prior experimental evidence regarding differential EEG activation was available for blocks, tonal memory, and mental rotations. Although this evidence indicates that the former two tests were RH dominant (Doyle, Ornstein, & Galin, 1974), for mental rotations the evidence is mixed (cf. Furst, 1976, and Ornstein, Johnstone, Herron, & Swencionis, 1980). Our own data indicates that EEG alpha asymmetry on this task depends upon an interaction of subject's sex and the reference electrode used in recording EEG (Warrenburg & Pagano, 1981).

TABLE 7
Performance Test Battery

Group		Test performance scores[a]								
		Critical thinking appraisal	Uncued free recall	Cued free recall	Uses fluency	Uses originality	Tonal memory	Mental rotations	Hidden patterns	Blocks
Novice meditators (N = 14)	mean	72.3	36.8	12.7	21.4	1.0	69.6	42.5	35.8	85.7
	s.e.	2.4	4.0	1.8	1.9	0.5	4.4	3.0	2.1	3.4
Long-term meditators (N = 15)	mean	74.2	44.8	12.9	21.6	1.1	82.9	38.0	37.0	87.9
	s.e.	2.3	3.9	1.7	1.9	0.5	4.4	3.0	2.1	3.3
Non-meditators (N = 16)	mean	75.9	42.7	19.6	23.1	1.9	65.6	43.8	39.1	87.0
	s.e.	2.3	3.9	1.7	1.9	0.5	4.3	2.9	2.0	3.3

[a] Percentage correct for all scores except uses (fluency and originality) which are reported as number of items listed. These data have been adjusted to partial out the effects of recency of school attendance (see text).

composed primarily of students, whereas this was not the case for the LTM group. On the average, the former group had been out of school a shorter time than the LT-TM group ($p < .01$). Furthermore, length of time out of school correlated negatively with 8 of the 9 test scores, and significantly with overall test performance ($r = -.34$, $p < .05$). Consequently, length of time out of school was entered as a covariate in all subsequent group analyses, and the means presented in Table 7 have been adjusted accordingly.

The performance data were analyzed via multivariate analysis of covariance, which yielded a significant main effect for groups ($p < .03$) and a groups × sex interaction ($p < .02$). The overall analysis was followed by univariate analyses of covariance for each test measure. Only two test measures revealed significant group main effects: tonal memory ($p < .03$) and cued verbal memory ($p < .02$). Planned mean comparisons between groups for the tonal memory test indicated better performance by the LT-TM group than both the Nov-TM ($p < .02$) and Non-Med groups ($p < .005$). The latter two group means did not differ reliably ($p > .10$). These results replicate our previous two experiments on tonal memory.

For cued verbal memory the Non-Med group scored higher than either the Nov-TM ($p < .01$) or LT-TM groups ($p < .02$), and the latter two means did not differ significantly ($p > .10$). Thus, of the 7 tasks studied only 2 showed main effects for groups: LT-TM subjects outperformed both of the other control groups in tonal memory, considered to be a RH dominant task, and both meditator groups performed worse than the non-meditators on cued verbal memory, a LH dominant task.

We also observed a group × sex interaction for tonal memory ($p < .05$) and users' originality ($p < .03$).[4] The tonal memory interaction was due to higher performance by Nov-TM females (80.7%) than Nov-TM males (58.3%), whereas the two sexes did not differ in the other two groups. Indeed, Nov-TM females performed virtually the same as LT-TM subjects (82.9%). In an effort to assess the possible effects of subject selection in explaining significant group effects, we contacted subjects in the Nov-TM group 3 to 5 months after they had begun meditating. Of the 16, 9 were still meditating regularly (maintainers) and 7 had stopped altogether or practiced infrequently (dropouts). Six

---

[4] The group × sex interaction for uses originality was unpredicted, and is in conflict with results of a large scale study that found men scored higher than women on a similar test to the uses test (Wilson & Vanderberg, 1978). We looked at individual subjects' data for the 8 female Non-Med subjects forming the higher scoring group. There we found that 3 subjects received extremely high scores (7 to 9), whereas 5 subjects were comparable to the rest of the entire sample (0 to 3). Due to the apparently idiosyncratic nature of these 3 high scores, we are unable to interpret this result meaningfully.

of 7 dropouts were male, whereas 7 of 9 maintainers were female, a pattern of sex differences that is significant ($p < .05$) by Fisher's exact test. Consistent with this pattern, and that of higher tonal memory scores for Nov-TM females, is the finding that Nov-TM maintainers scored higher in tonal memory ($\overline{X} = 76.1$, $N = 8$) than dropouts ($\overline{X} = 60.6$, $N = 6$). This is not a statistically significant difference, but the small sample sizes of the Nov-TM subgroups preclude powerful statistical testing. Nonetheless, this large mean difference combined with the pattern of sex differences indicates that subject selection was probably responsible for the tonal memory effect. A similar pattern, however, was not obtained for cued verbal memory with Nov-TM maintainers performing essentially the same (12.6%) as dropouts (12.9%).

In addition to the battery of performance tests, we administered a battery of personality self-report scales (described in detail in the next section on *Personality Traits*), one of which pertains to our hypothesis linking meditation and attention. This scale, called *absorption*, tests "primarily a capacity for episodes of absorbed and 'self-altering' attention that are sustained by imaginative and 'enactive' representation" (Tellegen, 1977, p. 2).[5] Absorption correlates moderately with hypnotic susceptibility, and high absorbers have been shown to have a more "flexible attentional style (with) greater mode specific cortical (EEG) patterning during selective attention" (Davidson, Schwartz, & Rotman, 1976, p. 611). In a prior cross-sectional study of meditators and non-meditators (Davidson, Goleman, & Schwartz, 1976), higher absorption scores were obtained in longer term practitioners of meditation.

We computed correlations between absorption and each of the performance scores. Only the correlation with tonal memory was significant ($r = .35$, $p < .025$). Dividing subjects into meditators ($N = 27$) and non-meditators ($N = 16$), this correlation became highly significant for meditators ($r = .52$, $p < .005$) but nearly zero for non-meditators ($r = .05$, n.s.). Comparisons between groups in absorption were not significant, although group means for the LT-TM (22.8), Nov-TM (21.4) and Non-Med groups (19.9) were ordered as found by Davidson *et al.* (1976). In a *post hoc* analysis, we combined Nov-TM maintainers ($\overline{X} = 25.5$) with the LT-TM group, and Nov-TM dropouts ($\overline{X} = 19.1$) with the Non-Med group, in order to test the difference between "adherent meditators" and "non-meditators" using larger samples. The resulting mean for adherent meditators (24.7, $N = 23$) was significantly higher ($p < .03$) than that for non-meditators (20.6, $N = 22$). Likewise, the variance of the former group (30.3) was significantly lower ($p < .05$) than that of

---

[5] We are indebted to Dr. Jonathon C. Smith (Roosevelt University) for introducing the absorption scale to us.

the latter (64.0), and was also less ($p < .05$) than that of Tellegen's standardized sample (56.3). Length of practice of meditation in the LT-TM group was not associated with higher scores on either tonal memory ($r = -.08$), cued verbal memory ($r = -.04$) or absorption ($r = -.02$). Cued verbal memory did not correlate with tonal memory ($r = .10$).

B. EEG Alpha Asymmetry during Performance

EEG laterality index (R/L) means (Cz reference) obtained during each task for the 3 groups are shown in Table 8.[6] These data were first averaged for the 3 verbal and 3 spatial tasks separately. We then conducted a group × sex × conditions ANOVA that included 4 repeated measures: verbal, spatial, tonal memory, and eyes open baseline (EOB). The conditions main effect was significant ($p < .001$), and was due to the verbal condition yielding a higher index (more LH dominant) than each of the other conditions. The latter 3 conditions did not differ significantly. Neither the groups main effect nor groups × condition interaction were significant (p's $< .10$). Similar analyses for the nose-referenced data likewise yielded a conditions main effect ($p < .0001$)

TABLE 8

Integrated Alpha Asymmetry Ratio (R/L) Means by Task and Group (Vertex Reference)

				Task condition					
Group		Uses	Verbal memory	Critical thinking appraisal	Eyes open baseline	Tonal memory	Blocks	Mental rotations	Hidden patterns
Novice	X̄	1.083	1.057	1.062	1.023	1.005	1.024	0.972	0.990
meditators	SD	.128	.119	.068	.119	.119	.086	.100	.058
($N = 9$)									
Long-term	X̄	1.142	1.103	1.043	1.024	1.060	1.068	1.017	1.055
meditators	SD	.166	.168	.092	.115	.151	.139	.121	.164
($N = 10$)									
Non-	X̄	1.193	1.147	1.055	1.062	1.046	0.993	1.030	0.975
meditators	SD	.247	.237	.099	.151	.100	.084	.152	.085
($N = 14$)									
Overall	X̄	1.147	1.109	1.053	1.040	1.039	1.024	1.010	1.003
mean	SD	.195	.190	.086	.132	.121	.103	.126	.114
($N = 33$)									

[6] We have also analyzed these data using asymmetry indices calculated via the formula $(R - L)/(R + L)$, and we obtained essentially identical results.

and no groups effects. As with the vertex-referenced data, the verbal condition (1.053) yielded a more LH dominant index than the EOB (1.009) or spatial (.993) conditions, which did not differ between themselves. An interesting discrepancy from the Cz reference data, however, was that the tonal memory index (1.032) fell between the verbal and spatial means and did not differ significantly from either.[7]

Bennett and Trinder (1977) reported that, compared to non-meditators, long-term TM meditators manifested greater task-induced shifts in asymmetry from verbal to spatial (blocks) and musical (tonal memory) tasks. Although their subject characteristics were similar to ours, these authors recorded from temporal, rather than parietal sites (Cz reference) using a percent–time alpha, rather than integrated alpha measure. It is possible that these methodological differences resulted in our discrepant findings. Our conflicting results for the two references sites regarding tonal memory are puzzling and point out that more basic work needs to be done concerning the EEG alpha asymmetry technique. Neuropsychological evidence regarding tonal memory convincingly indicates that (in non-musicians) this task requires RH specialization.

C. Does TM Induce a Shift in Hemispheric Dominance?

Of the nine test performance measures obtained in this experiment, only two yielded significant group main effects. The absence of generalized group differences on task performance scores of left and right hemisphere functioning clearly fails to support the general form of the meditation–laterality hypothesis: meditation does not appear to globally facilitate RH-specialized task performance, nor to globally impair LH-specialized task performance. Moreover, judging from the EEG asymmetry data, meditation does not appear to produce a relative state shift in hemispheric dominance during meditation or during performance.

Two test scores, however, did differentiate between meditator and non-meditator groups—tonal memory and cued verbal memory. Long-term meditators outperformed non-meditators on the former test, but the converse was true on the latter test. Our three-group analyses indicate that the practice of meditation, *per se*, is probably not responsible for these effects. Rather, the most parsimonious explanation of our results is that a self-selection process produced the obtained pattern of performance scores. The cued verbal memory and tonal memory test results support this view. Both the Nov-TM and LT-TM groups were worse than the Non-Med group in cued verbal memory. The lack of

---

[7] See footnote, p. 182.

difference in the performance of the two meditator groups strongly suggests that this effect is *not* due to the practice of meditation, but rather is due to some special characteristic of these meditator subjects. This conclusion is based on the reasonable assumption that a few weeks of TM practice in the Nov-TM group is not sufficient to cause a performance decrement which then persists indefinitely in meditators without changing in magnitude. The tonal memory results are somewhat more complicated but lead to the same conclusion, as explained below.

Whether or not our self-selection hypothesis is correct, we are still faced with the issue of explaining what this pattern of results actually means. In the introduction to this section we offered the hypothesis that, as the meditator continues to practice, alteration in attentional processes during the meditation state extend to periods outside of those involving explicit practice of TM, thereby becoming a generalized trait of the meditator. We predicted that this trait would facilitate RH information processing of non-linguistic, gestalt-patterned stimuli, and possibly impair LH information processing of linguistic, sequentially ordered stimuli. Quite to the contrary, our data suggest that persons who maintain long-term adherence to TM were predisposed, *prior to learning TM*, to utilize their attention to become totally absorbed in a non-verbal mode.

Our reasoning stems from several findings in these data. First, novice and long-term meditators who had maintained regular practice were significantly higher in absorption and tonal memory than the non-meditators and dropouts. Second, there was a highly significant correlation between absorption and tonal memory that applied only to meditators, indicating the existence of a special trait or syndrome. Further support for this "special trait" hypothesis comes from the finding that adherent meditators have a lower variance in absorption compared to both the non-meditator–dropout group and also to the general population. Third, the lack of association between length of practice in LT-TM meditators and either tonal memory or absorption indicates that this attentional trait probably did not develop as the result of meditation practice. From these data we conclude that absorbed attention may be an important prerequisite for successful long-term practice of meditation.

As described previously, absorption is the ability to have "episodes of absorbed and 'self-altering' attention that are sustained by imaginative and 'enactive' representations" (Tellegen, 1977, p. 2). In these episodes "the available representational apparatus seems to be entirely dedicated to experiencing and modeling the attentional object, be it a landscape, a human being, a *sound* [italics added], a remembered incident, or an aspect of one's self" (Tellegen & Atkinson, 1974, p. 274). This trait description defines well both the skills necessary to meditate and also to perform well on the tonal memory test. Such a skill would clearly be very important in the task of sustaining the memory of a 4 to 6 note tonal pattern for several seconds. Likewise, this trait should facilitate success in becoming absorbed in the covert repetition of the mantra in an easy, passive manner. If true, this trait should thereby promote the meditation experiential state as well as long-term adherence. It is also worth noting anecdotally that the LT-TM group rated the tonal memory task as easier for them than either of the other two groups ($p < .05$), when asked afterwards to make this rating on a 7-point Lickert scale.

Recent research by Qualls and Sheehan (1979; 1981a, b; in press) confirms that absorption is an important individual difference variable in predicting success in learning to achieve states of pronounced relaxation. High absorption scorers were able to relax more deeply when allowed to direct their attention towards their own strategies without biofeedback, than when explicitly required to attend to a biofeedback signal. Low absorbers displayed the converse pattern. However, when high absorption scorers were encouraged to utilize imagery during biofeedback conditions, they were able to incorporate the biofeedback signal into their own imaginative strategy and to achieve maximal relaxation. This latter result underscores the *active* attentional processing ability of high absorbers. We will return to a discussion of absorption in meditators in the next section (*Personality Traits*).

How do the cued verbal memory results fit into the attentional trait hypothesis we are offering? The cued and uncued verbal memory tests were designed according to previous research (Birnbaum & Eichner, 1971; Tulving & Pearlstone, 1966). The methods followed for uncued recall are essentially those of free recall: Subjects simply write down all the items they can remember. The cued recall portion of the test follows next, in which a list of all the category names is supplied to the subject (e.g., Indian tribes). Additional items recalled are then listed by the subject. Memory researchers treat cued recall similarly to recognition; that, is results from these tests are thought to reflect retrieval processes substantially *less* than do uncued recall tests. Additional items recalled with cueing are those that were attended to, encoded, and stored in memory, but that were inaccessible to retrieval prior to cueing. That is, words recalled with cueing are those that were successfully stored but subsequently forgotten. As with prior research, our findings that both meditator groups were lower in cued recall, but *not* uncued recall, can be interpreted to indicate reduced memory storage for these two groups. As with tonal memory, altered verbal memory storage may reflect altered attention, encoding, and/or storage processes. This finding is consistent with prior research from our laboratory that found meditators poorer in visual iconic memory, a test involving quick recall of briefly exposed digits (Frumkin & Pagano, 1979).

If this verbal memory deficit is due to altered attention, the above results would "mirror" those for tonal memory. Although we realize this interpretation is speculative, it suggests that meditators are predisposed to be less attentive to verbal, LH-processed information, as well as more attentive to non-verbal, RH-processed information. Since the act of meditation involves *dis*-attending to distracting verbal thoughts as well as attending to the mantra, these parallel attentional traits would appear to greatly facilitate meditation.

In summary, our original hypothesis that meditation globally facilitates RH- and impairs LH-dominant information processing was not supported. Rather, our performance differences are most likely due to characteristic traits of meditators prior to learning meditation. We have inferred that these traits may reflect (1) reduced attention to LH-processed, verbal information, yielding poorer cued verbal memory, and (2) enhanced attention to RH-processed, (nonverbal) information, as displayed in superior tonal memory and a more pronounced personality trait of absorption. Both tonal memory and absorption were higher in all meditators who maintained practice for at least 3–5 months, as compared to non-meditators and dropout novice meditators. Based on these data, we propose that absorbed attention to nonverbal stimuli, and reduced attention to verbal stimuli, facilitate the practice of meditation and long term adherence.

Thus, in originally hypothesizing that meditation produces a shift in "hemispheric dominance" we may have put the cart before the horse. We realize that only a fully longitudinal study of persons learning meditation can conclusively answer research questions of this type. Such an experimental design allows the investigator to distinguish genuine effects of meditation *per se* from self-selection and dropout factors. These cross-sectional findings may be disappointing to those who expected, as we did, to find general cognitive effects attributable to meditation practice. On the other hand, this information may be quite useful to clinicians who wish to use meditation as an adjunct to psychotherapy for anxiety reduction. Anxious clients who score highly on the absorption and/or tonal memory tests are probably better candidates for meditation than those who do not.

III. PERSONALITY TRAITS

Certainly one of the most important reasons that TM has become so popular in the last decade is its beneficial effects in terms of lowering self-reported "stress" or anxiety (Smith, 1976; Zuroff & Schwarz, 1978), and of enhancing the converse qualities of well-being or "self-actualization" (Seeman, Nidich, & Bantan, 1972), and internal locus of control (Hjelle, 1974). We looked for these effects in the three groups of subjects

(LT-TM, Nov-TM, and Non-Med) who were tested for hemispheric dominance, as described in the last section. These subjects completed seven self-report personality scales. Five of these were from the Differential Personality Inventory (Tellegen, 1977); absorption, stress, well-being, social desirability (SD), and acquiescence. The remaining two scales were locus of control (Rotter, 1966) and test anxiety (Sarason, 1978). Each of the scales has been widely employed and well-validated in a variety of previous psychological studies. The absorption, stress, well-being, and locus of control scales were the four substantive scales of interest, and acquiescence, SD and test anxiety were included as validity moderator scales.

The seven scales were first analyzed via multivariate discriminant analysis comparing the 3 groups of subjects. The overall analysis was significant ($p < .05$) and was followed by (1) a priori group mean contrasts for each of the 4 substantive scales and (2) one-way ANOVAs for each of the 3 validity scales. These data are presented in Table 9. Since the absorption results were described in the previous section, we will not repeat them here. As predicted, long-term TM meditators indicated less stress ($p < .025$), more well-being ($p < .05$), and a more internal locus of control ($p < .025$) than non-meditator controls. The long-term TM group was also lower in stress than novice meditators ($p < .025$). The two meditator groups did not differ significantly on either of the other two scales (p's $> .10$), nor did the novice TM and non-meditator groups differ on these three scales (p's $> .10$) (see Table 9).

Results of the validity scales were interesting, in that although groups did not differ in test anxiety ($p < .10$), they did differ in acquiescence ($p < .02$), and at borderline significance in SD ($p < .07$). The

TABLE 9
Personality Trait Scales

Group		Absorption	Stress	Well-being	Locus of control	Social desirability	Acquiescence	Test anxiety
Nov-TM	$\overline{X}$	2.14	11.6	19.4	8.7	10.9	15.9[c]	14.5
(N = 14)	SD	7.3	6.2	4.7	5.0	1.7	2.4	8.0
LT-TM	$\overline{X}$	22.8	6.3[b]	20.7	6.9[a]	11.2[a]	14.5	11.3
(N = 15)	SD	4.7	4.1	3.9	3.7	1.7	1.8	7.4
Non-med	$\overline{X}$	19.9	11.0	16.8	10.9	9.6	13.6	10.3
(N = 16)	SD	7.6	6.8	7.5	5.1	2.2	1.9	6.8
Standardized	$\overline{X}$	19.8	12.0	18.2	8.3	9.9	14.8	18.2
sample	SD	7.5	6.6	5.6	4.0	2.4	2.5	6.9

[a] LT-TM and Non-med groups differed, $p < .05$.
[b] LT-TM group differed from both Nov-TM and Non-med groups, $p < .025$.
[c] Nov-TM group differed from Non-med group, $p < .01$.

novice group was higher in acquiescence than non-meditators ($p < .01$) and was also higher than long-term meditators at near-significance ($p < .09$). Unlike the results for absorption described in the last section, in which novice TM maintainers were substantially higher than novice TM dropouts, means of each of the other six personality scales differed by less than 1 point between maintainers and dropouts.

Results for the SD and acquiescence scales pose an intriguing pattern, since novice meditators stand above the other two groups in acquiescence, and both the long-term and novice groups score higher than non-meditators in SD. The latter scale, like the Marlowe-Crowne scale of the same name (Crowne & Marlowe, 1964) taps defensiveness in reporting negative qualities about one's self (i.e., the tendency to "avoid looking bad" across the content of various scales; c.f. Weinberger, Schwartz, & Davidson, 1979). Despite long-term meditators' higher SD scores, SD did not correlate significantly with any other scale (r's $< \pm .21$), hence SD cannot be invoked as an "explanation" of the results on the substantive scales. This conclusion is supported by Zuroff and Schwartz (1978) and Smith (1978) who also found that SD did not predict self-reported anxiety reduction in two longitudinal studies of TM. We must note, however, that neither this latter study of TM, nor the one by Smith (1976; 1978) reported groups effects in SD. Acquiescence is a scale designed to reflect specifically the test-taker's tendency to answer "true," regardless of item content, and more generally the tendency to be agreeable. However, as "true" for SD, scores on this scale did not predict those on the substantive scales (r's $< \pm .23$). Correlations between each pair of the 7 scales were generally low (r's $< \pm .37$), except for that between stress and well-being ($r = .61$, $p < .005$).

The strongest and least ambiguous finding in these data involve the stress scale. Long-term meditators scored lower than both non-meditators and novice meditators, and dropouts did not differ from maintainers. Thus, we can conclude that the practice of TM, rather than subject selection, produced the lower stress scores in the long-term group. Tellegen (1977) describes this scale as one closely related to Eysenck's Neuroticism Scale, and it reflects the trait of emotional upsetness, worry, and nervousness—that is, anxiety. Results for well-being and locus of control are obscured by the fact that the novice TM group fell intermediately between non-meditators and long-term meditators. From these data alone, we cannot conclude whether the latter group manifests higher well-being and a more internal locus of control due to the practice of TM or due to self-selection factors. As mentioned earlier, we included a group of novice practitioners (1–5 weeks of practice) under the assumption that such brief practice of TM would not have produced appreciable change in any of our dependent measures.

It is possible, however, that even this brief duration of practice resulted in some effect on two self-report scales (well-being and locus of control) but not on a third (stress). Let us turn to previous findings of other investigators in order to try to better comprehend these results.

The self-reports of lower stress by long-term meditators, as compared to both novices and non-meditators, are consistent with results from a number of studies of TM utilizing both cross-sectional (Ferguson & Gowan, 1976; Hjelle, 1974) and longitudinal procedures (Ferguson & Gowan, 1976; Raskin *et al.*, 1980; Smith, 1976; Zuroff & Schwarz, 1978). Prior research on self-reported increases in self-actualization likewise suggests that our findings for well-being are due to a relatively rapid change that occurs in meditators even within five weeks of practice. Three longitudinal studies have reported increases in self-actualization over a six-week (Ferguson & Gowan, 1977) and two-month period (Nidich, Seeman, & Dreshin, 1973; Seeman *et al.*, 1972). Each of these studies observed no change in a no-treatment control group (not interested in learning TM) that was tested twice over the same interval of time as the group learning TM.

Prior research findings concerning locus of control are in conflict, however, regarding whether, and how quickly, this scale responds to TM practice. Stek and Bass (1973) observed no significant differences on this measure, nor on a self-actualization scale, between four groups of subjects exhibiting differential interest in learning TM. Another cross-sectional study by Hjelle (1974) did observe differences on these same scales between long-term TM meditators and persons about to learn TM. Results from three longitudinal studies of meditation appear to be in conflict. Marlatt, Pagano, Rose, and Marques (in press) obtained near significant increases in internal locus of control with six weeks of mantra meditation practice. (This study will be described in more detail in Section IV.) However, neither Zuroff & Schwarz (1978) nor Zaichkowsky & Kamen (1978) found a significant effect on this scale in 2–3 month longitudinal studies of TM. Despite the lack of a treatment effect for locus of control, Zuroff & Schwartz did observe a positive correlation ($r = .53$) between internality on this scale and anxiety reduction. The correlation between internal locus of control and stress in our study ($r = .37$) was not as substantial, but was significant ($p < .01$), and in the same direction as that obtained by Zuroff and Schwarz.

In summary, then, we can say with some confidence that practice of TM promotes healthier self-reports of lowered stress and anxiety on the one hand, and increased well-being and "self-actualization" on the other. Conclusions regarding locus of control must await further research that resolves the currently conflicting literature.

Although the salutary effects of TM on self-report are important in their own right, these results generate two additional questions of equal consequence: (1) Can such paper-and-pencil scales be corroborated by other types of assessment procedures?, and (2) Do alternative relaxation procedures promote equivalent results? In a previous section (*Psycho-physiological State Effects*) we discussed our research that discerned a generalized trait of gerater somatic relaxation for practitioners of progressive relaxation (PR) compared to long-term TM meditators. We also noted that, conversely, our TM subjects reported feeling less tense than PR subjects during the more stressful first laboratory session. Interestingly, two other treatment outcome studies comparing meditation to modified and abbreviated versions of PR also obtained greater effects on self-reported anxiety for the meditation group (Carrington, Collings, Benson, Robinson, Wood, Lehrer, Woolfolk, & Cole, 1980; Zuroff & Schwarz, 1978). However, the anxiety reduction advantage for TM was not corroborated by behavioral assessment, heart rate measurement, or, indeed, any other self-report measure in the Zuroff and Schwarz study. It is of further interest that the specificity of the TM Group's advantage over PR in self-reported anxiety supports the Davidson & Schwartz (1976) multiprocess model of relaxation described earlier. Unfortunately, these differential effects for TM and for PR were not corroborated by two other treatment outcome studies of similar design, as described below.

Raskin *et al.* (1980) compared TM, modified and abbreviated PR, and EMG biofeedback-assisted relaxation in the treatment of highly anxious subjects, obtaining no significant differences on any self-report scale. Marlatt *et al.* (in press) likewise failed to obtain differential effectiveness of mantra meditation and abbreviated PR treatments in heavy social drinkers. In an attempt to resolve the above conflicting results, we have carefully scrutinized each of these studies for possible methodological sources of the discrepancy. We found no single factor that could be responsible, however (e.g., dependent measures, duration or type of training, subjects tested, etc.). Most likely an interaction of factors account for these differences in outcome. The lack of synthesis here points out the difficulties often encountered in comparing studies from different laboratories. Such discrepancies further underscore the value of programmatically replicating one's own experimental results prior to drawing important empirical and theoretical conclusions.

A pair of studies by Smith (1976, 1978) are undoubtedly the most illuminating on TM and personality traits to date. Smith compared TM (Study 1) and a mantra meditation technique closely resembling TM (Study 2) to "placebo-expectancy" control groups (and also to a no-treatment group in Study 1). In the first experiment the expectancy group was taught to practice "periodic somatic inactivity" (PSI), which involved the same instructions and trainer conviction as TM, with one exception. Practitioners were told to "let your mind do whatever it wants. Whatever you do mentally will have little or no impact on the effectiveness of the technique" (p. 631–632). The rationale given for PSI was highly credible to naive subjects, and emphasized a scientific-sounding, mechanistic interpretation involving classical conditioning of relaxation "signatures" into a person's circadian rhythms.

These instructions were modified for the expectancy group in the second study. Subjects were again told to sit quietly with eyes closed, but this time they were instructed: "Deliberately pursue a sequence of cognitive activity that has a positive direction and is comprehensive. That is, simply engage in thought activity that you intend to be positive, that is, good, desirable, interesting, or anything the word positive means to you" (p. 634). Included in this category were fantasy–daydreams, story-telling and listing of "positive" items or traits. Subjects were pre-tested and then posttested after 6 months (Study 1) or 2 months (Study 2). Attrition rates were quite comparable for the TM and PSI groups in Study 1 (50–60%) but were somewhat less so for the meditation (48%) and "positive ideation" groups (30%) in Study 2. Perhaps surprisingly, all of these four groups manifested nearly identical decreases in self-reported anxiety over the course of the experiment. Smith interpreted his findings as indicating that the crucial therapeutic component of TM is not the TM exercise (TM mantra). Rather, he concluded that the combination of expectation of anxiety relief plus a daily sitting regimen is sufficient to produce anxiety reduction in motivated subjects. In Section IV, we will describe our own research that yields further support for this conclusion.

Despite virtually identical mean changes in trait anxiety, the patterns of personality variables that predicted anxiety reduction from, and adherence to, meditation were totally different from those for PSI. Supporting our own research findings, Smith (1978) found that those who benefited from TM scored highly on a scale that clearly taps the same dimension as absorption: Factor M (Autia) from the Cattell 16 PF Questionnaire. Quoting Cattell, Smith describes this scale as reflecting the "tendency to be 'imaginatively enthralled by inner creations,' 'charmed by works of the imagination,' and *completely absorbed'* [italics added] in the momentum of their own thoughts, following them 'wherever they lead, for their intrinsic attractiveness, and with neglect of realistic considerations' . . . and a capacity to dissociate and engage in *'autonomous, self-absorbed relaxation'* [italics added]" (pp. 274–5). Individuals who score high in Autia also "tend to be unconventional and interested in 'art, theory, basic beliefs' and 'spiritual matters.'" TM meditators who benefited were more anxious, but had *not* previously considered psychotherapy. They scored higher on Sizothymia, which indicates that persons are characteristically "'reserved, detached, critical, cool, aloof' and 'stiff.' Emotionally they are 'flat' or 'cautious.' They tend to like working along with things or words rather than with people" (p. 274). Six month adherence to TM was predicted by high self-criticism and low psychosis scores, and, curiously, also by *having* previously considered psychotherapy.

The profile of the successful PSI practitioners on the other hand is of those who "have 'exact calculating' minds and tend to be emotionally detached and disciplined, ambitious, and esthetically fastidious. They tend *not* to be gregarious or to get 'warmly emotionally involved with others'" (p. 276). PSI dropouts "score higher on 16 PF factors related to anxiety . . . However, they do not score higher on Psychoticism or lower on Self-Criticism" (p. 277).

As Smith points out, major components of the personality profiles of successful TM meditators and PSI practitioners are "matched" quite well with the pretreatment rationale offered by the trainer for the mechanism underlying the beneficial effects of each respective technique. Orientation meetings for TM provide a distinctly religious, philosophical rationale that relies heavily on artistic metaphors of calm stillness and detachment. Moreover, the actual initiation ceremony involves a Yogic ritual. Since the rationale and ritual are both mandatory, it is clear that this process exerts strong self-selection pressures on those who choose to start TM, as well as those who adhere and benefit from its practice. As mentioned above, the PSI treatment rationale was logical, scientific, and mechanistic. Clearly, each of these rationales should appeal particularly to individuals manifesting the respective personality traits described. Other research (cited by Smith, 1978) confirms the potent mediating effects of treatment credibility in psychotherapy. For meditation and relaxation treatments this conclusion is supported by some (Kirsh & Henry, 1979) but not all researchers (Zuroff & Schwarz, 1978; Borkovec, Grayson, & Cooper, 1978; Marlatt *et al.*, in press). On this basis we recommend future investigators to incorporate credibility measures in all treatment outcome studies of meditation or relaxation.

In an exploratory attempt to discover possible personality and/or performance trait correlates of the physiological state variables described previously (EEG alpha and theta activity), we computed correlations between these two sets of variables as follows. The eight personality and performance traits that differentiated groups (stress, absorption, locus of control, well-being, social desirability, acquiescence, tonal memory, and cued verbal memory) were correlated with the following physiological measures in the combined meditator group: parietal and frontal integrated alpha activity during meditation (mean of first 5 minutes), parietal and frontal alpha asymmetry (overall mean), SCFs during meditation (20 minute mean), theta bursts (75 μV) during meditation, and changes in each of these variables (except alpha asymmetry) from baseline to meditation. Out of the 40 correlations computed, two would be expected by chance ($p < .05$). In fact, we obtained two that were significant: change in parietal alpha amplitude with acquiescence ($r = .50$, $p < .03$), and parietal alpha asymmetry with cued verbal memory ($-.57$, $p < .006$).

IV. Clinical Outcome Effects

The last study that we shall describe investigated the effect of meditation and progressive muscle relaxation on alcohol consumption (Marlatt, Pagano, Rose, & Marques, in press). In this study, we employed the meditation technique developed by Beary and Benson (1974) instead of TM. We chose this technique because it was similar to TM (repetition of a mantra-like word in a quiet and relaxed setting), and the technique allowed us to make random assignment of subjects to groups.

The study was divided into three phases: a baseline period (2 weeks), a treatment period (6 weeks), and a follow-up period (7 weeks). During baseline, all subjects reported their daily alcohol consumption on detailed recording forms. At the end of this period, each subject was scheduled for a laboratory session in which he completed pretreatment personality measures, the Spielberger, Gorsuch, and Lushene (1970) State–Trait Anxiety Inventory and the locus of control subtest (Rotter, 1966), and participated in a taste-rating task as a further measure of his alcohol consumption rate. The taste-rating task was developed by Marlatt (Higgins & Marlatt, 1973), and provided an unobtrusive measure of alcohol consumption. Following these tests, subjects were randomly divided into four groups, with the restriction that groups would be matched based on their alcohol consumption during the first week of the baseline period. The four groups were: Benson meditation ($N = 10$), abbreviated progressive relaxation ($N = 8$), a control group for nonspecific effects (a reading group termed "bibliotherapy," $N = 9$), and a no-treatment control ($N = 14$).

Subjects in the first two groups were taught their appropriate relaxation technique, and instructed to practice it for two 20-minute sessions each day during the 6-week treatment period. The bibliotherapy group was instructed to read relaxing, enjoyable material in the same regimen, but not to use this time to do homework or class assignments. Daily records of the time spent in relaxation/reading sessions and the subjective level of relaxation experienced after each session were completed by these subjects throughout the treatment period. All groups, including the no-treatment control groups, continued to keep daily records of alcohol consumption. At the end of the treatment period, the personality measures and taste-rating task were again administered.

During the follow-up period, the daily record-keeping procedures were continued, but practice of the relaxation techniques was optional for the trained subjects. At the end of this period, subjects were asked to complete a follow-up questionnaire, which assessed their personal observations and conclusions about the study. A $4 weekly payment was made to each subject throughout the study, contingent upon receipt of his daily records of alcohol consumption.

The subjects were 44 males who were paid volunteers. All were undergraduates at the University of Washington and qualified as heavy drinkers according to Cahalan's national-drinking-habits survey (Cahalan, Cisin, & Crossley, 1969). The study was described to these subjects as a preliminary investigation into the effects of practicing relaxation techniques on the drinking of alcoholic beverages. Care was taken to emphasize the experimenters' uncertainty about what those effects would be, to avoid creating an expectation or demand that drinking would decrease after relaxation training. Of the original sample, 41 subjects (93%) completed the treatment phase of the study; their mean age was 23.5 years.

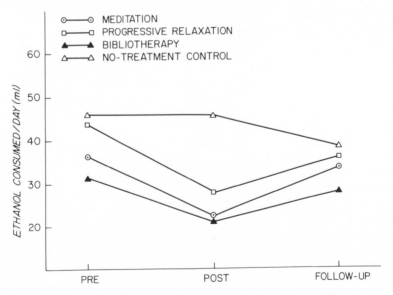

FIGURE 4. Mean alcohol consumption during baseline, treatment, and follow-up periods.

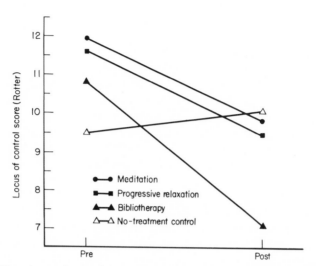

FIGURE 5. Mean locus-of-control scores during baseline and at end of treatment periods.

Although there are many aspects of this study, some of which have been mentioned in a previous section, for the purposes of this section we discuss only the alcohol consumption and locus of control results. These results are shown in Figures 4 and 5. The repeated measures ANOVA on alcohol consumption (Figure 4) revealed no significant effect for groups ($p > .10$). However, there was a significant trials effect ($p < .005$) and a groups × trials interaction, that attained borderline significance ($p = .09$). This latter effect was due to significant decrements in alcohol consumption in the meditation group ($p < .05$), the progressive relaxation group ($p < .025$), and the bibliotherapy group ($p < .03$), whereas no significant effect was found for the no-treatment control group. Individual comparisons yielded no significant differences, however, among the three relaxation groups. Thus, subjects who regularly practiced a relaxation technique showed similar decreases in alcohol consumption, whether they practiced meditation, muscle relaxation, or the nonspecific relaxation technique, bibliotherapy. Similar results during treatment were obtained for locus of control (cf. Figure 5). Two-way ANOVA revealed no signficant effect for groups ($p > .10$). However, significant effects were found for the trials factor ($p < .005$), and for the groups × trials interaction ($p < .025$). Individual t tests showed significant decreases in test scores (indicating a shift toward internal locus) for the progressive relaxation group ($p < .025$) and the bibliotherapy group ($p < .005$) and a decrease of borderline significance in the meditation group ($p = .07$). The no-treatment control group showed a nonsignificant increase in test scores. These results show that the regular practice of a relaxation technique, including the nonspecific control procedure of bibliotherapy was associated with shifts toward a more internal locus of control. There were no significant differences between relaxation procedures on this measure.

During the follow-up period, consumption rates increased so that during the last two weeks, group means were not significantly different from either pretreatment or posttreatment levels. It is important to note that almost all of the subjects chose to discontinue regular practice of their techniques during the follow-up period. Only 22% of these relaxation subjects indicated retrospectively that they expected treatment to decrease their drinking.

The pre to post-treatment changes indicate that each of the three techniques were effective in reducing alcohol consumption. This is an important result which potentially has important practical consequences. However, the fact that most subjects chose to discontinue practice of their relaxation technique again raises the important question of long-term adherence (i.e., how to foster maintained practice of techniques which, although beneficial, are often discontinued over time). A second point illustrated here concerns the uniqueness of meditation— all three treatments produced similar decrements. As in Smith's (1976, 1978) treatment outcome studies, our three relaxation groups followed the same twice-daily regimen involving bodily rest and "time-out" from worldly activities. Unlike Smith's subjects, however, our groups were given a neutral expectancy set regarding treatment effects on alcohol consumption. Furthermore, subjects were not seeking therapy; they were merely participating in a paid research project. Retrospective analysis of the subjects' expectancies indicated that only a small minority of the subjects expected the treatment results that actually were obtained. Given the fact that subjects neither sought nor expected the obtained treatment outcome, the health-promoting nature of our results are even more remarkable. They suggest that a motivated, positive expectancy may not be necessary for practitioners of relaxation techniques to profit from their regimen.

It is certainly intriguing to speculate that the crucial therapeutic ingredients of a relaxation regimen (TM, in particular) may actually have less to do with a person's motivation and expectation than with the relatively nonspecific rest that comes from taking time out from daily affairs. This, of course, is the position of Benson (1975; Benson *et al.*, 1974) who declares that all effective relaxation techniques "merely" provide conditions for the body's automatic, integrated "relaxation response" to occur. Benson cited four basic elements of a relaxation technique that are usually necessary in order to elicit the relaxation response:

(1) a quiet environment, (2) decreased muscle tonus, (3) a mental device, consisting of a constant stimulus that aids the practitioner in shift away from ordinary, rational thought processes, and (4) a passive attitude toward that mental device (i.e., not worrying about how well one is performing the technique, plus a disregard of distracting thoughts).

Although we clearly need further research on these matters before we can draw definitive conclusions, the more recent studies of Smith (1976, 1978) and Marlatt et al. (in press) suggest that for salutary relaxation effects to occur, the practitioner may not need to employ a repetitive mental device. These studies demonstrated that activities as disparate as pleasure reading, generating positive daydreams, and sitting quietly without engaging in any specific mental activity were each just as effective as mantra meditation. Indeed, it appears that balancing one's lifestyle by taking time out daily to enjoy restful activity may be the most important common element to various relaxation therapies. If such a regimen is followed it could create a self-sustaining process that (1) elicits the relaxation response; (2) insures that the practitioner disengages herself or himself from worldly affairs; (3) enables the practitioner to engage in pleasurable activity; and (4) fosters the self-attribution that the practitioner is able to control his or her own life, at least regarding points (2) and (3) above. Furthermore, once this self-regulating regimen begins to yield positive benefits (e.g., anxiety reduction, enhanced well-being, decreased alcohol consumption), these perceived changes probably contribute to the self-attribution of greater internal locus of control. In its extreme form this process could produce a "positive addition" (cf. Glasser, 1975).

V. Conclusion

In our introduction, we described how we have come to study Transcendental Meditation from the vantage of three questions: (1) What physiological changes characterize the state obtained during meditation? (2) Do the state effects of meditation generalize to times outside meditation practice, thereby becoming traits of meditators? (3) Are there predispositional factors that influence a person's response to meditation, both in a short-term and long-term perspective? On the one hand, our view of the current state of meditation research causes us to emphasize commonality and "common sense." The investigations we have conducted in our own laboratory, as well as those we have reviewed, lead to the following conclusions regarding the above three questions.

A. State Effects

The state of somatic relaxation obtained during the practice of a variety of meditation or relaxation techniques (including self-instructed relaxation while sitting with eyes closed) is qualitatively and quantitatively very similar when these techniques are practiced under optimally relaxing conditions by healthy normal subjects. Our conclusion is essentially in agreement with Benson's (Beary & Benson, 1974; Benson *et al.*, 1974) construct of a "relaxation response," with two exceptions: (1) We did not find this state to be "hypometabolic," and (2) Benson did not offer important qualifications regarding subjects or conditions of practice.

B. Trait Effects

Generalized trait changes do occur in TM meditators as a result of meditation practice, but they are far from "unique." Comparative treatment outcome studies of meditation and other relaxation techniques strongly suggest that persons gain considerably benefit "merely" by balancing their lifestyles with a regimen of taking time out daily to engage in an enjoyable, restful activity. Whether such a person meditates, practices muscle relaxation, or engages in positive daydreaming or leisure reading appears less important than their behavior of actually setting the time aside and engaging in some sort of enjoyable, restful activity in a regular disciplined way. One exception of emerging from recent research. Meditation may result in greater physiological reactivity to stressful stimuli, yet faster recovery. More reserach is clearly needed on this point.

The type of evidence we have regarding beneficial effects are primarily in the realm of self-reported changes. The practice of TM for one or more months leads practitioners to report that they feel less "stress" and more "well-being" than they felt prior to learning TM. These self-reports appear to be genuine reflections of what the practitioner actually perceives about herself or himself, rather than the result of a positive response bias on the part of meditators. Long-term meditators also reported a more internal locus of (personal) control than nonmeditators, but the data are not clear concerning the source of this effect (i.e., the relative contribution of self-selection and/or authentic practice effects).

In terms of trait effects that do not rely on global self-report scales, we have obtained evidence from a treatment outcome study that meditation reduces alcohol consumption in heavy social drinkers. Once again, this beneficial effect was not "unique" to meditation, but was obtained for a progressive relaxation and leisure reading treatment as well. We have found no indication that TM produces a "shift" in dominant hemisphere information processing from a primarily "linear" (LH) to a more "holistic" (RH) mode. This conclusion was drawn from both EEG and cognitive performance measures of hemispheric processing.

We regret to report that our search for a unique or dramatic effect directly attributable to meditation thus far has not been successful. In this area many practitioners have made sweeping claims about the effectiveness of their techniques. Frequently, this is based on subjective experience, and often the claims are "shored up" on the basis of "research." All too often, this research turns out to be not very rigorous—really only of pilot nature. This has been especially true within the TM movement. Our experience has been that when good scientific methodology has been used, the claims made have been extravagent and premature.

We would also like to point out that although our work involved TM, Becker and Shiparo (in press) have recently reported a similar finding in attempting to replicate the often quoted and influential reports of Kasamatsu and Hirai (1969) and Anand et al. (1961b). These studies have been used to substantiate physiologically the different state of attention produced during Zen as compared with Yoga meditation. Kasamatsu and Kirai reported that the EEG alpha suppression response did not habituate to repeated click stimuli in three Zen masters, but did habituate in control subjects. In contrast, Anand et al. reported that four Yogis showed no alpha suppression responses to a variety of external stimuli while performing Raj Yoga meditation. Unfortunately, these studies were incompletely reported and did not employ appropriate control groups and statistical procedures. In what appears to be a very carefully controlled study, Becker and Shapiro attempted to replicate and extend this prior research. The study included Zen, Yoga, and TM meditators and two attention control groups. The results failed to replicate this earlier pilot work. All groups showed initial alpha suppression and all groups showed similar rates of alpha suppression. We would like to clearly indicate that we do not intend to denigrate the practice of meditation. We think meditation may be an important and beneficial activity. Instead, we call for a vigorous and *rigorous* scientific validation of the effects of meditation with replication studies being conducted in various laboratories. We also feel it very important that research be conducted in some laboratories which are independent of the meditative discipline itself.

Although we have mainly discussed general group findings, it is important as well to emphasize that in our own research we have observed abundant individual differences in the magnitude and pattern of state effects of meditation. Some meditators on some days fall asleep rather quickly, and remain asleep during most of their meditation. Others show many transitions between Stage 1 (drowsiness) and Stage W (wakefulness). This is reflected in individual alpha amplitude data, as well, with some individuals increasing in alpha abundance during meditation, eventhough group means showed substantial and highly significant decreases. Large variations were observed in the occurrence of theta bursts, an unusual EEG activity that was present in a subset of both meditators and nonmeditators. Likewise, somatić physiological changes from baseline ranged considerably (e.g., between $+1\%$ and -8% oxygen consumption, and $+2$ and -8 beats per minute in heart rate). We have already noted that the original sample of 20 subjects whose oxygen consumption data were reported by Wallace *et al.* (Wallace, 1970a,b; Wallace *et al.*, 1971; Wallace & Benson, 1972) appear to have been a very unusual group. Data from seven of his subjects fell to values less than 15% below their predicted basal metabolic level, whereas none of those in our study did so (Warrenburg *et al.*, 1980).

In our exploratory attempts to uncover sources of individual differences we have discovered one relationship among trait variables, namely, the correlation between tonal memory and absorption. Our results strongly suggest that this association is due to a predispositional trait of persons prior to learning TM. The issue of long-term adherence has repeatedly come to the foreground in research on treatment outcome studies using meditation or relaxation techniques, since attrition rates are typically substantial during the first few months of practice. Our finding that subjects high in absorbed attention are more likely to continue regular practice should, therefore, be useful to professionals interested in the clinical application of meditation. The research findings of Smith (1978) and Qualls and Sheehan (1979; 1981a,b,c) confirm those from our laboratory in highlighting the absorption trait as a positive predictor of response to meditation. This research emphasizes that both the attentional abilities of persons prior to initiation as well as the therapeutic rationale (set) offered are important components in determining adherence to and benefit from meditation.

Smith's (1976, 1978) finding that two highly similar self-regulation techniques can produce virtually identical outcome effects in heterogeneous groups, but that distinct and identifiable subgroups derive particular benefit from each respective technique, should provide clinical researchers with a major impetus for similar investigations using other therapeutic treatments. The search for other predispositional factors mediating successful outcome from health-promoting regimens may well prove to be far more fruitful than the search for *the* technique that has the *most* dramatic or unique effect. Furthermore, the search for predictable patterning of the effects obtained from different techniques should likewise permit a more well-formulated basis for making treatment decisions. We are optimistic that this approach of emphasizing specificity of treatments for individuals will allow us to continue refining the application of behavioral methods in psychology and medicine.

ACKNOWLEDGMENTS

We wish to express our indebtedness to the following colleagues with whom we have had the opportunity to collaborate on this research: Mr. Lynn Frumkin, Drs. Michael Hlastala, Alan Marlatt, Janice Marques, Richard Rose, Marcella Woods, and Mr. Robert Stivers. Many undergraduate assistants, too numerous to name, also made substantial contributions to this work. Moreover, we want to thank the Seattle chapter of SIMS for their cooperation in helping us to obtain participant meditators.

REFERENCES

AGNEW, H. W., JR. WEBB, W. B., & WILLIAMS, R. L. The first night effect: An EEG study of sleep. *Psychophysiology*, 1966, 2, 263–266.

ANAND, B. K., CHHINA, G. S., & SINGH, B. Studies on Shri Ramanand Yogi during his stay in an air-tight box. *Indian Journal of Medical Research*, 1961, 49, 82–89. (a)

ANAND, B. K., CHHINA, G. S., & SINGH, B. Some aspects of electroencephalographic studies in Yogis. *Electroencephalography and Clinical Neurophysiology*, 1961, 13, 452–456. (b)

BANQUET, J. P. Spectral analysis of the EEG in meditation. *Electroencephalography and Clinical Neurophysiology*, 1973, 35, 143–151.

BEARY, J. F., & BENSON, H. A simple psychophysiological technique which elicits the hypometabolic changes of the relaxation response. *Psychosomatic Medicine*, 1974, 36, 115–120.

BECKER, D. E., & SHAPIRO, D. Physiological responses to clicks during Zen, Yoga and TM meditation. *Psychophysiology*, in press.

BENNETT, J. R., & TRINDER, J. Hemispheric laterality and cognitive style associated with Transcendental Meditation. *Psychophysiology*, 1977, 14, 293–296.

BENSON, H., BEARY, J. R., & CAROL, M. K. The relaxation response. *Psychiatry*, 1974, 37, 37–46.

BENSON, H., STEINERT, R. G., GREENWOOD, M. M., KLEMCHUCK, H. M., & PETERSON, N. H. Continuous measurement of oxygen consumption and carbon dioxide elimination during a wakeful hypometabolic state. *Journal of Human Stress*, 1975, 1, 37–44.

BIRNBAUM, I. M., & EICHNER, J. T. Study versus test trials and long-term retention in free-recall learning. *Journal of Verbal Learning and Verbal Behavior*, 1971, 10, 516–521.

BOALS, G. F. Toward a cognitive reconceptualization of meditation. *Journal of Transpersonal Psychology*, 1978, 10, 143–182.

BORKOVEC, T. D., GRAYSON, J. B., & COOPER, K. M. Treatment of general tension: Subjective and physiological effects of progressive relaxation. *Journal of Consulting and Clinical Psychology*, 1978, *46*, 518–528.

CAHALAN, D., CISIN, I. H., & CROSSLEY, H. M. *American drinking practices: A national study of drinking behavior and patterns*. New Brunswick, N. J.: Rutgers Center of Alcohol Studies, *6*, 1969. (Monograph)

CARRINGTON, P., COLLINGS, G. H., BENSON, H., ROBINSON, H., WOOD, L. W., LEHRER, P. M., WOOLFOLK, R. L., & COLE, J. W. The use of meditation–relaxation techniques for the management of stress in a working population. *Journal of Occupational Medicine*, 1980, *22*(4), 221–231.

CHASE, R. A. The effect of temporal lobe lesions on some auditory information processing tasks in man. In F. L. BARLEY (Ed.), *Brain mechanisms underlying speech and language*. New York: Grune and Stratton, 1967.

CORBY, J. C., ROTH, W. T., ZARCONE, V. P., & KOPELL, B. S. Psychophysiological correlates of the practice of Tantric Yoga meditation. *Archives of General Psychiatry*, 1978, *35*, 571–577.

CROWNE, D. P., & MARLOWE, D. *The approval motive*. New York: Wiley, 1964.

DAS, N. N., & GASTAUT, H. Variations de l'activite electrique du cerveau, du couer et des muscles squelettiques an cours de la meditation et de l' extase yogique. *Electroencephalography and Clinical Neurophysiology* (Suppl. No. 6) 1955, 211–219.

DAVIDSON, J. M. The physiology of meditation and mystical states of consciousness. *Perspectives in Biology and Medicine*, 1976, *19*, 345–379.

DAVIDSON, R. J., & GOLEMAN, D. J. The role of attention in meditation and hypnosis: A psychobiological perspective on transformations of consciousness. *The International Journal of Clinical and Experimental Hypnosis*, 1977, *25*, 291–308.

DAVIDSON, R. J., & SCHWARTZ, G. E. The psychobiology of relaxation and related states: A multi-process theory. In D. MOSTOFSKY (Ed.), *Behavior modification and control of physiological activity*. Englewood Cliffs, N. J.: Prentice-Hall, 1976.

DAVIDSON, R. J., GOLEMAN, D. J., & SCHWARTZ, G. E. Attentional and affective concomitants of meditation: a cross-sectional study. *Journal of Abnormal Psychology*, 1976, *85*, 235–238.

DAVIDSON, R. J., SCHWARTZ, G. E., & ROTHMAN, L. P. Attentional style and the self-regulation of mode-specific attention: An electroencephalographic study. *Journal of Abnormal Psychology*, 1976, *85*, 611–621.

DEIKMAN, A. J. Deautomatization and the mystic experience. Reprinted in C. TART (Ed.), *Altered states of consciousness*. New York: Wiley, 1969.

DIMOND, S. J., & BEAUMONT, J. G. Experimental studies of hemispheric function in the human brain. In S. J. DIMOND & J. G. BEAUMONT (Eds.), *Hemisphere function in the human brain*. New York: Halsted Press, 1974.

DOYLE, J. C., ORSTEIN, R., & GALIN, D. Lateral specialization of cognitive mode: II. EEG frequency analysis. *Psychophysiology*, 1974, *11*, 567–578.

EHRLICHMAN, H., & WIENER, M. S. EEG asymmetry during covert mental activity. *Psychophysiology*, 1980, *17*, 228–235.

ELSON, B. D. HAURI, P., & CUNIS, D. Physiological changes in Yoga meditation. *Psychophysiology*, 1977, *14*, 52–57.

FENWICK, P. B. C., DONALDSON, S., GILLIS, L., BUSHMAN, J., FENTON, G. W., PERRY, I., TILSLEY, C., & SERAFINOWICZ, H. Metabolic and EEG changes during Transcendental Meditation: An explanation. *Biological Psychology*, 1977, *5*, 101–118.

FENZ, W. D., & EPSTEIN, S. Gradients of physiological arousal in parachutists as a function of an approaching jump. *Psychosomatic Medicine*, 1967, *29*, 33–51.

FERGUSON, P. D., & GOWAN, J. TM—some preliminary findings. *Journal of Humanistic Psychology*, 1976, *16*(3).

FRENCH, J. W., EKSTROM, R. B., & PRICE, L. A. *Kit for reference tests for cognitive factors*. Atlanta: Educational Testing Service, 1963.

FRUMKIN, L., & PAGANO, R. The effect of Transcendental Meditation on iconic memory. *Biofeedback and Self-Regulation*, 1979, 4(4), 313–322.

FURST, C. J. EEG alpha asymmetry and visuospatial performance. *Nature*, 1976, 260, 254–255.

GALIN, D. Implications for psychiatry of left and right cerebral specialization. *Archives of General Psychiatry*, 1974, 31, 572–583.

GEVINS, A. S., ZEITLIN, G. M., DOYLE, J. G., YINGLING, C. G., SCHAFFER, R. E., CALLAWAY, E., & YEAGER, C. L. Electroencephalogram correlates of higher corital functions. *Science*, 1979, 203, 665–667.

GLASSER, W. *Positive addiction*. New York: Harper & Row, 1975.

GLUECK, B., & STROEBEL, C. Biofeedback and meditation in the treatment of psychiatric illness. *Comprehensive Psychiatry*, 1975, 16(4), 303–321.

GOLEMAN, D. Meditation and consciousness. An asian approach to mental health. *American Journal of Psychotherapy*, 1976, 30, 41–54.

GOLEMAN, D. J., & SCHWARTZ, G. E. Meditation as an intervention in stress reactivity. *Journal of Consulting and Clinical Psychology*, 1976, 44, 456–466.

HEBERT, R., & LEHMANN, D. Theta bursts: An EEG pattern in normal subjects practicing the transcendental meditation technique. *Electroencephalography and Clinical Neurophysiology*, 1977, 42, 397–405.

HECAEN, H., & ALBERT M. L. *Human neuropsychology*. New York: Wiley, 1978.

HIGGINS, R. L., & MARLATT, G. A. Effects of anxiety arousal on the consumption of alcohol by alcoholics and social drinkers. *Journal of Consulting and Clinical Psychology*, 1973, 41, 426–433.

HIRAI, T. *The psychophysiology of Zen*. Tokoyo: Igaku Shoin, Ltd., 1974.

HJELLE L. A. Transcendental Meditation and psychological health. *Perceptual and Motor Skills*, 1974, 39, 623–628.

KANAS, N., & HOROWITZ, M. J. Reactions of transcendental meditators and non-meditators to stress films. *Archives of General Psychiatry*, 1977, 34, 1431–1436.

KASAMATSU, A., & HIRAI, T. An electroencephalographic study on the Zen meditation (zazan). In C. TART (Ed.), *Altered states of consciousness*. New York: Wiley, 1969.

KIRSCH, I., & HENRY, D. Self-desensitization and meditation in the reduction of public speaking anxiety. *Journal of Consulting and Clinical Psychology*, 1979, 47, 536–541.

LEHRER, P. M. Psychophysiological effects of progressive relaxation in anxiety neurotic patients and of progressive relaxation and alpha feedback in non-patients. *Journal of Consulting and Clinical Psychology*, 1978, 46, 389–404.

LUTHE, W. (Ed.). *Autogenic therapy* (Vol. VI). New York: Grune and Stratton, 1969.

MARLATT, G. A., PAGANO, R., ROSE, R. M., & MARQUES, J. Effects of meditation and relaxation training on alcohol use in male social drinkers. In D. SHAPIRO & R. WALSH (Eds.), *The science of meditation: theory and experience*. New York: Aldine, in press.

MATARAZZO, J. D. *Wechsler's measurement and appraisal of adult intelligence* (5th ed.). Baltimore: Williams & Wilkins, 1972.

MILNER, B. Laterality effects in audition. In V. B. MOUNTCASTLE (Ed.), *Interhemispheric relations and cerebral dominance*. Baltimore: Johns Hopkins Press, 1962.

MORSE, D. R., MARTIN, J. S., FURST, M. L., & DUBIN, O. L. A physiological and subjective evaluation of meditation, hypnosis, and relaxation. *Psychosomatic Medicine*, 1977, 39, 304–324.

NARANJO, C., & ORNSTEIN, R. E. *On the psychology of meditation*. New York: Viking Press, 1971.

NEBES, R. D. Hemispheric specialization in commissurotomized man. *Psychological Bulletin*, 1974, 81, 1–14.

NIDICH, S., SEEMAN, W., & DRESHIN, T. Influence of Transcendental Meditation: A replication. *Journal of Counseling Psychology*, 1973, 20, 565–566.

ORME-JOHNSON, D. W. Autonomic stability and Transcendental Meditation. *Psychosomatic Medicine*, 1973, *35*, 341–348.

ORME-JOHNSON, D., & FARROW, J. T. *Scientific research on the Transcendental Meditation program: Collected papers* (Vol. 1). Livingston Manor: Maharishi European Research University Press, 1977.

ORNE, M., & WILSON, S. On the nature of alpha feedback training. In G. E. SCHWARTZ & D. SHAPIRO (Eds.), *Consciousness & self-regulation* (Vol. 2). New York: Plenum, 1978.

ORNSTEIN, R. E. *The psychology of consciousness*. New York: Viking Press, 1972.

ORNSTEIN, R., JOHNSTONE, J., HERRON, J., & SWENCIONIS, C. Differential right hemisphere engagement in visuospatial tasks. *Neuropsychologia*, 1980, *18*, 49–63.

PAGANO, R. R., & FRUMKIN, L. R. The effect of Transcendental Meditation on right hemispheric functioning. *Biofeedback and Self-Regulation*, 1977, *2*, 407–415.

PAGANO, R., ROSE, R., STIVERS, R., & WARRENBURG, S. Sleep during Transcendental Meditation. *Science*, 1976, *191*, 308–310.

QUALLS, P., & SHEEHAN, P. Capacity for absorption and relaxation during electromyograph biofeedback and no feedback conditions. *Journal of Abnormal Psychology*, 1978, *88*, 652–662.

QUALLS, P., & SHEEHAN, P. Role of the feedback signal in electromyograph biofeedback: The relevance of attention. *Journal of Experimental Psychology: General*, 1981, *110*(2), 204–216. (a)

QUALLS, P., & SHEEHAN, P. Trait-treatment interactions: reply to Tellegen. *Journal of Experimental Psychology: General*, 1981, *110*(2), 227–231. (b)

QUALLS, P., & SHEEHAN, P. Imagery encouragement, absorption capacity, and relaxation during electromyograph biofeedback. *Journal of Personality and Social Psychology*, 1981, *4*(2), 370–379. (c)

RASKIN, M., BALI, L., & PEEKE, H. Muscle biofeedback and Transcendental Meditation. *Archives of General Psychiatry*, 1980, *37*, 93–97.

REITAN, R. M. *Manual for administration of neuropsychological test batteries for adults and children*. Indianapolis: Author, 1969.

ROTTER, J. B. Generalized expectancies for internal versus external control of reinforcement. *Psychological Monographs*, 1966, *80*(1, Whole No. 609).

SARASON, I. G. The test anxiety scale: Concept and research. In C. D. Spielberger & I. G. Sarason (Eds.), *Stress and anxiety* (Vol. 5). Washington, D.C.: Hemisphere Publishing Co., 1978.

SCHOICKET, S., LEHRER, P. M., CARRINGTON, P., & WOOLFOLK, R. L. *Psychophysiological effects of progressive relaxation and clinically standardized meditation*. Paper presented at the Tenth Annual Meeting of the Biofeedback Society of America, San Diego, California, 1979.

SCHUMAN, M. The psychophysiological model of meditation and altered states of consciousness: A critical review. In J. M. DAVIDSON & R. C. DAVIDSON (Eds.), *The psychobiology of consciousness*. New York: Plenum, 1980.

SCHWARTZ, G. E. The facts on Transcendental Meditation: Part II. "TM relaxes some people and makes them feel better." *Psychology Today*, 1974, *7*(11), 39–44.

SCHWARTZ, G. E., DAVIDSON, R. J., & GOLEMAN, D. J. Patterning of cognitive and somatic processes in the self-regulation of anxiety: Effects of meditation versus exercise. *Psychosomatic Medicine*, 1978, *40*, 321–328.

SEEMAN, W., NIDICH, S., & BANTA, T. Influence of Transcendental Meditation on a measure of self-actualization. *Journal of Counseling Psychology*, 1972, *19*, 184–187.

SHEPARD, R. N., & METZLER, J. Mental rotation of three-dimensional objects. *Science*, 1971, *171*, 701–703.

SMITH, J. C. Psychotherapeutic effects of Transcendental Meditation with controls for expectation of relief and daily sitting. *Journal of Consulting and Clinical Psychology*, 1976, *44*, 630–637.

SMITH, J. C. Personality correlates of continuation and outcome in meditation and erect sitting control treatments. *Journal of Consulting and Clinical Psychology*, 1978, *46*, 272–279.

SPERLING, O. The information available in a brief visual presentation. *Psychological Monographs*, 1960, *47* (11, Whole No. 498).

SPIELBERGER, C. D., GORSUCH, R. L., & LUSHENE, R. E. *Manual for the State–Trait Anxiety Inventory*. Palo Alto, Calif.: Consulting Psychologist Press, 1970.

STEK, J., & BASS, B. A. Personal adjustment and perceived locus of control among students interested in meditation. *Psychological Reports*, 1973, *32*, 1019–1022.

TEBECIS, A. A controlled study of the EEG during Transcendental Meditation: Comparison with hypnosis. *Folia Psychiatrica et Neurologica Japonica*, 1975, *29*, 305–315.

TELLEGEN, A. *Manual for differential personality inventory*. Unpublished manuscript available from author, 1977.

TELLEGEN, A. Practicing the two disciplines for relaxation and enlightenment. *Journal of Experimental Psychology*, 1981, *43*(2), 165–176.

TELLEGEN, A., & ATKINSON, G. Openness to absorbing and self-altering experiences ("absorption"), a trait related to hypnotic susceptibility. *Journal of Abnormal Psychology*, 1974, *83*, 268–277.

TULVING, E., & PEARLSTONE, Z. Availability versus accessibility of information in memory for words. *Journal of Verbal Learning and Verbal Behavior*, 1966, *5*, 331–391.

WALLACE, R. K. Physiological effects of Transcendental Meditation. *Science*, 1970, *167*, 1751–1754. (a)

WALLACE, R. K. *The physiological effects of Transcendental Meditation*. Los Angeles: Maharishi International University Press, 1970. (b)

WALLACE, R. K. TM: Meditation or sleep. *Science*, 1976, *193*, 719–720.

WALLACE, R. K., & BENSON, H. The physiology of meditation. *Scientific American*, 1972, *226*, 84–90.

WALLACE, R. K., BENSON, H., & WILSON, A. F. A wakeful hypometabolic physiologic state. *American Journal of Physiology*, 1971, *22*, 795–799.

WALLACH, M. A., & KOGAN, N. *Modes of thinking in young children: A study of the creativity–intelligence distinction*. New York: Holt, Rinehart & Winston, 1965.

WALRATH, L. C., & HAMILTON, D. W. Autonomic correlates of meditation and hypnosis. *American Journal of Clinical Hypnosis*, 1975, *17*, 190–197.

WATSON, G., & GLASER, E. M. *Critical Thinking Appraisal: Manual*. New York: Harcourt, Brace and World, 1964.

WARRENBURG, S., & PAGANO, R. Sex differences in EEG asymmetry predict performance on visuospatial tasks. *Psychophysiology*, 1981, *18*, 171–172. (Abstract)

WARRENBURG, S., & PAGANO, R. R. *Meditation and hemispheric specialization: Absorbed attention in long-term adherence*. Manuscript submitted for publication, 1982.

WARRENBURG, S., PAGANO, R., WOODS, M., & HLASTALA, M. A comparison of somatic relaxation and EEG activity in classical progressive relaxation and Transcendental Meditation. *Journal of Behavioral Medicine*, 1980, *3*(1), 73–93.

WEINBERGER, D. A., SCHWARTZ, G. E., & DAVIDSON, R. J. Low-anxious, high-anxious, and repressive coping styles: Psychometric patterns and behavioral and physiological response to stress. *Journal of Abnormal Psychology*, 1979, *88*(4), 369–380.

WENGER, M. A., & BAGCHI, B. K. Studies of autonomic functions in practitioners of Yoga in India. *Behavioral Science*, 1961, *6*, 312–323.

WILSON, J. R., & VANDENBERG, S. G. Sex differences in cognition: Evidence from the Hawaii family study. In T. E. MCGILL, D. A. DEWSBURY, & B. D. SACHS (Eds.), *Sex and behavior*. New York: Plenum, 1978.

YOUNGER, J., ADRIANCE, W., & BERGER, R. Sleep during Transcendental Meditation. *Perceptual and Motor Skills*, 1975, *40*, 953–954.

ZAICHKOWSKY, L., & KAMEN, R. Biofeedback and meditation: Effects on muscle tension and locus of control. *Perceptual and Motor Skills*, 1978, *46*, 955–956.

ZUROFF, D. C., & SCHWARZ, J. C. Effects of Transcendental Meditation and muscle relaxation on trait anxiety, maladjustment, locus of control, and drug use. *Journal of Consulting and Clinical Psychology*, 1978, *46*, 264–271.

Author Index

Subject Index